The
Enduring
Covenant

The Enduring Covenant

The Education of Christians and the End of Antisemitism

Padraic O'Hare

TRINITY PRESS INTERNATIONAL
Valley Forge, Pennsylvania

Trinity Press International, P.O. Box 851, Valley Forge, PA 19482-0851
Trinity Press International is a division of the Morehouse
Publishing Group

Printed in the United States of America

Library of Congress Cataloging-in-Publication Data
O'Hare, Padraic.
   The enduring covenant : the education of Christians and the end of antisemitism / by Padraic O'Hare.
      p.   cm.
   Includes bibliographical references and index.
   ISBN 1-56338-186-9 (alk. paper)
   1. Christianity and antisemitism. 2. Christianity and other religions — Judaism. 3. Judaism — Relations — Christianity. 4. Christian education. 5. Judaism (Christian theology) — Study and teaching.   I. Title.
   BM535.045   1997
   261.2'6–dc20   96–42304
                                                                          CIP

97   98   99   00   01   02   10   9   8   7   6   5   4   3   2   1

*For Peggy and Brian
with gratitude and love.*

*"God is greater than religion . . .
faith is greater than dogma."*

— Rabbi Abraham Heschel

Contents

Acknowledgments

Gratitude is extended to the following people for a variety of reasons — for sustaining friendship, for the witness in their lives to the Jewish "genius" that is spoken of in these pages, for the inspiration of passionate and deep scholarship, for commitment to Jewish-Christian relations, and for specific and invaluable help with this manuscript: Sherry Blumberg, Mary C. Boys, Robert Bullock, Sheila Decter, Eugene Fisher, Audrey Galligan, Martin Goldman, Robert Goldstein, Marge and Jenny Handverger (and the late "Mister" Ed and Fanny Handverger), Maria Harris, Suzannah H. Heschel, Joseph Kelley, Leon Klenicki, Richard and Ann Landau, Ruth Langer, Sara Lee, Lawrence Lowenthal, Michael McGarry, CSP, Peter McGrath, SJ, William Miller, Gabriel Moran, Carol Ochs, Philip Perlmutter, Anni Pucilowski, Jane Redmont, William Rogers, Edith and Henry Ross, Murray and Charlotte Rothman, Richard Santagati, Harold and Ruth Simons, Brita and Krister Stendahl, Margot Stern Strom, Margot and Thayer (Ted) Warshaw, Helen and Walter Wertheimer, and Leonard Zakim.

Special thanks to Rabbi Langer and Professor Moran, Bishop Stendahl, and to Dr. Ochs for reading and giving excellent counsel on sections of the manuscript.

My gratitude is extended to the Lilly Endowment, through whose generous support I was afforded the time to engage in this research. Special thanks to Craig Dykstra, the Vice President for Religion at the Lilly Endowment. He has brought extraordinary character, intelligence, and vision to the work of supporting scholarly and pastoral developments across barriers of race, economic class, ethnicity, and religion. The funding that enabled this book to come to fruition is but a modest outcome of his vision and that of his colleagues.

Finally, I wish to express my gratitude and love to my mother, Dorothy O'Hare. What reverence I have for "others" is in large measure the result of the example of her genius for friendship and capacity for empathy, gifts for which I cannot adequately express my appreciation.

Introduction

In the preface to *Jewish-Christian Dialogue: A Jewish Justification*, David Novak writes: "No matter how abstract a theory about any type of human relationship becomes, the theorist must regularly return to the experiences that elicited his or her concern for it. Without that regular return, the theory loses contact with its own human content." Novak proceeds to describe his first memorable contact with a Christian. It took place on a train in the 1940s when Novak was eight years old. He met a man, whose name Novak has long since forgotten, who turned out to be a retired Methodist minister. The kindly old gentleman asked Novak what he liked to read; Novak responded that he liked to read the Bible. The gentleman asked if his favorite biblical hero was David; Novak answered that his favorite person was Abraham. They spoke briefly of Father Abraham before Novak's parents came looking for him. Novak concludes: "I sensed too that he was Abraham's son.... Then and there we were equals; each of us accepted the other exactly as he was."

I have asked a number of Christian friends and colleagues about the origin of their passion for reparation and reverence between Jews and Christians. I have heard some stories of first encounters, but never have I heard an adequate explanation of the passion. Its source, like my own, is not a sense of responsibility, though that is certainly present. The passion is not exhausted by appreciation for individual Jews or Judaism as such, though appreciation and friendship abound. I have concluded that the source is ineffable. Later in this book I quote Dom Bede Griffiths, who speaks of each individual as a "capacity" of the Holy One, as a light refracted from the Light. It must be, mysteriously, that for some, the expression of divine "capacity" is this passion.

I have said facetiously on many occasions that I was led to Jewish-Christian relations by a love of "deli," or again by the insuperable joy I experience from the movies of Mel Brooks. I have stopped saying this, embarrassed that it sounds reductionistic, and perhaps insulting. Still — enjoying good food and laughter in the face of tears — perhaps it is not reductionistic after all.

I, too, have a first encounter indelibly etched in my memory. It is of a face, a gentleness, a solicitude for a little Gentile boy who truly shared with an old, Jewish delicatessen worker — what else — a love of "deli." The delicatessen was called the Colony Deli. It is long since gone from Eighty-Second Street off Roosevelt Avenue in Jackson Heights, Queens, New York. I went in often for the hot dogs. But one afternoon the "old" gentleman (I was around eleven or twelve, I think; perhaps he was the age I am now) told me about Challah, the bread of Sabbath Seudah. I don't remember any of his words about the bread, its preparation, or the importance attached to it. I remember only that he somehow did convey the importance of the bread and the wonders of the Sabbath, and that by doing so he graciously invited me into a strange, alluring world, though perhaps I am manufacturing and imposing portentous meanings and effects on this encounter and on the talk of bread for the Friday night Sabbath meal. Still, Jews and Christian both believe that the ineffable, as Rabbi Abraham Heschel has said, is manifest not only in great things but in ordinary things such as a morsel of bread.

This book emerges from that ineffable passion, from those origins, however obscure their meaning and dim the details. It arises as well from fifteen years of sustained and satisfying engagement in Jewish-Christian relations, into which I was invited by friends and colleagues, Martin Goldman and Michael McGarry, CSP. The book is divided into six chapters. In chapter 1 I survey what the philosopher Jules Isaac called the history of the "teaching of contempt." Terrible memories — bitter for Jews, shameful for Christians — are raised here. I have only recently been reminded (by Margot Stern Strom) of how volatile Christian hearers can become when faced with the facts of this history, when faced with our sustained theological justification for subordination and misery for Jews, leading, inevitably if indirectly, to twentieth-century genocide.

Chapter 2 deals with genuine religious pluralism and dialogue. It is an insistent plea that such pluralism rests not on civility or tolerance, nor least of all on "liberal" indifference. Reverencing those on paths of holiness other than one's own is demanded by who God is! The chapter evokes the witness and scholarship of exemplars of such interreligious reverence, Abraham Joshua Heschel and Krister Stendahl. And it situates within authentic Catholic theological anthropology a theological justification for the proposition — as Bishop Stendahl has said — that "from God's perspective we are all minorities."

Chapter 3 is the most arduous piece of writing I have done. (I trust it will not be any reader's most arduous "read.") It is a short Christology, as it would be called in traditional systematics. The purpose of the chapter is to demonstrate the possibility and necessity of teaching in a way utterly devoid of triumphalism and exclusivism our beliefs about Jesus Christ and the experience for Christians of Jesus Christ as the Near Presence of the Holy One. It is at the same time a catechesis of Jesus Christ that is richer for Christians than the classical Christology that still dominates in many places. The chapter places the focus on eucharistic practice.

Chapter 4 is an essay on the religious educational theory of my teacher Gabriel Moran. By distinguishing between "teaching religion" and "teaching religiousness," by acknowledging the many relational experiences that constitute education and the many graces of ordinary life that support and sustain "religiousness," and, finally, by insisting that the purpose of religious education is to form holy people, Moran provides the only conceptualization of religious education practice that is adequate for our purpose. His is a theory of practice in which interreligious reverence is intrinsic, because it is a theory devoid of triumphalism and apologetic intent.

Chapter 5 is an appreciation of Judaism, of the religious worldview and life that emerges from what is here called "the genius of Judaism." It is a perilous venture not only because something as complex, diverse, and rich as Judaism is virtually impossible to encapsulate in an essay, book, or whole library of books, but also because of the danger of casting the meaning of certain Jewish experiences and beliefs in the mold of unexamined Christian assumptions. My justifications for the effort are based on the admiration I have felt for Judaism and many Jews of my acquaintance, some of whom I count as friends, and the need to debunk persistent stereotypes.

The concluding chapter focuses on practice, on (1) elements of a paradigm shift to which Christian religious educators (and Jewish, Muslim, and other religious educators, as well) must give themselves if reverential convergence of peoples on different paths of holiness is to occur; (2) principles for such practice; and (3) select examples of religious education programs for interreligious reverence, especially between Jews and Christians.

When I conceived the ideas for this book and began writing, the book had but one purpose: to speak about a practice of religious education that eliminates anti-Judaism. I have written often and appreciatively of late about the richness of Eastern religious traditions. So it is not surprising to me that as I wrote, a more broadly conceived practice for interreligious reverence became more prominent in the pages of the manuscript. But what did surprise me in the course of composing this book was how obvious it became to me that triumphalist religion destroys the very clues to holiness that the religious community seeks to pass on to its members. What I have come to believe is that every time we unearth a defensive and xenophobic practice or pattern of speech in our religion and set it aside, we are doing something that adds to the health of our religious community, to its capacity to assist people to become holy.

Chapter One

Anti-Judaism, Antisemitism: History, Roots, and Cures

In this chapter I will define Antisemitism,* distinguish it from anti-Judaism, show the intimate relationship between the two, and link both to ecclesiastical triumphalism, glorification of the church as the one place of salvation, and of its hierarchs as absolute arbiters of truth. The triumphalist attitude is the linchpin of theological anti-Judaism and often of Antisemitism among Christians.

Further, I will clarify the links between persistent anti-Judaism and the way Christians understand the Second Testament, early church origins, and early Judaism. The history of Christian anti-Judaism and Antisemitism, including contemporary developments, will be assessed and some preliminary remarks on what Christians need to reform in our thought and teaching will be offered.

Definitions

For the moment, I accept as a working definition of Antisemitism that offered by Edward Flannery in the introduction to the 1985 edition of his pioneering work, *The Anguish of the Jews*. For Flannery, three elements constitute Antisemitism: hatred, contempt, and stereotype.[1] We shall see, however, that some of the contemptuousness displayed century after century by Christians toward Jews, as well as some of the stereotyping, is fueled more by theological conviction and not by hatred. This is not to claim that where there is genuine theological conviction, hatred cannot also be present. The purpose here is not to exculpate Christians or any other people

---

*Advocates for the use of the term "Antisemitism" (rather than "anti-Semitism") include Professor Yahuda Bauer of Hebrew University in Israel. The argument for this new usage is that the prior usage subtly grants the existence of something called "Semitism," in response to which one might well assume a posture of opposition. There is, however, no such ideology or entity as "Semitism." Thus the new usage.

whose imaginations, language, and other images contain and carry anti-Judaism. Nor is the distinction that will be made between Antisemitism and anti-Judaism too fine a point, a bit of Gentile preciousness. Both anti-Judaism and Antisemitism predate Christianity. For example, in his authoritative study, *The Origins of the Inquisition in 15th-Century Spain*, Benzion Netanyahu traces Antisemitism and anti-Jewish stereotype to a tract, "A History of Egypt," written by the Egyptian priest Manetho in 270 C.E. Netanyahu calls the work "the first written Antisemitic piece to come down to us from antiquity...[one full of] the most atrocious lies and the most absurd libels,... " a diatribe occasioned by the alliance of Jews in Egypt with the Persian overlords.[2] But Christianity is unique in that its anti-Judaism, born of theological conviction, is virtually identical to its classic expression of its own self-understanding, which is to say its understanding of Christianity replacing Judaism. And this Christian understanding of itself has achieved an orthodox status with vast numbers of confessants. The foundation and formulation of the self-understanding of vast numbers of Christians cannot helpfully be reduced in all instances to hatred.

The second reason the distinction between anti-Judaism and Antisemitism is so important is in a way the opposite of the first. If the first proceeds from sympathy, however guarded and realistic, the second proceeds from a rigorous attention to just how insidious it is to confront a majority (Christians) whose corporate self-understanding is in such large measure founded on being anti-Jewish in theological conviction. It is not only the haters who have to be confronted but those who do not hate but are still anti-Jewish. The best way to confront this problem is to make the distinction but also to show the links between anti-Judaism and Antisemitism, as I hope to do, and by doing so to help the anti-Jewish to change their hearts.

A final reason for the distinction is related to the marked virulence of Christian Antisemitism. Having noted that Antisemitism predates the Christian *adversus Judaeos* tradition, Rosemary Radford Ruether nevertheless makes this chilling point: "Hatred between groups which have no stake in a common stock of religiously sanctioned identity symbols can scarcely be as virulent as hatred between groups whose relations express a religious form of 'sibling rivalry.' "[3] Hatred founded on such volatile motives needs to be assessed and countered with passion but also with precision.

I leave it, therefore, to the reader to distinguish between contemptuousness and stereotyping driven by sincere (but destructive) theological conviction, and that motivated by hatred. And I propose, not uniquely, that Antisemitism is hating Jews just because they are Jews. Surely everything that emerges from racial Antisemitism, what Netanyahu traces to the Inquisition in Spain, is hateful. The reader will judge whether there is, in addition, but not unrelated to such hatefulness, a distinct anti-Judaism. For the present, let us consider anti-Judaism without reference to hate and return to the larger question.

The essence of theological anti-Judaism lies in Christian replacement theology, quite literally Christians' understanding of themselves as replacing Judaism in the affections of God, the Holy One. Mary Boys points to the etymology of the term *supersessionism,* which names the many tenets of this ideology, noting that it derives from the Latin verb *supersedere,* "to sit upon."[4] Boys identifies eight tenets that define supersessionism: (1) revelation in Jesus Christ supersedes the revelation to Israel; (2) the New Testament fulfills the Old Testament; (3) the church replaces the Jews as God's people; (4) Judaism is obsolete, its covenant abrogated; (5) post-exilic Judaism was legalistic; (6) the Jews did not heed the warning of the prophets; (7) the Jews did not understand the prophecies about Jesus; (8) the Jews were Christ killers.[5]

Clark Williamson and Ronald Allen speak of theological anti-Judaism in somewhat different terms, though their treatment is consistent with Boys's. In *Interpreting Difficult Texts: Anti-Judaism and Christian Preaching,* they identify six defining features of this oppositive theological ideology: (1) that Jews and Judaism represent everything bad about religion; (2) that the cleavage between promise and denunciation in the prophetic books of Hebrew Scripture is represented by Christianity (promise) and Judaism (denunciation); (3) that Christianity embodies salutary universal values; and Judaism, destructive particularistic prejudices; (4) that the "Old Adam" (Judaism) embodies law and the letter of the law; and the "New Adam," Christ Jesus, and the Christians embody spirit and grace; (5) that the Jews have been rejected for their crimes; and (6) perhaps their most interesting contribution, that anti-Judaism itself is a comprehensive *model* for understanding both Judaism and Christianity.[6]

Finally, one of the most detailed examinations of anti-Judaism in the polemical texts of the Christian Scripture and early church life is Jules Isaac's famous list of eighteen points in the appendix of his

historic monograph of 1947, "Has Anti-Semitism Roots in Christianity?"[7] Isaac states the case positively, offering propositions for
correcting anti-Jewish stereotyping and ignorance about the Second Testament and the early days of Jewish Christianity. By putting
the propositions in a negative key, we have an exhaustive catalog
of the erroneous foundations of theological anti-Judaism.

Isaac's points are these: (1) There is awesome ignorance among
Christians of the Hebrew Scriptures, and (2) ignorance, therefore,
of the classical Jewish religious values that constitute so much
of the spirituality, the faith path, set out in the Christian Scriptures. (3) Christians undervalue, indeed, dismiss the religious and
moral significance of Jewish monotheism; (4) deny the vibrancy of
first-century Palestinian Judaism from which Christianity emerged;
(5) ascribe the dispersion of the Jewish people after the destruction of the Second Temple to divine retribution; (6) ignore certain
"editorial tendencies" (as Isaac gently puts it) in the Christian
Scriptures, editorial liberties casting many of Jesus' Jewish contemporaries in the worst light; (7) fail to link Jesus and his teaching
to Jesus' own Judaism and fail to appreciate the "Jewishness" of
Jesus. (8) Related to item 7, Christians ignore the fact that Jesus
remained a Jew, "under the law," preaching in synagogue and temple for his whole life; (9) deny that Jesus understood his mission as
directed to his own Jewish compatriots; (10) deny the acceptance
and receptivity of many Jews to Jesus; (11) assume the Jews of
Jesus' time rejected him as Messiah when he was presented to them
as the Messiah; (12) assume the Jewish leaders of Palestine represented the Jewish people when, in fact, as Isaac says, they were the
"representatives of an oligarchic caste bound to Rome and detested
by the people"; (13) interpret certain texts so that Jesus is perceived as rejecting Israel, when, in fact, Jesus always distinguished
the people of Israel from "evil shepherds"; (14) falsely accuse the
Jews of killing God; (15) assert that those who participated in the
death of Jesus had the support of the people; (16) assume erroneously that the Jewish people had a legal role in the proceedings
against Jesus; and (17) assume, erroneously yet again, that all or
most of the Jews of Jesus' time resided in Palestine.

The eighteenth in Isaac's list is perhaps the most touching point
of this awful catalog of ignorance and prejudice. Isaac concludes
his appendix by noting that even if, as is polemically portrayed at
the end of the Gospel of Matthew, there were a scene in which
a mob of his fellow Jews screamed to Pilate about Jesus, "his
blood be upon us and our children," for Rabbi Jesus, "Father for-

give them,... " consistent with the traditions of forgiveness Jesus learned as a Jew, would prevail. There would be no justification for centuries of contempt and violence or for a whole intellectual structure such as theological anti-Judaism.[8]

So, the foundations of theological anti-Judaism! But for all the destructive consequences of this oppositional ideology, it is not yet Antisemitism. Christopher Leighton's effort to distinguish between the two is instructive. He associates the origins of anti-Judaism with the origins of Christianity; and Antisemitism with modern nationalism and racial theories. But his is a useful analysis even if one accepts a much earlier date for the origins of racial Antisemitism, as Netanyahu proposes.

Anti-Judaism, Leighton writes, "took hold in the early church as the Christians were struggling to explain the Jewish rejection of those messianic proclamations that centered on Jesus...when Christians were straining to establish their own claim to Divine Election. This defensive posture was bolstered by a replacement theology."[9]

In contrast, "Anti-Semitism stemmed from a revolutionary vision of redemption in which the national character could only be fully realized when purged of the corrupting influences of the 'Jewish nation,...' [a vision in which] the idea of national character was gradually reinforced by pseudoscientific theories that identified the Jewish people as a degenerate race. Antisemitism squeezed the Jewish people into a biological category."[10]

The work of definition is not sufficiently served, however, by leaving matters thus: Antisemitism is hateful; anti-Judaism is a matter of sincere conviction and as such is not an expression of hate, though it is a cause of contemptuousness based on, among other factors, stereotypes. In a clear reference to "supersessionist anti-Judaism," E. Roy Eckhart first implies that there are at least two kinds of anti-Judaism, and then labels the theological kind, the supersessionist or replacement ideology, "the Christian crime."[11] One does not have to be a racial Antisemite to hate Jews. Theological anti-Judaism gives rise to hatred and not only to benign hope that Jews will see the light and convert. It is crucial, therefore, to state clearly that theological anti-Judaism gives rise to hateful anti-Judaism and to Antisemitism. Consider one Christian and one Jewish commentator on the connections. First Bernhard Olsen: "One vital point about this unbelievable cruelty for which we Christians must take responsibility is this: that Hitler's pogrom [sic] was but the crown and pinnacle of a long history of hatred toward the Jew, participated in (if not initiated by) those whose duty it was to teach their children the truths of Christianity."[12]

And from Eliezar Berkovits: "Without the contempt and hatred for the Jews planted by Christianity in the hearts of the multitude of its followers, Nazism's crimes against the Jewish people could never have been conceived, much less executed."[13]

Christian theological anti-Judaism and the hateful behaviors and beliefs to which it gives rise must be traced to their most elemental source. And that source is ecclesiastical triumphalism, specifically expressed in this instance in what Eckhart calls "supersessionist triumphalism."[14] For a definition, consider Olsen's words: "Many anti-judaistic expressions reflect the idea that the 'church' is the ultimate institution, that to which prime loyalty is demanded and which needs to be defended, idealized and idolized."[15]

Triumphalism emanates from an essential feature, not a marginal and easily dispensed feature, of organized Christianity. Acknowledging this allows us to see the work of purifying Christianity of anti-Judaism and removing this powerful prop for Antisemitism. The great liberation theologian Gustavo Gutiérrez is speaking of triumphalism when he says, "The church must cease considering itself as the exclusive place of salvation and orient itself toward a new and radical service of people."[16] It is, therefore, as we shall have occasion to consider at length in chapter 3, to the heart of Christian doctrine, the doctrine of Jesus Christ, that we must journey to excise triumphalism and its anti-Jewish effects.

One may doubt whether many Christians, or many Christian leaders, are willing to make the journey. One need not ignore the exceptional progress in Jewish-Christian relations during this generation to acknowledge that progress exists in perilous tension with a steady stream of apodictic claims and oppositive use of doctrine from many Christian quarters. With droll British understatement, Norman Solomon muses, "It may be doubted that the refutation of triumphalism is the soundest foundation on which to base a relationship with Christians. Evidently, it makes them feel uncomfortable."[17]

However uncomfortable it may be for conscientious Christians to admit, it is hard to avoid an affirmative answer to Johannes Metz's question: "Does there not break through within Christianity, again and again, a dangerous triumphalism connected with saving history, something the Jews above all have had to suffer from in a special way?"[18]

It is only a little consoling to modify Emil Fackenheim's painful rebuke and say *a certain kind of Christianity* is ruptured by the Holocaust. Fackenheim writes: "Christianity is ruptured by the Holocaust and stands in need of *tikkun* ["healing," "repair," "mending"].... Surely the Christian good news that God saves in Christ is itself broken in *this* [Fackenheim's emphasis] news."[19]

Writing about ignorance of the history of Christian inspired and led anti-Judaism and Antisemitism, Flannery supplies a second reason for confronting triumphalism. It may never be substituted for the first reason — the need for repentance and reparation of relationships — but it can bolster Christians in this painful process. Flannery says that such ignorance "blocks the way to Christian self understanding...[and] denies [Christians] an opportunity to confront a capital sin of the Christian...and to undertake the *metanoia* this requires."[20]

There can be no easy consolation for thoughtful Christians, who embrace responsibility (though not necessarily guilt) for the evil generated by church triumphalism. Nor can there be forgiveness for institutional church leaders apart from strenuous effort[21] to excise the disease. There is some relief, however, when one contemplates how the history of contempt could have occurred. Here it is the great Rabbi Heschel who comes to our aid. Though the whole hateful reality of Christian anti-Judaism and its links to Antisemitism are unique in scope and outcome, the triumphalism that has fueled that reality is not. Triumphalism is endemic to religion. As Heschel says: "Religion as an institution, the Temple as an ultimate end, or, in other words, religion for religion's sake, is idolatry. The fact is that evil is integral to religion, not only to secularism. Parochial saintliness may be an evasion of duty, an accommodation of selfishness. Religion is for God's sake. The human side of religion, its creeds, rituals and instructions is a way rather than a goal. The goal is to 'do justice, to love mercy and to walk humbly with thy God.' When the human side of religion becomes a goal, injustice becomes a way."[22]

Christian Origins and the Second Testament

There is now a vast literature on the Second Testament and primitive Christianity. Were it to pervade Christian understanding, a more factually accurate picture of first-century Palestinian Judaism — of the Jesus movement as a Jewish movement, of the early evolution of belief about Jesus, and of the nature of polemics in the

Second Testament — would emerge, and a Christian replacement theology of Judaism might disappear.

But as Williamson and Allen note, this theology, supersessionism, functions as a comprehensive model of Christian self-understanding. It is a *classic*, born, as noted above, of the desire to account for the divine election of the members of the new movement, the movement of Jews called "Christians."

In one of its meanings, one associated with philosophical and theological hermeneutics, a "classic" is a text, person, event, or in this case an interlocking set of explanations of the nature of things, an ideology, with "excess of meaning."[23] The profundity of the classic is such that when the text, for example, is encountered deeply by people seeking insight in their concrete, existential situations, new meaning can emerge. The process is primarily one of "dynamic analogy":[24] ideas live, stories instruct in conversation with human experience. Such encounter with a classic text is not primarily a matter of bringing scholarly understanding to bear, though such understanding is not antithetical to encounter.

In the case of a supersessionist explanation for much of what appears in the Second Testament and much that is recalled and given prominence in the early life of the church, "classic" takes on a different meaning. Here we are confronted with a classic *orthodox* explanation. It is golden; it does not admit of new meaning; it is calcified. It is this classic — supersessionist — explanation that confronts professional religious educators, theologians, and exegetes when they invite traditionally educated Christians to reinterpret the story of the Jews in the study of early Christian origins. Reinterpretation includes a great deal of factual correction.

Added to the power of the supersessionist explanation is an anti-intellectual suspicion of scholarly ideas as they pertain to religion. When these are joined to the deeply oppositional character of religion in its conventual forms (which will be addressed more fully in chapter 2), the work of bringing an accurate portrayal of these times, texts, events, and developments — the work of purging Christian religious education of anti-Judaism — is seen as monumental work.

Still, we know a great deal on the basis of which supersessionism must eventually fall. We know that the first followers of Jesus of Nazareth were Jews who did not understand themselves as leaving Judaism to found a "new religion." We know that for them Jesus, now risen from the dead, is not God but the eschatological prophet sent to herald the end times.[25] When the world does not end, the belief of the Christian Jews evolves, and Jesus becomes for them the Lord sitting at the right hand of the Holy One. And this belief evolves so that by the end of the period when the canonical writings are developing, Jesus Christ is understood as the pre-existing divine Son of God. We know that during this evolution, another is taking place, the one James Charlesworth designates as the transition from the "Palestinian Jesus Movement" (ending ca. 70 C.E.) to later "Christianity."[26] We also know a great deal about Jesus' Jewishness, his reverence for the people of Israel and for the Law, and the distinction he always drew, as noted above, between the people and some corrupt leaders. Most important for rectifying anti-Jewish perceptions, we know a great deal about the social context of the anti-Jewish polemical texts of the Second Testament, that, in the words of Philip Cunningham, "a contextual awareness discloses that . . . polemic is the product of human conflict and does not represent timeless truths about God."[27]

When reconstructing early Christian origins and the Second Testament in ways that are at once more factually accurate and more contextually sensitive, and that at the same time diminish the influence of supersessionist attitudes, it is instructive to consider the Gospel of John and the Pauline writings among the latest and the earliest canonical writings respectively.

In his essay "The Problem of 'the Jews' in John's Gospel,"[28] Daniel Harrington notes that the overall portrayal of the non-Christian Jews of Jesus' times is as fools, persecutors, and finally executors of Jesus. The foolishness of the Jews is communicated through the series of debates that are constructed between Jesus and "the Jews." The Jews are also depicted as persecuting Jesus and his followers over Sabbath healing, as feared by Jesus' followers, and as wanting to kill Jesus.

Considering the Jews' foolishness, Harrington points out that the debates staged in the composition of John's gospel are a *literary device* designed to highlight Jesus' teachings. The portrayal of the Jews as fearsome, as persecutors, as desiring and eventually effecting the death of Jesus — the whole seamless, unremittingly negative portrayal — can be ascribed to sociological, political, and theological factors rooted in the situation and in the perspective of John and his community.

Harrington ascribes the sociological pressure to depict the Jews in negative fashion to the devastating situation of the Jews after the destruction of the Second Temple, ca. 70 C.E., and the Roman persecution that followed Jewish rebellion. In the process of reconstructing the religious and cultural fabric of Judaism, four normative views emerge about authentic Judaism and the path it should take. These are apocalyptic, nationalistic, rabbinic, and Christian. Harrington says: "The composition of John's gospel should be viewed against this background and the rival claims among Jews to carry on the tradition of Judaism. The negative portrayal of the Jews in John's gospel is part of an intra-Jewish quarrel."[29]

Charlesworth agrees with this assessment of the reason for the negative view of the Jews, noting: "It seems...that the hostile portrayal of the Jews in John was occasioned by a harsh social situation: Jews leveling invective at other Jews. John emerges out of an historical situation marred not by non-Jews versus Jews, but by some Jews fighting with other Jews. If this is an accurate perception, as many specialists on John now conclude, then it is misleading to base a Jewish Christian dialogue on a document which is the bi-product of a social crisis; and it is misinformed, and unjust, to justify distrust of Jews on the basis of alleged 'anti-Judaism' in the Gospel of John."[30]

According to Harrington, the political reason for the negative picture of the Jews is the result of the same marginal situation of all the Jews in the Roman Empire after the fall of Masada (ca. 73/74 C.E.). Given their extreme marginality, the loss of even a shred of self-rule, and suspicion and subjugation within the empire, "John and the other Evangelists to various extents, shifted the responsibilities for Jesus' death from the Romans to the Jews,... explain[ing] away the embarrassing circumstances of Jesus' death and connect[ing] the Jews of Jesus' day with the rivals of his own community."[31]

Finally, with reference to John's theological orientation, Harrington maintains that the extremely negative characterization of the Jews is a function of John's own proclivity for "dualistic metaphors," imagery dominated by the categories of light and darkness, the non-Christian Jews serving as embodiments of darkness.[32]

With reference to Paul and the problem of supersessionism, we can choose no better guide than Krister Stendahl. In his broadly admired and influential study, *Paul Among Jews and Gentiles*, Bishop Stendahl definitively lays to rest an interpretation of Paul's life, ministry, and theology that lends itself so formidably to supersessionism. By the end of Stendahl's treatises, the idea that Paul means to replace Judaism with Christianity, that this is his mission or that his conversion is of this nature, is effectively repudiated.

Regarding replacement, Stendahl says: "It should be noted that Paul does not say that when the time of God's kingdom comes, Israel will accept Jesus as the Messiah. He says only that the time will come when 'all Israel will be saved' " (Romans 11:26).[33]

Regarding Paul's own life, his experience on the road to Damascus, Stendahl insists that the idea that this represents a change of "religion" is incoherent. "It appears that a Jew, so strong in his Jewish faith that he persecutes Christians, himself becomes a Christian.... [But] here is no change of 'religion' that we commonly associate with the word conversion."[34] On the contrary, Stendahl argues that Paul's conversion consists in accepting a challenging new mission but not a mission entailing abandonment of Judaism. Paul understands himself as "called" in the same sense as the prophets, identifying himself in Galatians 1:13–16, as Stendahl notes, with Isaiah and Jeremiah as "called from birth."

Paul's conversion is not from Judaism; his mission is not to speed its replacement: "Serving the one and the same God, Paul receives a new and special calling in God's service. God's Messiah asks him as a Jew to bring God's message to the Gentiles."[35]

Though Paul in the first letter to the Thessalonians is angry and frustrated and cries out that "God's wrath has come upon [the Jews who killed both the Lord Jesus and the prophets] at last" (1 Thessalonians 2:14–16), Stendahl evokes the mature Paul who says, "Has God rejected his people? By no means" (Romans 11:1).

The expert contextualizing of the seeming "anti-Judaism" in John's Gospel and the illuminating theological and psychological assessment of Paul and his mission ought to persuade traditionally educated Christians that the image of the hard-hearted and superseded Jews who refused to follow Jesus has no place in a positive theological account of who the Christians are and who they are in relation to the Jews. But given the classic status of this account, its influence is hard to excise. It takes first an appreciation that the context Harrington and others are reconstructing is not so foreign to our own experience of rivalry about the orthodox position, and that such interpretations are neither cynical nor reductionistic. Second, it is necessary to be open to the violence done Jews by the supersessionist perspective, and the perspective's corrosive influence on Christianity. Finally, this contextualizing has the desired effect only if one's way of reading and praying "sacred" literature is free of fundamentalism.

Harrington offers a clear and compelling case that placing John in the context of the conflicts of late first- and early second-century

Judaism within the empire — bracketing, if you will, the polemic texts so their negativity is not sacralized — in no way reduces claims about the presence of the Holy Spirit. One needs to see those times as like our own and, of course, to believe that inspiration is available in our own. Harrington writes: "Quarrels within a religious movement are often bitter. In our own day, Jews argue about who is a Jew, Catholics debate about the proper interpretation and implementation of Vatican II, and Liberal and Fundamentalist Protestants repeat the 'battle for the Bible.' Such modern analogies can help us appreciate the context in which John talked about the Jews. A Jew himself, John wrote in a highly emotional setting in which the future of Judaism was at stake. John was convinced that the Christian way was correct and the early rabbinic way was not."[36]

Whether one accepts the righting of the picture of primitive Christianity and rejects supersessionism depends not simply on scholarly evidence. To a greater extent it depends on truly feeling the horror to which these distortions led and still lead. Later in this chapter I will sketch an outline of the history of contempt, distortion, invective, and violence emerging from these roots of the classic Christian self-understanding vis-à-vis the Jews. For now, I note simply my own experience as a teacher: though painful for honest and kind Christians to admit as credible, when they allow the history of Christian anti-Judaism and Antisemitism into their minds and hearts, they change.

Finally, the exegetical and theological work noted above, the work of Harrington and Stendahl and so many other richly instructive scholars, means absolutely nothing to a fundamentalist Christian. Biblical fundamentalism holds to direct divine dictation of every part of speech in Scripture and therefore to the doctrine of inerrancy and the proposition that everything in Scripture is as true as everything else. The efficacy of a more accurate depiction of early church origins and the Second Testament in changing anti-Jewish religious attitudes rests on the capacity of the Christian exposed to such exegesis to discern that the truths of Scripture, as the Second Vatican Council constitution on revelation said, are "the truths of our salvation," the truths that bring "new being," holiness in all its personal and social expressions and effects. There can be no saving truth in the assertion that God — who is love — replaces — one people with another. This conduces to xenophobia.

Early Judaism Understood

The supersessionist mentality and replacement theology rest on one-dimensional, factually inaccurate, and stereotypical ideas about first-century Palestinian Jews and Judaism. The catalog of inaccuracies includes these: (1) that a single ruling elite held power within Palestinian Judaism; (2) that its leaders implacably opposed Jesus and his followers; (3) that all Palestinian Jews waited in a culturally monotone and legalistic mire for a messiah understood in but one way; (4) that all the Jews opposed Jesus; (5) that the Roman authorities reluctantly allowed them to assuage their blood thirst and kill Jesus; (6) that a univocal and uncreative Pharisaic party gained ascendancy after Jesus' death and, evolving into Rabbinic Judaism, has led Jews subsequently along narrow, legalistic lines.

As the rejection of theological anti-Judaism requires an accurate portrayal of primitive Christianity and a more informed reading of the Second Testament, it also requires some appreciation of the Palestinian Judaism of which the Jesus Movement was a part, and of the real nature of Pharisaic Judaism.

Of first-century Palestinian Judaism, James Charlesworth writes: "There was not one ruling all powerful group in early Judaism; many groups claimed to possess the normative interpretation of Torah, Jerusalem and Temple...; [Palestinian Judaism] also spawned and sustained other varieties of Judaism, most notably the Samaritans and the Essenes. Palestinian Judaism was neither dormant nor orthodox; it was vibrantly alive and impregnated with the most recent advances in technology, art, literature, astronomy.... There were not four sects but at least a dozen groups and many subgroups. We should not think in terms of a monolithic first century Palestinian Judaism."[37]

A comprehensive reconstruction of Palestinian Judaism of the first century is beyond the scope of this chapter. Let two relatively straightforward corrections serve to make the point. They are simple facts, but they correct destructive Christian errors about the Jews of Jesus' time. They deal with nineteen centuries of Christian assertions that the Jewish people bear corporate responsibility for the death of Jesus, and that the Pharisees of Palestinian Judaism have been the paradigm through the ages of religious hypocrisy and legalism.

My own early religious socialization as a Catholic Christian was to a large extent free of overt theological anti-Judaism. Despite the fact that I am old enough to have heard the "perfidious" Jews prayed for during Holy Week, the sufferings of Jesus were in every instance, if my memory serves me well, associated with my own sins and shortcomings, not the evil intent and acts of some ancient Jews. I recognize one of many estimable features of my religious upbringing in Eugene Borowitz's treatment of G. C. Berkouwer's biblical exegesis. Expecting to find pronounced Anti-semitism in Berkouwer's writings, Borowitz notes with satisfaction that instead, "he systematically applies a universalizing hermeneutic to passages that speak of the Jews as opponents of the Christ and the Church."[38] I remember this well: "Never mind blaming the Jews for the suffering of Jesus Christ; it is your own sins that nail him to the cross."

At the same time, two scenes from Scripture stand out as vividly as these childhood teachings: in Matthew, "the Jews" cry out, "His blood be upon us and our children" (27:25), and in John, responding to a reluctant (weak-willed but not evil) Pilate, "the Jews" cry, "Crucify him, crucify him" (19:15). It did seem to me that *all* "the Jews" were crying out, and that poor Pilate was being bullied.

James Charlesworth makes a simple but important point related to blaming all the Jews for the death of Jesus. He notes that the largest number of Jews living contemporaneously with these events lived not in Jerusalem but in Alexandria, that perhaps less than 60,000 Jews lived in the Holy City and upwards of 200,000 in Alexandria.[39]

As to Pilate, his image undergoes "softening" as the Christian movement seeks tolerance in the empire, a motive which Harrington notes in his discussion of the context of the Gospel of John, as noted above. Yet in his own day, Pilate was accused of "corruptibility, violence, robberies, ill-treatment of the people, grievances, continuous execution without trial, endless and intolerable acts."[40] Pilate was, in fact, removed as governor of Judea for excess cruelty by, of all people, the brutal emperor Caligula.

Regarding the Pharisees, of which there are estimated to have been at least seven parties, when we search the literary device of setting them up time and again as foils in conversation with Rabbi Jesus, thus allowing Jesus to give his message, what do we find? In the most historical of the texts of the Second Testament, the Acts of the Apostles, we find only two Pharisees mentioned by name. These are Paul and Gamaliel. Of Paul, Eugene Fisher writes (citing Acts 23:6–8 and 26:5), "Paul always considered his claim to having been a Pharisee to be a title of honor...and used methods of reading and interpreting Scripture that appear to have been common to the Pharisees."[41]

The Pharisee Gamaliel cautions the Jewish authorities that the Jesus Movement may or may not be of God. If the movement is not of God, it will perish; but if so, it will flourish, regardless of what the authorities do (5:33–39). Fisher describes Gamaliel as "open to God and God's will, seeking truth, observing the commandments of the Torah, and teaching others the way of God's love by example and saving deeds."[42] Even more pointedly, Fisher notes that Gamaliel's reasoning was typically Pharisaic: "The lives of the Apostles were saved by a classical example of Pharisaical reasoning, which is to say reasoning permeated with piety, wit and compassion."[43]

Can we, as Krister Stendahl asks, "liberate ourselves from the historicism of the first century?"[44] We can if we free ourselves from error regarding the facts of Palestinian Jewish life of the time. But beyond correcting their errors, Christians will have to acknowledge, as the great Rabbi Heschel once said, that "God is not a monopolist," that the Holy One speaks to many people, that many lead comparably holy lives within comparably rich paths of faithfulness. With reference to first-century Judaism and emergent (Jewish) Christianity, Jacob Neusner has provided a clue (to which I will return in chapter 5), suggesting in his book *Jews and Christians: The Myth of a Common Tradition* that after the Second Temple, Judaism was preoccupied with sanctification and Christianity with salvation. The distinction will, I hope, suggest not only comparable strengths as paths to holiness but the richness of genuine interreligious dialogue based on reverence for people on paths of faithfulness other than one's own.

The History of Contempt[45]

Understanding the full burden for Jews of their history with Christians and the burden for Christians of responsibility — and often guilt — requires a picture of the steady devolution of relations. This common history begins with separation; becomes disdain; expresses itself in efforts at conversion, isolation, and deprivation; and reaches its nadir in our century with the unique genocidal horror, the Shoah.

Jesus of Nazareth lived and died a Jew; likewise Paul, who understood himself as a Jewish missionary to the Gentiles. The early polemic enshrined in the Second Testament is not disputation between members of rival religions but intramural contending over the road of faithfulness for Israel. And yet there is separation between the schools. Edward Flannery sees the earliest roots of separation in Peter's acceptance of the centurion Cornelius for baptism without requiring circumcision (Acts 10) and in the dispute between Peter and Paul at Antioch (Galatians 2:11–21). A trajectory of separation between Jews and Christians is firmly established at the Council of Jerusalem, at which the acceptance of Gentiles who have not fulfilled the law of Israel is canonized (Acts 15:5–11).[46]

There is relatively peaceful coexistence between Jews and Christians in the empire for three centuries. Some accounts of Jewish persecution of Christians in these centuries are available, though many of them are suspect, and the historian Marcel Simon maintains, "The few sure cases of active hostility do not, it seems, go beyond the realm of individual and local actions. It cannot be a question of a general conspiracy of Judaism nor of a determining role, but merely of actions of some Jews, who abetted or stimulated active hatred."[47]

During this period, however, the calumnies that will serve for centuries as rallying cries for persecution of Jews are first articulated. Marcion calls for the rejection of the Hebrew Scriptures as, in Franklin Littell's words, the text of a "particularistic" and "materialistic" people.[48] Cyprian, writing in the middle of the third century, expresses the conviction that the Jews are a punished and replaced people in need of conversion. With chilling foreshadowing, he writes of the "final solution" (though not with such intent): "Now the peoplehood of the Jews has been canceled; the destruction of Jerusalem was a judgement upon them; the gentiles rather than the Jews inherit the kingdom; by this alone the Jews could obtain pardon of their sins, if they wash away the blood of Christ slain in his baptism and, passing over into the Church, should obey its precepts."[49] Even earlier, in the second century, the most lethal of all anti-Jewish religious rhetoric is expressed. In the middle of the century, Melito, bishop of Sardis, first says that the Jews collectively are a deicide people.[50]

The fourth century is definitive for relations between Christians and Jews for centuries to come. As Jacob Neusner writes: "In the beginning of the fourth century Rome was pagan; in the end Christian. In the beginning Jews in the Land of Israel administered their own affairs; in the end their institution of self-administration lost the recognition it had formerly enjoyed. In the beginning Judaism enjoyed entirely licit status and the Jews the protection of the State; in the end Judaism suffered abridgement of its former liberties, and the Jews of theirs."[51]

In the year 313 c.e., Emperor Constantine in the Edict of Milan laid down toleration of all religions; in 323, the church was afforded a position of primacy among the religions of the lands occupied by the Romans; and in 329, the emperor himself was baptized a Christian. The reasons are complex, but the story of Constantine's vision is well known. Having achieved a great victory at the Milvian Bridge in the year 313, Emperor Constantine ascribed the outcome to the God of the Christians. A contemporary account says: "He [Constantine] said that about noon, when the day was already beginning to decline, he saw with his own eyes the trophy of a cross of light in the heavens, above the sun, and bearing the inscription, 'Conquer by this' [*in hoc signo vincit*]. At this sight he himself was struck with amazement, and his own army also, which followed him on this expedition and witnessed the miracle."[52] Thus is born the alliance that moved Heschel to write seventeen centuries later, "The Church is often closer to the State than it is to God."[53] And much Jewish suffering issues from this alliance.

There follows the patristic age, a period of detailed elaboration of orthodox Christian doctrine that achieves classic status, the age of the writings of the great early fathers of the church. Theological anti-Judaism's fundamental themes are established and solidified in these writings. Before this period, earlier writers such as Origin and Irenaeus rail against the Jews. In a second-century tract, "The First Homily," Origin speaks of the Jews as "given to flesh and blood." In a contemporaneous writing, "Against the Heresies IV," Irenaeus associates the Jews with Cain. But three fathers of the patristic period — Ambrose, Chrysostom, and Augustine — will serve to show in dramatic ways the steady ideological consolidation of replacement theology during this time.

Ambrose was bishop of Milan; he lived from 339 to 397 and was a major influence on that colossus of Western Christianity, indeed Western civilization, Augustine of Hippo. Ambrose is associated with one of the most chilling early events or texts foreshadowing twentieth-century events. In Letter 40, Ambrose takes issue with the Emperor Theodosius's intention to require Christians of Callinicun to finance the rebuilding of a synagogue burned down by Christians. Ambrose defends the act, writing that what has been done is not so blameworthy, "and less so when it was a synagogue that was burnt, a place of unbelief, a home of impiety, a refuge of insanity, damned by God Himself."[54]

John Chrysostom (347–407) is perhaps the most often quoted father when giving examples of anti-Jewish rhetoric. In or out of context, his flaying of the Jews is breathtaking. A characteristic passage from the "Oration Against the Jews" asserts: "It is because you killed Christ. It is because you stretched out your hand against the Lord. It is because you shed the precious blood, that there is now no restoration, no mercy anymore and no defence. Long ago your audacity was directed against servants, against Moses, Isaiah and Jeremiah. If there was wickedness then, as yet the worst of all crimes had not been dared. But now you have eclipsed everything in the past and through your madness against Christ, you have committed the ultimate transgression. This is why you are being punished worse now than in the past.... If this were not the case God would not have turned his back on you so completely.... You who have sinned against Him and are in the state of dishonor and disgrace."[55]

Chrysostom is quoted only a little less often than Augustine. Given his preeminence among the Western fathers and the range of continuing influence of his thought, the violent anti-Jewish rhetoric in Augustine's writings is especially noteworthy. Consider two passages, both from Augustine's "Reply to Faustus the Manichean": The Church admits and avows the Jewish people to be cursed because after killing Christ they continue to till the ground of an earthly circumcision, an earthly Passover.... In this way the Jewish people, like Cain, continue tilling the ground, in the carnal observance of the Law, which does not yield to them its strength because they do not perceive in it the grace of Christ.[56] No one can fail to see that in every land where the Jews are scattered, they mourn for the loss of their kingdom and are in terrified subjection to the immensely superior number of Christians.... To the end of the seven days of time the continued preservation of the Jews will be proof to believing Christians of the subjugation merited by those who, in the pride of their kingdom, put the Lord to death.[57]

(The antiquity and centrality of the idea that God uses the "wandering [and suffering] Jews" as an instrument to educate humanity regarding the effects of faithlessness makes it all the more startling to consider the distinctly *theological* meaning of Vatican de jure recognition of the State of Israel. John Pawlikowski writes: "The Vatican action... puts a final seal on the process begun at Vatican II to rid Christianity of all vestiges of 'displacement theology' and the implied notion of perpetual Jewish wandering."[58])

Reference to the anti-Jewish content of the Fathers is usually accompanied by two qualifications. First, these violent passages must be seen in the context of continuing Jewish missionary activity, a little-known feature of early Rabbinic Judaism to which, again, the historian Marcel Simon gives testimony, indicating that it is a significant factor through the fifth century of the common era. Such activity is expressed, for example, in the Ebionite movement to merge faith in Christ with Jewish monotheism. Chrysostom's invective is often enough dismissed by noting the fact that he was addressing himself to Christians, by and large, Christians who were continuing to participate in Jewish communal life in the middle of the fourth century. The other qualifying point is to acknowledge the rhetorical style of the day, simply that it was a passionate and, by today's standards, overheated form of oratory.

Such qualifications are important, especially as they certify that pointing to these theologians as evidence of early anti-Judaism is not done in an anachronistic vacuum. The subsequent history of church treatment of Jews, however, ensures that these qualifications are not exculpatory.

Parallel in time to these writings, there is a consolidation through Roman law of the marginal and prejudiced place of Jews in the empire as well as early and especially violent examples of what will become a pattern of pogrom and expulsion in later centuries.

Through laws passed during Constantine's lifetime, Jews are forced, given the odium of the task, to function as tax collectors, as *decurion*. Considering the ruinous economic situation of the times, through this constraint Jews begin to become associated with the economic plight of Christians.

Constantine also forbids intermarriage between Jews and Christians, for fear that Christians might convert to Judaism, not based on myths of racial purity. Under Theodosius a century later, it becomes a capital offense for a Christian and a Jew to marry; his code equates the act with adultery.

(If we "fast forward" to the twentieth century, we have a bracing view of the continuity of the teaching of contempt and of hatred. In 1913, seven years before being elected to the United States Senate, Tom Watson, a racist and nativist demagogue of the early century, wrote: "Every student of sociology knows that the black man's lust after the white woman is not much fiercer than the lust of the licentious Jews for the gentile."[59])

In 413 C.E. a group of monks sweep through Palestine, destroying synagogues and massacring Jews at the Wailing Wall. In the following year, after 700 years in the city, Jews are expelled from Alexandria by the bishop, Cyril. In 425 Jews are required by law to observe Christian feasts and fasts and to listen to sermons designed to persuade them to convert to Christianity. The Theodosian Code of 439 forbids Jews to own slaves, thus profoundly limiting their economic options. In 534 the Code of Justinian "further depressed the status of the Jews by discarding many laws protecting their civil and religious rights, while retaining and extending their restrictions."[60] The explicit acknowledgment of Judaism as a legal religion is dropped, Jews are forbidden to celebrate Passover before Easter, and the reading of Torah scrolls in Hebrew is proscribed.

With the turn of the second millennium of the common era, from medieval through early modern times, patterns of expression of anti-Judaism and Antisemitism, echoed with horrifying effect in contemporary times, are set. Broadscale violence is validated in the minds of the people by marauding Crusaders. The hateful anger of medieval Christian peasants is fed by fanciful tales of Jewish perfidy and felony, and the peasants' murderous revenge grows beyond the power of bishops and popes to stem. Rumors of Jewish acts such as ritual murder of Christian children are set in the popular imagination and repeated to the present time. The use of powerful religious symbolism in liturgical contexts to fortify affective repulsion toward Jews is codified in a way that Christians, in small numbers and isolated circles, still practice. Wholesale ghettoizing and special identification of Jews is carried out. The association of the Jews with disease becomes more pronounced. Vast populations of medieval Jews are expelled from "host" countries. The association of Jews with bad blood, which provides a foundation for racial Antisemitism, begins. The use of religious pretexts for exploiting the wealth of some Jews moves forward. And the poisonous view of Jews among German peoples grows.

The most profound expression of murderous violence directed at Jews prior to our own century is the pogroms that occurred in association with the Crusades, commencing in 1096. The manner in which violent Antisemitism spills over the artificial boundaries of Christian theological anti-Judaism in the eleventh and the twelfth centuries is well captured by Marc Saperstein: "There are grounds for seeing anti-Jewish violence of the crusades as symbolic, if not symptomatic, of a profound change. The massacres revealed that lower levels of Christian society could not be counted upon to behave toward the Jews as official doctrine taught, that popular antipathy could be stirred up by the lesser clergy and spill over into violence unsanctioned by king or pope."[61]

The medieval period also witnesses the growth of chimera about the Jews, fanciful rumors of evildoing on their part. The most famous of these is the story of young William of Norwich, who disappears at Easter, on March 25, 1144. The rumor is spread that the child has been kidnapped by Jews, ritually murdered, his blood drained and used as part of the Passover meal. A century later, in 1255, young Hugh of Lincoln is rumored to have met a similar fate. Thus arises the "blood libel." Such lies stir violent feelings among the Christian peasantry. They combine with the peasants' preoccupation with the devil and the terror induced by plague to portray the Jew in popular imagery and Christian iconography as the devilish, plague-carrying conspirator who, in league with lepers, poisons all the wells of Europe.[62] This imagery is fortified by the powerful symbolism of the liturgy: "With the development of liturgical drama at the turn of the millennium, the possibilities of inculcating hatred of the Jew through popular representation of him as the enemy of salvation was greatly extended."[63]

The most famous strictures against medieval Jews enacted by an ecumenical council of the church are those decreed by the Fourth Lateran Council (1215). As Raoul Hilberg has shown, the decrees and laws promulgated at this council and similar ones, as well as many regional synods throughout the medieval period, foreshadow the Nazi Nürnberg Laws. They place Jews in ghettos, require explicit dress, including a golden "Jewish badge," a reminder that the Jews [sic] betrayed Jesus for gold.

Jews are expelled from England in 1290, from France in 1390, and from most German cities between the fourteenth and sixteenth centuries. Most famous is the expulsion of the thriving, culturally rich Jewish communities in medieval Spain, an act preceded by ten years of inquisition. It is in Spain, beginning in 1482 with the Spanish Inquisition, that Torquemada relentlessly pursues the hunt for insincerely converted Jews, Merranos, successfully urging the expulsion of all Jews ten years later so that the disingenuously converted can more easily be ferreted out. Here, too, is the idea of *mala sangre*, "bad blood," codified in the sixteenth-century Spanish "laws of purity of blood." This is a significant benchmark in developing ideas of racial purity.

The extraordinary cruelty and exponential excess of the Spanish Inquisition provide examples of the use of religious pretext for avarice, and of envy toward the material prosperity of some Jews. Edward Flannery writes that "so brutal became the efficiency [note the word 'efficiency'] of the Torquemadan and later tribunals that the Holy See . . . intervened on several occasions, . . . [Pope Sixtus IV himself declaring that] avarice and lust for gain motivated the tribunal more than zeal for salvation of souls."[64]

Finally, on the cusp of modern times, the preeminent figure of religion and German nationalism, Martin Luther, compares the Jews to the devil — and now causes us to quake in the light of twentieth-century events in Germany. Raoul Hilberg, historian of the destruction of European Jewry, has said that he did not even know of the existence of Luther's *The Jews and Their Lies* until, as a lieutenant in the United States Army combing through Nazi archives in Berlin after World War II, he found a copy of the text among these records.

Hear Martin Luther: "We are even at fault in not avenging all this innocent blood of our Lord and of the Christians which they shed for 300 years after the destruction of Jerusalem and the blood of the children they have shed since then (which still shines forth from their eyes and their skin). We are at fault in not slaying them."[65]

Any sketch of anti-Judaism and Antisemitism during modern times is best begun by noting the ambiguities of emancipation movements and their failure to remove cultural roadblocks to Jewish participation in the societies of Western Europe after the French Revolution. In *The Ordeal of Civility,* John Murray Cuddihy documents the rejection of Eastern European Jewishness by bourgeois "polite" society of the West. Despite emancipation laws, the Osjuden who sought to take their place in Western European Gentile society were simply not "civil" in the prevailing, accepted fashion. They were too passionate, too crude; they were traditional, not modern. Cuddihy cites Irving Howe's whimsical observation that the Jews are the only people in recorded civilization whose historic destiny, as laid down by Western Christian Gentiles, was to be "nice."[66] At the end of the nineteenth century in his charter Zionist statement, "The Jewish State," Theodore Herzl argues that no matter what the Jews do, no matter how assimilated some Jews become, they are not accepted.

Against this background, German nationalism gives rise to virulent racial Antisemitism, as expressed, for example, in Wilhelm Marr's 1879 work, *The Victory of Judaism over Germanism.* And in France, Edward Drumont's *La France Juive* heaps vitriol on French Jews against the backdrop of reactionary Catholic longing for the order of the ancient regime and the charge that the Jews are the chief instruments of French anticlericalism and secularism. In Russia in 1905, the fraudulent "Protocols of the Elders of Zion" are produced. This fictitious document alleges the continuing plan for world dominance of the Jewish Elders.

In *Our Peace*, a well-received Catholic tract published in 1936, the French Jesuit theologian Gaston Fessard, SJ, in a chapter entitled "The Negative Mission and Destiny of the Jewish People," speaks of "the murderous race... eternally riveted at the crossroads where the destinies of mankind meet and intersect, in order to point out to passers-by the direction of history."[67]

Jules Isaac points with sadness to the ambiguity of even well-intentioned official Christian statements of this time, statements whose purpose is to repudiate Antisemitism. In *The Teaching of Contempt*, Isaac cites a March 25, 1928, decree of the Vatican Holy Office that reads in part, "The Apostolic See... condemns in an especial manner the hatred against the *once chosen by God* [emphasis added] that hatred, namely, which nowadays is commonly called anti-semitism."[68]

And pronounced Antisemitism is evident in early- and mid-twentieth-century United States, the theological influences clear, for example, in the rhetoric of William Pelley, the 1936 presidential candidate of the Christian Party: "We Americans now have a political party openly and fiercely anti-Jewish. The newly organized Christian Party now gives us an opportunity to register effective protest to the way in which Jews are taking over our industry, our property and our money."[69]

In midcentury United States, there is no more instructive embodiment of the lethal interplay of theological anti-Judaism (the teaching of contempt) and rabid Antisemitism than the popular "radio priest" of the 1930s, the Rev. Charles Coughlin. Speaking of the "Protocols of the Elders of Zion," Coughlin proclaims, "We cannot ignore the news value of their strikingly prophetic nature." Charged with Antisemitism, Coughlin's retort is to urge "a Christian front which will not fear being called anti-Semitic because it knows the term 'anti-Semitism' is only the pet phrase of castigations in Communism's glossary of attacks." And finally, of the Jews' spiritual inferiority he says: "Because Jews reject Christ, it is impossible for them to accept his doctrine of spiritual brotherhood in the light in which the Christian accepts it."[70]

Consider finally the testimony in the extraordinary scholarship of David Wyman, for example, in his chilling study, *The Abandonment of the Jews,* documenting the United States' actions toward Jews during World War II. The instructiveness of Wyman's study of the deep-seated Antisemitism of United States' culture, of our leaders' refusal to rescue European Jews in the 1940s, the and of violence toward Jews in this country throughout the war is heightened by knowledge of his personal response to what his scholarship revealed. Wyman is a son of the "American" heartland, son of a Methodist minister. Nothing in his upbringing prepared him for what his research revealed. To hear him say that in official, if implicit, American policy during World War II, the rescue of European Jews is considered a "problem," is to confront real, though quiet, moral outrage.

Wyman demonstrates conclusively that powerful forces in the United States government during the war conspired to prevent the rescue of Jews. He notes that given the indifference of President Roosevelt and Secretary of State Cordell Hull, rescue becomes the portfolio of Assistant Secretary of State Breckinridge Long. And Long writes in his diaries at this time of being "under persistent attack from the 'Communist,' extreme radical, Jewish professional agitators, [and] 'refugee enthusiasts' as well as the 'radical press' and 'Jewish radical circles.' "[71]

Wyman's meticulously researched picture of virulent Antisemitism during war time in the United States, as well as what he calls "passive anti-Semitism" — "uncrystallized but negative feelings about Jews" — is a fitting summary to this brief sketch of the history of the teaching of contempt and its effects. He writes, "It was during the war ... that anti-Jewish hatreds that had been sown and nurtured for years ripened into some extremely bitter fruits. Epidemics of serious anti-Semitic actions erupted in several parts of the United States." Wyman sights numerous examples of vandalism, public opinion polls showing broad anti-Jewish and Antisemitic prejudice and, precisely at the time of the Holocaust, examples of what he characterizes as "a small but noticeable flow of hate-filled letters to government officials and members of Congress" protesting the idea of rescuing Jews: "I am writing to you to protest against the entry of Jewish refugees into this country. ... Their lack of common decency, gross ignorance and unbelievable gall stamps them as undesirables even if they could be assimilated into a common society, which they cannot." And: "I see from the papers the 200,000 refugee Jews in Hungary will not live through the next few weeks. Thats too Dam Bad what in Hell do we care about the Jews in Hungary. What we want is the refugee Jews brought to this country returned where they come from." And finally: "Are we to harbor all the riff raff of Europe.... The Jews take over everything here."[72]

The Situation Today

The situation today is, of course, immensely complex. This summary will focus — on the negative side — on the continuing ambiguity of Christian leaders regarding theological understanding of Judaism and Christianity in relationship to one another, on continuing evangelical Protestant anti-Judaism, on the conflicts arising in the depiction of Jews in some African American nationalist movements, and on current attempts to deny the factuality of the Holocaust. On the positive side, the remarkable growth of conciliation between Catholics and Jews and the general deepening of Christian appreciation for religious Judaism are worth noting.

As this chapter is being prepared, *The Catechism of the Catholic Church* in English has been selling for several months. As the "Statement on *The Catechism of the Catholic Church* by the Catholic members of the Christian Scholars' Group on Judaism and the Jewish People" points out, the Catechism "asserts the irrevocable nature of the covenant between God and the Jewish people,...refers explicitly to Jesus' Jewish identity, and refutes any notion of collective guilt of the Jewish people in the death of Jesus. It speaks of the Hebrew scriptures as revelatory for Christians, and attests to the Jewish background of Christian liturgy."[73]

Still, the treatment of Jews and Judaism in what may become a widely influential document is disappointing. As the study group says, "the *Catechism* does not represent fully the developments in Catholic-Jewish relations since the promulgation of *Nostra Aetate*" or subsequent Vatican statements through 1985, nor the heartfelt sentiments of Pope John Paul II. The study group notes (1) that Judaism is often referred to in the past tense in the *Catechism*; (2) typological interpretation is employed through the text, encouraging the persistence of a supersessionist mentality; (3) Judaism of first-century Palestine is inadequately described, leaving open the continuing possibility of a sacralizing of polemical texts; (4) and the Shoah (the Holocaust) is not specifically referred to, despite, as the scholars' group points out, Pope John Paul II's words in 1986 that "this is the century of the *Shoah*."

One sees the problem of continuing reluctance to engage religious difference with absolute reverence for the path of holiness of the "other" in Cardinal Joseph Ratzinger's skeptical commentary at a conference in Jerusalem on Jewish-Christian relations. Delivered on February 2, 1994, Ratzinger's talk identifies such scholarly and religious efforts as those directed at confirming the Jewishness of Jesus, the culpability in his death of the Romans, and the Hellenistic influences in early Christianity as efforts "to mollify the issue," rather than authentic insights designed to cure Christian theological anti-Judaism.[74]

Writing in *Explorations,* William Willimon, Dean of the Chapel and Professor of Christian Ministry at Duke University, points to an even more disturbing development in conservative evangelical Christianity. He reports on the gratuitous anti-Jewish features of *The International Children's Bible,* published by Word Incorporated in 1988. Willimon notes that the children's Bible is "*more* [his emphasis] anti-Jewish than the original of other English versions. For instance, the King James Version renders John 11:53: 'Then from that day forth they took counsel together for to put him to death.' The International Children's Bible paraphrase: 'That day the Jewish leaders started planning to kill Jesus.' " Willimon goes on to note numerous similar examples, such as subheadings like "Jewish Leaders Try to Trap Jesus," "The Jews Against Jesus," and "Saul Escapes from the Jews."[75]

On another plane are the vitriolic Antisemitic features of certain elements of African American self-help, pride, and nationalist movements, and of aspects of Afrocentric studies. Luther's tract "The Jews and Their Lies" is sold at Nation of Islam gatherings, as are copies of "The Protocols of the Elders of Zion." Professor Anthony Martin of Wellesley College is only the best known of professors employing the pseudoscholarship of *The Secret Relationship Between Blacks and Jews,* a text noteworthy for proposing that colonial Jews dominated the slave trade. Characteristic of this tragic linking of African American progress with Antisemitism are the vitriolic statements of Khalid Abdul Muhammad, charges that ring with the calumnies of the centuries: "I called them [Jews] bloodsuckers. I'm not going to change that. Our lessons talk about the bloodsuckers of the poor in the supreme wisdom of the Nation of Islam. It's that old no-good Jew, that old imposter Jew, that old hooked-nosed, bagel-eating, lox-eating,

Johnny-come-lately perpetrating a fraud, just crawled out of the caves and hills of Europe, so-called damn Jew. . . . And I feel everything I'm saying up here is Kosher."[76]

Despite the viciousness of this rhetoric, the Antisemitic movement that occupies a privileged place of infamy today — indeed, in the whole sorry history of Antisemitism and the theological assertion that has fed it, prepared for it, or conditioned Christians to accept it — is the contemporary movement to deny the reality of the Holocaust. Despite tens of thousands of volumes of documentary evidence, despite Adolf Eichmann's insistence in 1961 that Reinhard Heydrich told him in 1941 that "the Fuhrer has ordered the physical extermination of the Jews," despite Hitler's own words at the end of January 1942 that "the result of this war will be the complete annihilation of the Jews,"[77] there exists in our time a powerful, effective, well-financed, and broad movement in the United States, Canada, and Western Europe to deny that the ultimate expression of the teaching of contempt and the Antisemitism to which it gave rise ever occurred.

One may question whether the potential critical mass of Antisemitic feelings lessens or whether it is only that social legitimization of the crassest expressions of such hatred fluctuates. Still, there can be no denying that since World War II in the United States and elsewhere, Antisemitism has been reduced and Christian theological anti-Judaism ameliorated to some extent. For all the confusion of anomalies such as greeting Kurt Waldheim and Yasser Arafat, approving the beatification of Edith Stein, or failing to negotiate the controversy about a Carmelite Convent at Auschwitz with sufficient sensitivity to either the Jewish community or the Carmelite nuns, it is nevertheless true that Pope John Paul II is a figure of historic proportions in the movement of Christians to repudiate contempt and live with real reverence and affection with Jews.

During the pontificate of Pope John Paul II, there have been many epochal statements, many moving events — for example, the first visit of a pope to the synagogue of Rome or the profoundly moving commemoration of the Shoah, Yom HaShoah, held within the Vatican in 1994. In some ways, a little-reported letter written in 1987 by Pope John Paul to the then president of the National Conference of Catholic Bishops in the United States best summarizes the progress and is most touching. In this letter, the pope's language comes as close as any official Catholic statement has to taking responsibility on behalf of Christians for the centuries of teaching contempt and for the Antisemitism these teachings have generated. Pope John Paul writes Archbishop John May of Saint Louis in May 1987: "There is no doubt that the sufferings endured by the Jews (in the *Shoah*) are also for the Catholic Church a motive of sincere sorrow, especially when one thinks of the indifference and sometimes resentment, which, in particular historical circumstances, have divided Jews and Christians."[78]

Though progress in stemming theological anti-Judaism should not be overemphasized, it is nevertheless real. Philip Cunningham's study of the treatment of Jews and Judaism in Catholic religious education curriculum materials, which builds on the 1961 study of Sister Rose Thering and the 1976 study of Eugene Fisher, is especially encouraging in this regard. In handling of Hebrew Scripture, the relations of Jesus and his Jewish contemporaries, the Pharisees, the crucifixion, and the relationship between the covenants, Cunningham finds great cause for hope, even while he points out that what flaws continue to exist result from "uncritical use of the Bible" and possible negative influences in lectionary-based programs (programs of catechesis for Christian children based on liturgical readings) when those programs are not handled with sophistication.[79]

What Is to Be Done?

A people whose classic expression of their self-understanding as a religious community is founded on replacing another people must learn nonoppositional religious sensibilities, must learn simply to revel in the joy of experiencing a particular path of holiness without also seeking to disprove or discredit the "others." Theological anti-Judaism must be rejected, in the words of Williamson and Allan, as contradicting the good news of God's unbounded love and therefore "simply incredible."[80]

Equally powerful is the reason that Roy Eckhart expresses for rejecting any vestige of this corrupting religious ideology. Speaking of theological anti-Judaism as "supersessionist triumphalism," Eckhart says, "A potential Christian ideological contribution to a future Shoah is implied [in supersessionist triumphalism] because traditional supersessionism remains abidingly central to the Church's message."[81]

What is required is, to use two shopworn words, *dialogue* emerging from a very deep commitment to *pluralism*. But the dialogue, precisely because it emerges from a profoundly pluralistic mentality, is more than polite agreement to clarify and then continue disagreeing. It is also more than agreeing to identify a limited agenda of matters about which there is agreement. Many very insightful commentators misunderstand, and sometimes mock, the profundity of the pluralist mentality required to achieve real reverence for the other, or to save one's people from corruption as well. Norman Solomon, for example, speaks of liberal theologians on both sides, Jewish and Christian, being able to reach "accommodations" because of their "relativist" positions, "denying that any *theology* [my emphasis] is ultimately superior to any other."[82] Of course, this is precisely the point of profound pluralism: that no formulaic expression about the practice of holiness of one people is superior to that of another. It is not "theology" that is revealed; it is the Holy One and a holy way of living. Religious ways either produce holy people or they do not. The superiority of language (theological expression) is beside the point. Real religious pluralism arises, as Rabbi Heschel knew, from "respect for each other's commitment and respect for each other's faith.... [It] is more than a political and social imperative. It is born of the insight that God is greater than religion, that faith is deeper than dogma, that theology has its roots in depth theology"[83] (of which Rabbi Heschel writes elsewhere: "Theologies divide us; depth theology unites us").[84]

Authentic religious pluralism leads to dialogue that transcends the false civility of reductionistic and antinomian liberals. Rather, as Emil Fackenheim says, "the heart of dialogue is to...risk self-exposure. If Jew and Christian are both witnesses, they must speak from where they are. But unless they presume to be on the throne of divine judgement, they must listen as well as speak, risking self-exposure just because they are witnesses."[85]

We turn to chapter 2, on religion and xenophobia, pluralism and dialogue, with these words of Rabbi Heschel: "This is the agony of history: bigotry, the failure to respect each other's commitments, each other's faith. We must insist upon loyalty to the unique and holy treasures of our own tradition and at the same time acknowledge that in this aeon religious diversity may be the providence of God."[86]

Chapter Two

Between Religions:
Xenophobia or Reverence?

In this chapter I will examine the foundations of religiously inspired prejudice, exclusivism, and absolutism; the "sacred violence" to which these give rise; and patterns of fundamentalism that carry the xenophobic feelings of oppositional religion.

In contrast to these influences and their destructive consequences stand genuine pluralism and dialogue. This pluralism is greater than civility or tolerance born of indifference. It arises from what one author calls "depth dialogue" — part of conversion from individual and group narcissism, the ultimate expression of hubris; conversion from believing and acting as if we possess the Holy One and others are alienated from the Source of Being. Turning away individually and collectively from such dangerous and unhealthy arrogance is true change of heart.

The need to reject religiously inspired xenophobia and to embrace interreligious reverence and dialogue is evoked in contemporary theology of religions; the inspiration to do so is part of the essence of the Catholic ethos when it is freed from historical ecclesiastical patterns of opposition, exclusion, absolutism, and violence. These ideas will also be examined.

Introduction

The critique of religion is common under the influence of the modern mentality, but it has been present in human discourse since the time of the Hebrew prophets. Religious people themselves distinguish between authentic and inauthentic manifestation of religiousness. ("Religiousness" itself is sometimes used to signify something authentic; "religion," or more often "religiosity," is reserved for negative appraisal.) For example, Paul Tillich distinguishes between the "church" and the "spiritual community."

The ecclesiologist[1] Avery Dulles distinguishes between the "institution" and the "community of disciples"; the theologian Rosemary Haughton, between "Mother Church" and "Sophia" (more about this below). In none of these instances does the theologian cited intend to deny to the first manifestation (church, institution, mother church) any and all validity or virtue. This is not the case, however, with the critique of the great Calvinist theologian of our century, Karl Barth. Distinguishing "religion" and "faith," Barth proclaims religion a work of the devil!

From a completely different vantage point, social psychologist Gordon Allport sheds light on the interplay of good and evil that seems constitutive of religion in his analysis of its relationship to prejudice: "The role of religion is paradoxical. It makes prejudice and it unmakes prejudice. While the creeds of the great religions are universalistic, all stressing brotherhood, the practice of these creeds is often divisive and brutal. The sublimity of religious ideals is offset by the horrors of persecution in the name of these same ideals."[2]

One does not have to be a sectarian[3] to acknowledge that there is something intrinsically disordered in religion, some elemental difference and conflict between religion and spirituality. Here spirituality means a way of life, expressed necessarily in communal living, in which one practices to revere what is holy, to yearn for what is good, and to act with compassion, gratitude, and joy. "Religion" connotes a seemingly irreducible element of exclusion and opposition. Norman Solomon captures the nagging reality of it with his usual serious playfulness: "Religion is a strange and potent thing. People that I played with, went to school with, share a whole language and culture with, in the marketplace, the concert hall, the laboratory, at the hustings, on the street, in all the facets of everyday life — we don't have to handle each other with kid gloves. But dress us up as theologians, professing the love of God and man, and the pursuit of peace, and put us in the conference hall labeled as Jews and Christians, and we hardly know each other. We are nervous, we tread softly lest we unleash hatred and suspicions. Is this the cost of spirituality?"[4]

The problem is stated with precision by Rabbi Heschel: "It is an inherent weakness of religion not to take offense at the segregation of God, to forget that the true sanctuary has no walls. Religion has often suffered from the tendency to become an end in itself, to seclude the holy, to become parochial, self-indulgent, self-seeking, as if the task were not to ennoble human nature but to enhance the power and beauty of its institutions or to enlarge the body of doctrine. It has often done more to canonize prejudice than to wrestle for truth; to petrify the sacred than to sanctify the secular."[5]

Christianity is not the only religion resting on an orthodox claim so absolute that reverence for the other seems remote; the change of heart of interreligious encounter born of genuine pluralism and dialogue, unlikely; exclusiveness and xenophobia, unabating. It is, however, one of the religions in which absolutism has flourished for many centuries. And the results of Christianity's absolutism have had the greatest impact on Jews and Judaism.

The essence of Christian absolutism rests on claims about Jesus Christ. Karl Barth is an exemplary figure: "Only one thing is really decisive for the distinction between truth and error.... That one thing is the name of Jesus Christ."[6] And Karl Rahner writes: "Because of Jesus Christ, Christianity understands itself as the absolute religion, intended for all men, which cannot recognize any other religion besides itself as of equal right.... Pluralism is a greater threat and a reason for greater unrest for Christianity than for any other religion.... The fact of pluralism of religions... [is the] greatest scandal and the greatest vexation for Christians."[7]

Radical Christocentrism gives rise to what Krister Stendahl calls "the structure of salvation as victory"[8] — Jesus Christ's victory over sin, humanity's victory over death through and only through Jesus Christ, the Christian church's victory over societies. It is the victory of the Christian religion. The idea of victory provides the impulse to spread a universal Christian claim. The combination of the universal claim as typified in the quote from Karl Barth, and the idea of salvation as victory give rise to what Stendahl calls "sacred violence": "Our universal claim makes it self-evident that God's hottest dream is that others become like us, believe as we do, and understand themselves as we do.... The hunger for oneness as conformity breeds sacred violence."[9]

Thus, for all the beauty of Christian faithfulness, all the human transcendence achieved in companionship with Jesus Christ as New Being, all the genuine spirituality of the Christian path of clues to a holy life — here in this radical Christocentrism, in a classic doctrinal understanding of salvation as victory, in the tradition of universalist Christian claims; here is religion as a source of brutality. It has been so in the past; it is so to an extent in the present. It could be so in the future.

Universalist absolutism thrives on the diminishment of the other, on ignorance of the other. E. P. Sanders speaks of this as the "comparison of reduced essences."[10] To sustain the arrogance of absolute claims, one must not let the full reality of the life of a Jew, a Muslim, a Hindu into one's conscious field. Sanders says, "A pattern of religion, defined positively, is the description of how a religion is perceived by its adherents to function."[11] But the universalists must not allow the "full fact" of personal experience, as William James called it, to penetrate their minds. James defined the "full fact" as "a conscious field plus its object as felt or thought, plus an attitude towards the object, plus the sense of a self to whom the attitude belongs."[12] It was a full fact about Jews and Judaism that Shakespeare put on the lips of Shylock: "Is a Jew not a man?"

But instead of growth in appreciation of the full fact of the path of holiness traveled by others — instead of the humility that other peoples' reverence, yearning for the good, and practice of compassion and gratitude should inspire in us, this absolutism — any absolutism inspired by religion — leads instead to fierce and lethal pride, even though Rabbi Heschel tells us authentic religion "begins... with the awareness of a reality that discredits our pride."[13]

Instead of the solidarity that a common religious worldview should inspire (the common view that all creation participates in a transcendent lure of holiness, compassion, and joy), we have instead the demonization of the other. As Krister Stendahl says, "Demonization is one of the plagues of religious traditions because you are dealing with an intense rhetoric intensified to the voltage of the divine."[14]

For Christianity, the fundamental fact of absolutism, the false pride on which it rests, and the demonization of the other to which it leads is the Holocaust. Christian theological anti-Judaism, as noted in chapter 1, is the necessary precondition, if not sufficient cause, of this unparalleled horror of human cruelty. And now, after the Holocaust, it is the fundamental fact of which all Christian theological reflection on how to be a faithful Christian must take account. It is the fact on the strength of which exclusive and absolute claims must fall. David Tracy asks: "How can we pretend to take history with theological seriousness and then ignore the Holocaust? If we do ignore it, then we should either admit the bankruptcy of all theological talk on history as the locus of divine action and human responsibility or admit that we will only allow the 'good' parts of our history [to] prove worthy of theological reflection."[15]

In our time, after the Holocaust but always mindful of it, and as a result as well of previously unparalleled encounter between people of the East and of the West, real change in the edifice of Christian triumphalism is occurring. Other cultural dynamics also undermine the exclusivism, absolutism, and prejudice of religion. And a rich area of theological discourse about pluralism and dialogue emerges.

Pluralism and Dialogue

"Pluralism," the great theologian of religions Raymundo Panikkar has said, "stands between unrelated plurality and a monolithic unity."[16] Panikkar's own experience of interreligious encounter, growing reverence, and the enrichment of his own Christian path of holiness through interreligious encounter is most instructive. He says: "I 'left' [Europe] as a Christian, I 'found' myself a Hindu, and I 'returned' a Buddhist, without having ceased to be a Christian."[17] Panikkar's openness to such encounter is based on his own Christian way — in the basic religious insight that the Holy One is either the God of all or of none, in the perception that the Holy One is not scandalously partisan. He writes: "The whole idea of belonging to a chosen people [in the triumphalist, exclusivist sense], of practicing the true religion, of being a privileged creature, struck me not as a grace but as a disgrace."[18] Such a preposterous notion, Panikkar adds, is founded on "an entire conception of truth based on the principle of property."[19]

True to the genius of the Catholic humanist spirit, Panikkar rejects Christian exclusivism by founding his theological assessment on both elemental human experience and classic doctrinal tradition. Narrow, sectarian Christian pride of place in the affection of the Holy One contradicts the experience and the teaching that God is love. But Panikkar says that his objection is not based on "God's goodness and justice" but on realizing "this idea [Christian exclusivism] contravenes the freedom and joy I would look for in a belief that enables the human being to grow to full stature."[20]

Langdon Gilkey speaks eloquently of the other basis for embracing genuine religious pluralism: a noble image of the Holy One. For Gilkey, the development of a broad, pluralistic feeling among many people on different religious paths, and specifically the replacement of Christian triumphalism with Christian reverence for others, represents "a shift in the balance between what were called the requirements of faith and those of love; or better put, a new assessment of how God views those requirements."[21]

So the religious pluralism that in some quarters is progressively if slowly replacing absolutism, exclusivism, prejudice, and violence is firmly rooted in the human experience of the Holy One and of the holiness of people on other paths. It is not simple civility, grudging tolerance, or the search for a common, homogenous doctrinal or practical core; genuine religious pluralism is not syncretism. As Paul Knitter writes: "The new vision of religious unity is not syncretism which boils away all the historical differences between religions in order to institutionalize their common core."[22]

In contrast to such ersatz pluralism, Knitter refers to growing interreligious reverence and dialogue, and the enrichment of each unique path of spirituality, as "unitive pluralism." "Unitive pluralism is a unity in which each religion, although losing some of its individualism (its separate ego), will intensify its personality (its self-awareness through relationship). Each religion will retain its own uniqueness, but this uniqueness will develop and take on new depths by relating to other religions in mutual dependence."[23]

It is hardly necessary to say that the growth of interreligious sensibilities, the expanding notion of what Gilkey calls the "rough parity" of religions, is a source of great anxiety for the greater portion of traditionally socialized members of religions, especially though not exclusively Christians. Gilkey acknowledges this, saying: "Ecumenical tolerance represents an impressive moral and religious gain, a step toward love and understanding. But it has its own deep risks, and one of them is this specter of relativity, this loss of any place to stand, this elimination [sic] of the very heart of the religions as ultimate concern."[24] It is as if all that is good in religion, ultimate concern leading to ultimate commitment, is tragically linked to the aspect of religion that causes evil: the exclusivity of the claim to what Gilkey calls the "absolute starting point," in effect, an absolute proprietorship of God.

Panikkar addresses the risk and ambiguity of genuine attitudes and behaviors of religious pluralism when he speaks of a "universal life," not universalist claims, of course, but the attitude that the Holy One is available to all, inspiring all people on all the paths of holiness. In this sense, he asks: "Can one lead a universal life in the concrete? Is it feasible to live by faith that is at once embodied — incarnational — and transcendent?"[25]

The answer of those inspired to let go of the religion of exclusion and absolutism, which leads to xenophobia, prejudice, and violence, is that such attitudes and behaviors must be rejected. In the case of Christianity, as noted earlier, we must rediscover that for all the legitimacy that some traditions attach to absolutism and exclusivist claims, parallel traditions exist that demand inter-religious convergence, reverence, even affection. As John Hicks notes: "Christians are gradually realizing that they, that Christianity, not only allows but requires, a recognition of the limitations of all historical revelation, of all human knowledge."[26]

It is, however, precisely in theological work, in the act of formu-lating what we take to be knowledge of the Holy One and what divine life in us requires (distinct from faithfulness, which is prac-ticing living the holy life) that the greatest blocks to full-hearted interreligious reverence arise. Thus, Gilkey claims that we cannot resolve what he calls the paradox of religious pluralism (that we remove our own "absolute starting point" but retain "ultimate concern") at the level of theological formulation. It is, he claims, only in *praxis,* in "doing dialogue," that we are "push[ed] and lure[d] into the middle of a maze we still can hardly enter into intellectually. [But] now in 'doing dialogue' we embody and enact this paradox.... We remain *there* [Gilkey's emphasis]: embodying stubbornly but relatively our unconditional affirmations."[27]

Raymundo Panikkar places true religious dialogue coming from profound feelings about religious pluralism in an epic context. He holds that Christianity has moved through four previous epochs: those of witnessing, conversion, crusade, and mission. For Chris-tians now is the era of dialogue![28]

Just as an attitude of genuine pluralism entails rejecting the search for a common core and transcends civility and tolerance, genuine dialogue is very much more than good-natured exchange of information about the intramural curiosities of one another's symbol systems and practices. Pluralism and dialogue are founded on a profound experience of the universal love of the Holy One and on the conviction that authentic human conversation is con-stitutive of human being and becoming. Genuine dialogue is, in the felicitous terms of Leonard Swidler, "depth dialogue" or "spir-itual dialogue." "In depth or 'spiritual' dialogue we experience the partner's religion or ideology from within,"[29] though here there is a need to urge caution. If depth dialogue is not simply clarifica-tion and acceptance of differences, neither is it, in the thoughtful phrase of a teacher of mine, "understanding me too quickly."[30] Even Panikkar says of the relationship with the partner in dialogue,

"I can never understand his position as he does.... To understand [as he does] is to be converted to the truth one understands."[31]

If depth dialogue is not simply trading information, neither is it knowing the full fact of the religious experience of our dialogue partners as they experience it. But the dialogue is something very deep and profound. To employ an overused and often abused term correctly, depth dialogue entails real "vulnerability," openness to fundamental change in one's life, one's feelings, thoughts, and actions. Vulnerability, in turn, presupposes very healthy, life-giving roots in one's path of holiness and the people of which one is primarily a part. Panikkar speaks of the vulnerability in quite stark terms. He was accustomed to advise students in his courses in history of religions "that if they were not open to the possibility of being converted during the semester, they should immediately drop the course."[32] (Such a statement implicitly raises the specter of centuries of effort to force conversions. At the same time, it dramatizes the openness of depth dialogue.)

John Cobb points to the same deep level of dialogue. Criticizing the subtle search for a common core in some seemingly genuine interreligious conversation, Cobb says that if those engaged in dialogue "wish to be open, they should simply be open."[33] And Swidler writes, "Everyone searching for religious meaning and truth, no matter how convinced by and committed to a particular tradition or position, if they would act with integrity must have a radical openness."[34]

The profundity of depth dialogue cannot be overstated. The dialogical imperative arises from the fundamental conviction of the great religions that to exist is to coexist.[35] Bernard Lonergan put it so: "Just as it is one's own self-transcendence that enables one to know others accurately and to judge them fairly, so inversely it is through knowledge and appreciation of others that we come to know ourselves and to fill out and refine our appreciation of values."[36] In the same spirit, John Dunne writes: "Passing over and coming back it seems is the spiritual adventure of our time."[37]

We will know that we are engaged in depth dialogue if we experience the other (person, path) inside us, if we experience "passing over," if — in the words of Panikkar — the dialogue becomes a very deep, internal soliloquy: "The real religious or theological task, if you will, begins when the two views meet head on inside oneself, when dialogue prompts genuine religious pondering and even a religious crisis at the bottom of a man's heart; when interpersonal dialogue turns into intrapersonal soliloquy."[38]

All that has been said above pertains to the essential spiritual work of depth dialogue, its dependence on people paying attention to the selves we are becoming, on doing "good work" on our own masterpiece. The existential core of depth dialogue depends on practice of faithfulness: gently striving to become ever more reverent of the Holy One; desirous of what is good; practicers of compassion, gratitude, and joy. There is, in addition, a broader context for dialogue. An indefatigable promoter of such convergence between Jews and Christians, Leon Klenicki, addresses these several features, basing his perspective on the conversion to real conversation already spoken of: "Dialogue requires search and patience. We need a period of meditation and reflection in order to consider the future. Patience is required to resolve doubts, to prevent the repetition of former situations, to prevent excessive dreams as a result of unreserved enthusiasm. Carefully committed reflection and critical consideration are indispensable in the search for our joint goal. The search into the meaning of God's special call is a search for the meaning of our faith encounter beyond syncretism and sporadic sympathies."[39] In such humanly demanding work, it is important above all for Christians — members of a majority religion — to remember that such work makes different demands on Jews.

Pluralism, Dialogue, and "Uniqueness"

Even after the spirit of pluralism and the practice of dialogue begin to take us beyond absolutist religious attitudes and superficial talk, there remains the nagging fear of loss of religious particularity, the fear, as Gilkey says, of the "specter of relativity." As Panikkar asks: "Can a religious people really be embodied...and transcendent?" The elemental issue at the heart of religious pluralism and interreligious dialogue is the question of uniqueness.

One of the most incisive studies of uniqueness is that by Gabriel Moran. In *Uniqueness: Problems and Paradox in Jewish and Christian Traditions*, Moran notes that the claim to uniqueness can be viewed as trivial or exalted. Triviality adheres to false claims of uniqueness. In the spirit of unmasking such claims, T. S. Eliot said, "All cases are unique and very similar to others."[40] Exaltation, in the sense of a vain glorious claim, is often associated with the Jewish idea of being a "chosen people," an association wholly at odds with the full fact, the theological meaning of chosenness, for Jews themselves.

Uniqueness is often contrasted with universality. As noted in chapter 1, early and late anti-Jewish theological rhetoric contains much talk of this "particularistic" people, this clannish people, the Jews, contrasted to the people who are Christian and their universal ideals and values. All religions in the West are criticized for uniqueness or particularity by those in thrall to the modern, rationalistic mentality. The Enlightenment is in large measure a search for a way to escape the barbarity of religious wars and authoritarian persecutions justified in the name of the particular and unique truth possessed only by this people, this chosen people, namely, the Christians. So the modern anthem goes: we will found the good society, and we will form the person of character, and we will promote virtues without the stories of religion, the lives of the saints, reference to the loving and just will of the Holy One. Personal and political comity will be based on the universal value of reason alone. What religion is permitted inside the margins of modern, rationalistic, secular life will be, in Locke's telling phrase, "religion within the limits of reason alone." Moran, as we will see in chapter 4, has spent a professional lifetime trying to wean religious educators, or anyone who will listen and read, from the preposterous notion that there is some universal, general, rational, homogeneous personal and communal path of noble life and society, insisting that all the paths are particular but need not inspire sectarian hatred. For now, it seems sufficient to note that even at a very sophisticated level, interreligious dialogue itself is constantly threatened by this universalism in the form of syncretism, the false idea of a universal and general path of holiness, a common core. The idea is imported into the conversation via the modern, rationalistic mentality.

The centerpiece of Moran's study of uniqueness, and its great strength, is his distinction between "exclusive" and "inclusive" meanings of uniqueness. In the exclusive view, everything is seen to be individual. In the inclusive view, one understands that the "real is relational."[41] For those who claim exclusive uniqueness, "the world is a world of individuals that only externally relate to one another."[42] So, in the sequence 33393, 9 is unique in the exclusive sense that it is not 3, though like 3, 9 is a number. And in the sequence 333M3, M is even more exclusively unique in that not only is it not a 3, it is not a number, though numbers and letters share "thingness."

Regarding the inclusive meaning of uniqueness, that based on the experience that all realities interpenetrate, Moran says, "In this way of being in the world, to be is to be in communion. The greater the receptiveness to others," Moran says, echoing Lonergan, "the more distinctive the self."[43] Moran offers the following example of inclusive uniqueness. Given the following letter combinations — a, ab, abc, abcd — "abcd," he writes, "is different from all the others because it includes all the others."[44]

But the reference to a uniqueness that is inclusive (abcd including a, ab, and abc) is not imperialistic. Moran has not slipped into a second-order absolutism that argues that our path of holiness is the one, true way, but other people are anonymously included in "the way" — our way — by the will of a loving God. The discussion of revelation that follows on Moran's explanation of these two uses of the claim of uniqueness makes clear that the inclusion of which he speaks is like the experience Panikkar speaks of having: being a Christian in a way that is deeply, existentially changed and deepened by experiencing clues to the practice of holiness provided by Hinduism and Buddhism. In the exclusive meaning, revelation is "exclusive possession of the truth." In the inclusive meaning "one discovers...revelation...from conversations with all other peoples...standing open to all knowledge."[45]

In Moran's inclusive sense of revelation, however, one experience does constitute a common core, a universal claim. But it is an experience that precedes all religion, even while it gives rise to all religions and is therefore not available as a stick for religious absolutists. The experience is pretheological in the sense Rabbi Heschel gives the terms, prereflective in the words of Karl Rahner. It is the experience of the Holy One who sets in our hearts, all hearts, the reverence for the Holy, the yearning for what is good, the practice of compassion, gratitude, and joy. The common core is the lure of faithfulness. Moran asserts quite boldly, therefore, "The phrase Christian faith makes no more sense than Christian grace.... Because there is one God, there is one revelation of that God, one faith in God, one redemption by God.... The Bible (and Qur'an) make it quite clear that there is only one God and that one's response to God is either faithfulness or infidelity,"[46] not Judaism or Christianity, Islam or Hinduism.

The inclusive sense of uniqueness, one fully consistent with the celebration of particularities, is based on the conviction that all seek faithfulness, but paths are particular. Because all seek faithfulness, the convergence of religions provides the opportunity for the enrichment of people on many paths through sharing clues about practicing holy life.

It is worth noting that among the Western, monotheistic religions, Judaism alone embraces inclusive uniqueness, rather than absolutism or an exclusive notion of uniqueness. It alone, as Krister Stendahl says, has no "extra ecclesiam nulla salus"; it alone "accepted the humility of particularism, of trying to be a 'peculiar people.' "[47] "Judaism is . . . a revelatory religion . . . that at the same time doesn't think that everybody has to be a Jew in order to be acceptable to God."[48]

But what to make of the Jewish idea of the "chosen people"? It cannot, of course, mean "only we are beloved of God," for every Passover Seder today includes the reading from Exodus in which the Holy One remonstrates with the joyous children of Israel, who are celebrating the destruction of the Egyptian soldiers in the Red Sea: "But God said: 'My children lie drowned in the sea, and you would sing?' " The Jewish theological idea of chosenness, as Moran points out, must be understood by reference to the experience of vocation, not the claim of superiority based on exclusive uniqueness: "To have a vocation is to feel called to something; one does not so much choose a vocation as feel chosen."[49] To feel chosen to be faithful in this peculiar way, this inclusively unique way, is not a claim of superiority; it is an act of humility. "The way to avoid claiming superiority to other[s] is to emphasize . . . uniqueness."[50] Stendahl sums up the point: "Christians have often ridiculed if not demonized this particularism and described it as an arrogance claiming that Jews in their tribalism consider God only concerned with Israel. Far from it. . . . In a plural world there is great wisdom in the awareness that the revelation that has come to me through Scripture and tradition calls me to be faithful in a manner that does not include but excludes the obligation of proving all others wrong or inferior."[51] In other words, my people and I have been chosen to be faithful in this inclusively unique way. You and your people have been chosen to be faithful in another way.

Absolute Claims and Historic Christian Witness

Still the influence of an exclusive understanding of uniqueness persists. The fear of relativity haunts. The contemporary convergence of religions produces anxiety over the possibilities of syncretism. Some worry that radical pluralism and depth dialogue are not true to the claims made in the name of Jesus Christ about Christianity, that these developments are propelled to such a great extent by the desire for social harmony and credibility, that something essential in the historic, Christian witness is lost. In chapter 3 of this book, Christian readers especially will have to confront challenging reflection on the doctrine of Christ and interreligious reverence. It is good to entertain a credible critical view of certain features of pluralism and dialogue at this point.

The credibility of the critical view is established with mention of the name Schubert Ogden. Ogden has criticized many of the leading figures in Christian theology of religions, or what he calls "pluralist theology." Among those criticized are Gordon Kaufman, John Hick, and Rosemary Ruether. Though supportive of pluralism and dialogue, Ogden fears an accommodation that is not true to orthodox Christian belief, one that is not justified by the classic Christian sources. He writes: "Any theology that wishes to remain Christian, like the witness on which it reflects, must not only be credible in terms of our contemporary life but also appropriate in terms of normative Christian witness."[52] Ogden goes on to criticize many of the contributors to John Hick and Paul Knitter's influential collection, *The Myth of Christian Uniqueness*: Kaufman, for uncritical historical consciousness; Ruether, for captivity to a feminist ideology; and Hick, for proposing the non sequitur that the evolution from exclusivism through inclusivism to pluralism is providential. Ogden challenges the bases set out earlier in this chapter as well. He is not persuaded that common human experience today invalidates Christian claims, nor is he persuaded by an argument based on who we think the Holy One is, because we Christians also bear witness throughout the centuries that the Holy One is definitively revealed in Jesus Christ.

It is clear that Ogden's critique is based on his concern that radical pluralism is motivated chiefly by the desire for social harmony. This is understandable, because there is a vigorous body of opinion within the theology of religions that identifies social justice and the capacity to join in common action across religious lines as the essential reason and rationale for interreligious convergence. As a discussion later in this chapter will make clear, I think it is wrong to give this motive the central place, even though the sorry history of violence and hatred between religions often leads to immobility and paralysis in the face of profound human suffering. But I also reject Ogden's implication that radical pluralism and depth dialogue are the fruits of modern accommodation, developments more beholden to multiculturalism than classical Christian understandings.

Returning to the critique of religion, consider that the theological basis of the critique (distinguished from the secular reductionist critique based on rationalism) is no less basic to Jewish and Chris-

tian self-understanding than what Tillich called the "prophetic
principle." The prophetic principle is based on the proposition
that only God is God. On the basis of the principle, as Tillich
argued, "there is a point at which...religion itself loses its importance."[53] That only God is God is a principle that "transcends
every particular religion and makes the exclusiveness of any particular religion conditional."[54] And "in the depth of every living
religion...that to which it points breaks through its particularity,
elevating it to a spiritual freedom and with it to a vision of the
spiritual presence in other expressions of the ultimate meaning of
man's existence."[55]

Ogden's criticism, though thoughtful, breaks down on the
strength of the basic belief that God is love. If what Kaufman
calls the "categorical pattern" of a religion — in this case Christianity, its "multiplicity of...institutions, practices and liturgies...
philosophies, theologies and myths" — or has been "destructive,
damaging or oppressive to humans and therefore evil,"[56] it must
fall because God is love! We will not chalk up reform to social
accommodation, to efforts to be nice with Christian orthodoxy
on the table as a bargaining chip. Like Saint Paul we insist that
"Christian witness" cannot be preserved at the price of idolatrous
absolutism. Krister Stendahl makes clear that for all his occasional
expressions of exasperation with other Jews, there is no warrant
in Paul's writings for absolutism or arrogant universalism. In Romans 11:25 Paul counsels, "Do not be wise in your own conceit."
In 1 Corinthians 4:4ff. he says, "It is the Lord who judges," and
later in that letter (13:5), he teaches, "Agape...does not seek its
own."[57]

Radical religious pluralism and depth interreligious dialogue are
genuine movements of the Holy Spirit. They spring from real religious faithfulness and, as Stendahl says, from knowledge of a secret
that the Jews know that we Christians should go and ask them
about: "The secret is quite simply this, that universalism is the ultimate arrogance in the realm of religion. It is by definition and
unavoidably spiritual colonialism and spiritual imperialism."[58]

Fundamentalism

Fundamentalism is a full-blown expression of idolatrous absolutism. It is the antithesis in our time of genuine religious pluralism,
depth dialogue, and the mutual reverence and enrichment that flow
from these engagements and attitudes. This startling, volatile, and

broadscale cultural, political, and religious movement — spread across the face of the globe, involving powerful and large minorities in virtually every religion — is by definition a movement to fortify lines of separation from the others, insisting on completely distinctive identity. Fundamentalist cohorts in every religion demonize those outside the true religion, fear and loathe what they take to be syncretism, and employ selective interpretation of the texts and beliefs of the past in a manner designed to demonstrate their own absolute and exclusive claims to faithfulness.

Regarding the separatist impulse of fundamentalists, Martin Marty and Scott Appleby write: "Fundamentalism appears as a strategy, or set of strategies, by which beleaguered believers attempt to preserve their distinctive identity as a people or a group ... [by] fend[ing] off outsiders who threaten to draw believers into a syncretistic, areligious or irreligious cultural milieu."[59]

The necessary demonization of those outside the pale, as well as coreligionists who are perceived as faithless accommodationists within, is a function of the social-psychological dynamics to which fundamentalists are in thrall. Of this feature of the movement, Patrick Arnold writes: "Psychological studies describe its [fundamentalism's] strongest adherents as 'authoritarian personalities': individuals who feel threatened in a world of conspiring evil forces, who think in simplistic and stereotypical terms and who are attracted to authoritarian and moralistic answers to their problems."[60] "Fundamentalists," Marty and Appleby point out, therefore "set and maintain boundaries...[and] identify and mythologize their enemies."[61]

(In the context of the United States, the rise of the Christian Right — its cynical coalition with unethical and even violent elements within the culture, and its exceptionally sophisticated apparatus for gaining power through electoral activity and political action committees — poses a threat not only to interreligious reconciliation but to civil liberties and domestic tranquility for Jews and others perceived as both other and demons.[62] Here, however, a distinction must be made between conservatives, for example, and some evangelical Protestants and fundamentalists. Arnold writes of the difference: "Conservatism may be described broadly as a philosophy that values established, traditional ideas and practices, and seeks to preserve a given community's historical heritage — especially in times of social change."[63] Though the line is somewhat permeable, in this country so-called moderate or progressive evangelical Protestants, though less fulsomely engaged in interreligious dialogue, are often active agents of social harmony and fervent advocates of civil liberties within the framework of their essential religious conservatism.)

Along with their separatism, their efforts to forge a distinct identity, and their identification of enemies within and without, fundamentalists also engage in "the selective retrieval of doctrine, beliefs of a sacred past."[64] Theirs is "captivity by what might be called the 'myth of the Golden Age.' Fleeing from the exaggerated evils of contemporary society, they seek the glorious days of their religious founders, an imaginary past edited of its actual errors."[65]

This feature of fundamentalism — selective and editorialized retrieval of meanings from ancient texts and doctrinal traditions — is as problematic for religious pluralism as the separatist and demonizing elements of the movement. As noted in the discussion in chapter 1 of classic orthodox interpretation of events and texts of the Christian past, interpretations that are exclusive, absolute, and triumphalist are most popular with the larger number of Christians, including, of course, fundamentalist Christians. Such interpretation is "golden; it does not admit of new meaning; it is calcified." Thus, for the fundamentalist Christian there is no salvation except through Jesus Christ. (Indeed, Robert Wuthnow and Matthew P. Lawson report that in a 1992 poll, 44 percent of adults in the United States affirm that salvation comes only through Jesus Christ.)[66] Jews rejected Christ; Paul turned his back on Judaism; Peter was the first pope (a Catholic variation); and so on. It is because of the extraordinary, negative power of such ahistorical, erroneous, but forcefully held convictions about the meaning of the texts and traditions of the religious past that Charles Davis links the spirit of religious pluralism to the capacity to be faithful without becoming obsessive about a "fixed content" of interpretation of the meanings of the religious past. He writes: "A post-conventional or universalistic religious identity is . . . realized when people, belonging to a religious tradition, but not tied to its fixed contents and forms, engage as free, autonomous persons in a process of unrestricted and unconstrained communication with others."[67]

Clearly the spirit of fundamentalism is the opposite of the spirit of religious liberalism. And religious pluralism and depth dialogue in our time are the products of the liberal spirit. Every factor noted thus far in this and the previous chapter that promotes interreligious reverence and mutual enrichment emerges from the genuine spirit of religious liberalism. Arnold points to the antipathy between fundamentalism and liberalism, noting that fundamentalists often save their greatest rage for "co-religionists who appear to have adapted all too well to modernity [a synonym for liberalism] through unholy compromise."[68] Against fundamentalism, a firm defense of religious liberalism, or the modern spirit in religion, must be made.

The modern or liberal impulse is the source for grounding religious loyalties in continuing human experience, subjecting inherited traditions of interpretation of religious beliefs to historical analysis, exploring the context of sacred texts, and rejecting the imposition of absolute interpretations by authoritarian and triumphalist ecclesiastical powers, in favor of freedom, open inquiry, and relativity (in the sense of openness to change and growth). In his exceptional study of models of theology,[69] David Tracy identifies these as the fruits of theological liberalism but also notes the fault line of this modern mentality in religious thinking. Theological work serves real faithfulness (reverencing what is holy, yearning for what is good, and being compassionate, grateful, and joyous) when its explanations of experiences of faithfulness take full account of both inherited message and contemporary situation. As a movement within the broader cultural epoch of modernity, liberal Christian theology has not, as a matter of historical fact, perfectly balanced the claims of both traditions (message) and contemporary experiences (situation). A larger theme of modernity, its rejection of traditional authority, easily spills over and influences liberal theological thinking. This can lead to insufficient care for past formulations. Or the liberal theologian, however ingenuous, may not always exercise the courage needed to acknowledge honestly that some traditional formulas of belief are simply evil, that they diminish people, and project what Martin Buber called an "oh so burdened" image of God.

For Tracy, the self-correcting expression of the liberal spirit in religion and in theology is "revisionism." The revisionist Christian theologian tries to help construe faithfulness with equal measures of appreciation and critical assessment of both inherited message and contemporary experience. Such a perspective allows people who are deeply and lovingly rooted in a religious path to engage with generosity and courage in interreligious dialogue, depth dialogue that actually changes people.

Peter Berger also has a helpful analysis and appreciation of liberalism. For him, one of the elements of the liberal spirit is what he calls "mellowness." Berger acknowledges that liberal mellowness is more likely to be practiced in periods of "relative normalcy."[70] In periods of personal and social crises, such as contemporary fundamentalists find themselves in, "fanaticisms tend to be more plausible."[71] But Berger makes a very telling observation about religious fanaticism, one wholly applicable to the discussion of contemporary fundamentalists. The remark addresses whether fanaticism (separatism, absolutism, the demonization of the other, the refusal of interreligious reverence) can actually survive experiencing the Holy One in one's life, whether religious liberalism may not be founded on a theophany rather than on disloyalty and accommodation: "One could even suggest that those who have truly encountered the 'reality of the unseen' can *afford* [Berger's emphasis] the mellowness of Liberality, both in their lives and in their thinking."[72] "Piety," Berger says, surely "requires certainty, but not fanaticism."[73]

Affirming the liberal impulse in religion, we should also label fundamentalism what it is: "immature religion." The term comes from the research of a preeminent social psychologist of religion, Gordon Allport. His study of mature and immature religion is itself influenced by the liberal spirit, especially the thought of Paul Tillich.

During a long career in which themes such as prejudice and the relationship of religion to both personality and prejudice were among his major preoccupations, Allport evolved the idea of "the Religion of Maturity." At every turn his research recommended to him the distinction between such religious attitudes and those of immature religion. He found the former open to experience, consistent with critical thinking, autonomous in motive, satisfying, integrative, and capable of growth and change. For Allport, immature religious attitudes are hostile, fearful, compulsive, archaic, and fanatical.

The six characteristics of "the religion of maturity," developed in his work *The Individual and His Religion*, are sketched below.[74]

1. *Differentiated,* by which Allport means the religiousness is rich, complex, and related to a multiplicity of interests and capable of sustaining a critical perspective. Failing this, immature religiosity is founded on "hostility, anxiety...[and] prejudice."

2. *Dynamic,* by which Allport means the religiousness is autonomous, not individualistic but emerging from one's internal-

ized "motivation power." Failing this, immature religiosity is "steered exclusively by impulse, fear . . . [and] . . . wish."

3. *Consistency,* by which Allport means the religiousness provides "a steady, persistent influence." Failing this, immature religiosity is "very likely to raise moral storms."

4. *Comprehensive,* by which Allport means religiousness that is satisfying and tolerant. Failing this, immature religiosity is compulsive and intolerant. Allport writes of this feature, "The religion of maturity makes the affirmation 'God is,' but only the religion of immaturity will insist 'God is precisely what I say He is. . . .' "

5. *Integral,* by which Allport means something quite specific: mature religiousness is "capable of balancing archaic expression and the modern mentality." Immature religiosity is not.

6. *Heuristic,* by which Allport means religiousness that can hold beliefs tentatively without loss of religious resolve. He writes: "It is characteristic of the mature mind that it can act wholeheartedly even without absolute certainty." In contrast, immature religion is fanatical. Religious fundamentalism is immature.

Further Theology of Religions

Though theological ideas are present thus far, the argument for interreligious reverence and an end to religiously inspired xenophobia will be enriched by a more focused assessment of the place of theological work in supporting such reverence and by further discussion on the work of theologians working in this field or whose reflection is relevant to it.

Writing in 1990, David Tracy says, "It is difficult to understand how any serious theologian in any tradition would not admit the challenge to ordinary theology of the issue of religious pluralism."[75] The tone of mild exasperation, the fact that the statement is made, suggests that not enough has changed among the members of the guild of theologians since 1971, when Robley Whitson wrote his masterful work, *The Coming Convergence of World Religions.* In that book, Whitson said: "A test of theological perception into the issue of unity can be made of Christian theologians by examining the manner in which they approach the relationship between Christianity and other religious traditions. A certain benignity is usually present, but it is very difficult to find much more. With rarest of exceptions, theologians do not seem ill at ease with their lack of knowledge of non-Christian religious traditions."[76]

The indifference of so many Christian theologians — and theologians in other religious communities — to religious pluralism is related to the function theological work most often serves within a religion. When based on an "orthodox model,"[77] theological expression intends to make clear and compelling the truth of belief statements already adopted by authoritative spokespeople (usually spokesmen) within institutional religion. In its neoorthodox variant, the intention is much the same, though these theologians will take more care than their orthodox counterparts to be compelling, to couch apologetics in existentially evocative terms. These are the two most common modes of theological work within institutional religion. Most traditionally socialized members respond to these kinds of expressions. Because the truths these theologians seek to advance usually trace their formulation to a time when what today is called religious pluralism was called flirting with false religion, and what today is called depth dialogue was then called a near occasion of sin (putting oneself in a situation in which one's "faith" might be tested beyond endurance), there is little to be expected from such theological work.

A simply liberal (rather than revisionist-liberal) mode of theological work can often be relativistic in a negative sense; its centrifugal tendency is to become "radical," by definition indifferent or hostile to traditional formulations. Such modes of theological work only cause orthodox and neoorthodox theologians and their constituencies, both hierarchies and "the people," to dig in their heels. Again theological discourse on religious pluralism is not advanced.

It is to reconstructed liberal theologians (revisionist in the sense that Tracy employs the term) and to their work that we must look for rich, substantial study and conversation about the relationship between interreligious encounter and the adequacy of our notion of the Holy One, our responsiveness to grace in common human experience, and our collaborative action to end absolutism, exclusivism, and separation. But in many religions, these theologians are an embattled minority. In Catholic Christianity, for example, the influence of the present "restorationist" papacy is nothing less than quasi-fundamentalist, and genuinely revisionist theologians, work-

ing in many fields including the theology of religions, are subject
to banning.

Still, when theological study and conversation are open to
historical evidence, mindful of traditions, and responsive to contemporary experience, and when they emerge from the theologian's
spirituality, theology can be a profound tool of human faithfulness. And it can be a rich resource for all the religious education
the community sponsors, including education for interreligious
convergence.

Consider first, from what Tracy calls "general theology," the
idea that theological thinking is directed at life, that it is not primarily a tool of traditionalism,[78] an instrument of institutional
conformity, a cudgel for imposing orthodoxy. In this spirit, Elizabeth Johnson, writing of theology itself, says: "Neither abstract
in content nor neutral in its effects, speaking about God sums up,
unifies and expresses a faith community's sense of ultimate mystery, the world view and expectations devolving from this and the
concomitant orientation of human life and devotion."[79]

Johnson's view is bolstered by that of Wilfred Cantwell Smith.
He distinguishes beliefs from faith and asserts: "Faith is not an entity. It is, rather the adjectival quality of a person's living in terms
of transcendence."[80]

And from Rabbi Heschel we learn that theology "must lay bare
what is involved in religious existence.... [It] must recover the
situations which both precede and correspond to the theological
formulations... [that] the primary issue of theology is pretheological; it is the total situation of man and his attitudes toward life and
the world."[81]

Theology evoking "ultimate mystery," theology encouraging
transcendence, theology construing the depths of religious existence — reverent life, life lived yearning for what is good, a life
of compassion, gratefulness, and joy — this is theology at the
service of interreligious convergence, genuine religious pluralism,
depth dialogue. Here the person thinking theologically escapes "religion" in the sense given to the word at the beginning of this
chapter. Aided by theological thinking and conversation, we escape
absolutism, exclusivism, separation, prejudice, and violence.

Turning again to some theological work on the implications
of religious pluralism for both the healthy self-understanding of
people in all religions and interreligious enrichment, notice should
be made of the work of Paul Knitter. Writing from a Catholic perspective, Knitter explains that historic Catholic tradition has from

its beginning at least rejected a theological understanding that excludes all but Christians from salvation. Knitter characterizes this Catholic tradition as "many ways, one norm." I will examine the Catholic perspective more fully later in this chapter. The idea of inclusion, wedged between exclusion and full-blown pluralism, is also central to the discussion in chapter 3 of religious pluralism and the doctrine of Christ. For now, it is sufficient to note Knitter's observation that Catholic history is a "teeter-tottering between two fundamental beliefs: God's universal love and desire to save and the necessity of the Church for salvation."[82] Knitter points out that as early as the Ecumenical Council of Arles in 473 C.E., the church condemned the idea that "Christ, Our Lord and Savior, did not undergo death for the salvation of all peoples... [that God] does not wish anyone to perish."[83] This position is not firm grounding for the radical religious pluralism for which we yearn. But it is an important theological wedge leading us to accept the idea that the Holy One lives in all people who seek holiness.

Also a Catholic theologian but writing from the perspective of philosophical theology, David Tracy has increasingly lent his prodigious insight to clarifying the relationship between interreligious dialogue and human knowing. As noted above, Tracy considers it virtually impossible to engage in theological study and discourse apart from honoring religious pluralism. He asserts further that Christian theological work is meaningless unless the Holocaust is confronted honestly. Tracy's position is based on the epistemological assertion that "to understand is to understand differently."[84] Reason, in the broad sense of human beings bringing all their resources of thought and feeling to bear on understanding, is "reason-as-dialogue."[85] It is worth noting that for all his originality and depth of learning, Tracy began his theological work under the guidance of Bernard Lonergan, who tells us, as noted above, "that it is through knowledge and appreciation of others that we come to know ourselves and to fill out and refine our apprehension of values."

Writing from a liberal Protestant perspective, Langdon Gilkey contributes a number of rich and novel points to theological clarification of the importance of pluralism and dialogue. His explanation of the rise of these values as related to the evolving priority of love over "defense of the faith" was noted earlier. Gilkey has also contributed the important insight that though providential developments leading to greater reverence for paths of holiness other than one's own owe much to the spirit of liberalism, which

relativizes religion and doctrine in the face of historical development, such affirmation is also present in neoorthodox Christianity.
One would not expect to find in traditional Christian piety this
implicit broadening of the base for embracing religious pluralism. But as Gilkey points out, "Participants in the neo-orthodox
movement continued with only a few qualifications, the ecumenical
spirit . . . [because] they accepted the relativity of doctrines, confes-
sions and laws — the realm of 'religion' in Barth's sense — and also
they seconded the priority of love over the demands of doctrinal
and legal exactness. . . . They recognized their own fallibility."[86]

Gilkey also makes the point that the acknowledgment of the
"rough parity" of religions and the rejection of triumphalism
echoes a broader cultural movement: "Western culture has recently
undergone precisely this same shift: from a position of clear superiority to one of rough parity."[87] Though Schubert Ogden might
argue that such a development is not linked intrinsically to "Christian witness," others might say that radical religious pluralism and
expanding depth dialogue are inevitable because "all the world
proclaims the Holy One."

This survey of selected features of theology of religions should
not close without noting the extent to which feminist theological
study and conversation implicitly and explicitly support and enrich
theological reflection on interreligious convergence and reverence.
Whether Christian feminist theologians are in explicit conversation with those in other religions or not, their work profoundly
influences this conversation. The reason for this is that feminist
theological thinking, among other things, is by definition reflection on the reality and destructiveness of exclusion, absolutism,
authoritarianism, subordination, and violence. It is theological
thinking pervaded with the demand that voices that have been
silenced be heard, that the experiences of those who have been
declared "other" be taken account of. Though the ethical focus of such theological thinking must continue to center, though
not exclusively so, on women, the defining concerns of feminist theological thinking are precisely the concerns of theology of
religions.

Consider, first, Elizabeth Johnson's criticism of the limitations
and distortions of classical God-talk. Though sacred texts are ap-
pealed to, the classical language is exclusive, but the sacred texts
contain many images of the Holy One. Though the mystery of the
Holy One proliferates in the sacred texts, classical language insists
on a literal God, our God, no one else's.[88]

When Dorothee Soelle rejects an idolatrous God-image framed in "male-dominated" culture, she is rejecting a "God" in whose image neither women nor people in "other" religions, are revered: "As a woman I have to ask why it is that human beings honor a God whose most important attribute is power, whose prime need is to subjugate, whose greatest fear is equality.... Why should we honor and love a being that does not transcend but only affirms the moral level of our male-dominated culture?"[89]

And when Rosemary Radford Ruether articulates the "critical principle" and the "prophetic principle" of feminist theology, she is giving expression to loyalties and commitments in the face of which neither misogyny nor religious triumphalism can stand:

Critical Principle: "Whatever denies, diminishes, or distorts the full humanity of women is, therefore, appraised as not redemptive. ...Whatever diminishes or distorts the full humanity of women must be presumed not to reflect the divine."

Prophetic Principle: "A rejection of every elevation of one social group against others as image and agent of God, every use of God to justify domination and subjugation."[90]

The Theological and Religious Purpose of Dialogue

There is one trend in contemporary theology of religions that though noble in purpose is shortsighted and could undermine the most profound result of embracing religious pluralism and engaging in interreligious dialogue. This trend is to identify the basic purpose of dialogue with forging solidarity in action for justice and peace.

Paul Knitter, in an essay entitled "A Liberation Theology of Religions," goes so far as to argue that the basic purpose of dialogue is mutual support for the "preferential option for the poor."[91] But the signature statement of this stance comes from Harvey Cox, who writes: "The whole meaning of the discussion among people from different religious traditions...the purpose of the conversation...becomes neither an end in its self nor a strictly religious [sic] quest, but a step in the anticipation of God's justice."[92]

One feels a certain self-consciousness in rejecting the idea that justice is the essential goal of interreligious dialogue. The end of religious wars and the strength interreligious solidarity affords to action for justice (*tikkun olam,* "healing the world") are noble aspirations on which to found commitment to religious dialogue and pluralism. But they are not yet the primordial basis for such commitments. The deepest expression of human hubris and the greatest source of human corruption and evil is to believe that the Holy One is mine and not yours, that the Holy One prefers my people to your people. Some values have to be embraced indirectly. First, in the felicitous phrase of Krister Stendahl, there must be "Holy Envy," conversion to the perspective that the Source really embraces you and your people: Holy Envy occurs "when we recognize something in another tradition that is beautiful but is not ours, nor should we grab it or claim it. . . . Holy envy rejoices in the beauty of the others."[93] Then, in our hearts' truly finding the other beautiful, there will be no hesitation to act when the beauty of any child of God is despoiled. But to make the common political agenda the basis of dialogue is to risk achieving less than full compassion. Thus David Tracy writes: "The praxis of interreligious dialogue itself, I believe, does not merely bear a 'religious dimension.' It is a religious experience."[94]

Heschel and Stendahl: Theology and Exegesis Serving Interreligious Reverence

I want to conclude this section, reviewing examples of theological work supporting religious pluralism and interreligious dialogue, by dwelling at some length on the work of two giants in the movement of reverence among peoples on different paths of holiness. These two are themselves men of great reverence and holiness. They are the late Jewish theologian and philosopher, Rabbi Abraham Joshua Heschel, and the distinguished Lutheran Scripture scholar, Bishop Krister Stendahl. Stendahl's work in biblical exegesis[95] and Heschel's work on theological method are powerful intellectual tools for the healing of religious xenophobia.

Chapter 1 and earlier sections of this chapter contain examples of the importance of Scripture scholarship for promoting religious pluralism and interreligious dialogue, examples of how such scholarly inquiry can disabuse members of religions influenced by exclusivism, prejudice, and triumphalism of an authoritative scriptural basis for such attitudes. Few figures have played as important and effective a role as Krister Stendahl in bringing the erudition of scriptural scholarship to the service of religious pluralism and interreligious dialogue. As pastor and scholar, teacher and dean of Harvard Divinity school, as bishop of Stockholm, in writing and lecturing (but in a special, challenging, nurturing and whimsical way, quietly — or better, privately — as mentor), Stendahl has occupied and continues to occupy a central place. One more example of his scholarly contribution will serve to make the point.

In an essay with a typically droll title, "From God's Perspective We Are All Minorities," Stendahl dismisses the idea that there is any warrant for religious triumphalism, in this case, specifically that there is justification for Christian theological anti-Judaism in Christian Scripture. He tackles three texts that have been interpreted as the bedrock of Christian absolutism, "Christian colonialism," as he calls it. And in addition, he brings to the service of interreligious reverence a contextual interpretation of one of the most beloved and appealing texts of Christian Scripture.

The first text, on the basis of which Christian exclusivism has traditionally been justified, is Acts 4:12, in which Peter makes the famous reference to "no other name," having healed in the name of Jesus in whose name alone is salvation. The second text is John 14:6: "I am the way, the truth, and the life. No one comes to the Father except through me." And the third text is part of the "missionary discourse" in the Gospel of Matthew, in which Jesus is depicted as saying, "Go therefore and make disciples of all nations" (Matthew 28:19). Of each text, Stendahl notes, "Words like that grow legs and walk out of their context."[96] The Matthian text will be considered first. In the spirit of Christian absolutism and universalism, the text becomes an engine for Christian missionary effort down the centuries. First, all are excluded who do not hear and accept that salvation is in the Christ, Jesus. In later centuries, inclusion, the possibility of salvation, is admitted but still this is only through the saving work of God in Christ. The way this missionary impulse fuels the often violent effort to convert Jews was noted in chapter 1. At the very least, this interpretation of the meaning of Jesus' charge to make disciples of all nations makes it impossible to fully embrace religious pluralism and interreligious dialogue that takes seriously the presence of the Holy One and the possibility that people on other religious paths might be holy. But Stendahl notes that taken in context, read in the light of the whole text of Matthew, this simply cannot be the meaning of the missionary discourse, for "Matthew is strictly for Israel," as the words of Jesus, recorded earlier in this Gospel make clear: "Do not go to any Gentiles ... " (Matthew 10:5).[97] What we see in this text is not a clarion call for one, universal, absolute, and Christian religion, but a call to spread the Christian interpretation of the proper path of Judaism. Like the texts of the Gospel of John as exegeted by Daniel Harrington (noted in chapter 1), the missionary discourse in Matthew "should be viewed against this background ... the rival claims among Jews to carry on the

tradition of Judaism." But Stendahl notes, "Once that structure
of religion came into the hands of Christianity and Islam, it was
coupled with universalism in such a manner that no one could be
acceptable to God who did not think and believe as Christians and
Muslims think and believe."[98]

With reference to Peter's pronouncement that there is "no other
name" through which there is salvation, which is to say, healing,
Stendahl points out that Peter makes a confessional statement responding to the accusation that he is a magician with his own
powers. Stendahl calls confessional language "caressing language
...express[ing]...devotion with abandon and joy."[99] Here is a
deeply personal and emotional confession of devotion — made in
the context of the accusation that Peter, who has been instrumental in a cure, is performing a miracle in his own name — and it
becomes a classic, exclusivist text of Christian Scripture. Words
grow legs, indeed! Stendahl's contextualizing of the text from John
follows a line similar to his work with the text in Acts. Here in
Jesus' farewell speech, in response to Thomas's heartfelt expression
of anxiety and confusion and his fear of being left bereft and losing his way, Jesus says to his beloved friends, "I am the way.... "
Stendahl rejects "tak[ing]...a passage from the most intimate and
tender conversation with the most intimate and closest circle of
disciples, from a context in which their hearts are full of forebod-
ing" and in which Jesus consoles them, and making it a text of
exclusion and absolutism.[100]

Finally, there is chapter 13 of the first letter of Paul to the
Corinthians, the magnificent ode to love and the works of love. Its
soaring poetry is well known: "Love is patient; love is kind. Love
is not jealous or boastful; it is not arrogant or rude. Love does not
insist on its own way," and so forth. Placed in context by Stendahl, this text is the anthem for interreligious reverence and depth
dialogue. This passage is not, in the first instance, about romantic
love; neither is it about charity and love in general. Paul writes this
against the backdrop of deep, angry, bitter religious dispute. This
text is a prescription for what must characterize those engaged in
religious differences. "The ode to love in First Corinthians is not
speaking about love in general but is Paul's solution to the problem of how diversity can be an asset instead of a liability."[101] If
Paul's paean to the primacy of love were to become the charter
document of interreligious relations, then all Christians would find
a way, as Stendahl has "to sing my song to Jesus with abandon
without telling negative stories about others."[102]

The late Rabbi Abraham Joshua Heschel (d. 1972) among other accomplishments was arguably the greatest single figure in twentieth-century interreligious conversation, convergence, and mutual reverence. A giant of philosophy and theology, a theologian of extraordinary poetic gifts, a master of Jewish mysticism, Heschel was, as well, in mid-twentieth-century United States, one of the leading figures in movements of peace and justice. On a world scale, he was one of the most important ecumenical figures of our times and exercised enormous influence in the Catholic Church's repudiation of centuries of official anti-Jewish teaching.[103]

Like many great theologians in many traditions before him and since, one of the issues included in Rabbi Heschel's ubiquitous range of interests was the role theology plays, or fails to play, in promoting faithful life, holy life. The concern is implicit in a classic definition of theology offered by Saint Anselm in the twelfth century, that theology is "faith seeking understanding," *fides quaerens intellectum*. Faithfulness is occurring; reverent response to the Holy One, compassionate engagement with others, takes place under the influence of grace, internally and communally, in the pattern of ordinary life. We seek at a point in the dynamic path of our lives to construe what is occurring: how to be faithful, how to form a faithful people. The work of construal, of expression, is theology. But theology, especially the theology in which experts in theology engage and the theological formulations that are available to the hierarchies, is a noble servant but a dangerous master. The tendency, in some religions more than others, is to substitute formula orthodoxy, the propositions of belief, for faithful life. Criticizing this tendency, Gustavo Gutiérrez, the great Peruvian theologian of liberation, says that theology, like philosophy for Hegel, must come out only in the evening. First, in the daytime, there is real justice and charity; the silence of contemplation and of *praxis;* transforming, which is to say faithful, living.[104] Gutiérrez borrows a phrase from Bernard of Clairvaux, insisting that to be faithful we must "drink from our own wells," pay attention to the opportunities, invitations, and challenges to live holy lives here and now, in present experience, in this place where we find ourselves.[105]

David Tracy also addresses this problem of theology in the context of the history of Christianity. He speaks of it as the separation of theology and spirituality: "I think that theology will be better off the more that theologians attempt to recover a relationship to traditions of spirituality and thus undo the separation of theology and spirituality that developed after medieval scholasticism.

...Unfortunately, that once helpful distinction became a fatal separation, one that intensified in the ever wider split between theory and practice in most modern thought. Surely, an absolutely crucial part of the undoing of that separation would be, in theology, spiritual attentiveness to the presence of God in all of life, including theological thought."[106]

Rabbi Heschel's way of speaking of theology as a servant of faithfulness is to distinguish "theology" and "depth theology": "The theme of theology is the content of believing; the theme of depth theology is the act of believing.... Theology declares, depth theology evokes.... Theology demands believing and obedience; depth theology hopes for responding and appreciation. Theology deals with permanent facts; depth theology deals with moments. ...Theology is like sculpture, depth theology like music. Theology is in books; depth theology is in the hearts. The former is doctrine, the latter is events."[107]

In many ways Heschel's notion of "depth theology" is akin to Amos Wilder's famous idea of "theopoetics." For Wilder, "Before the message there must be the vision, before the sermon, the hymn, before the prose the poem."[108] In the same spirit, Heschel says, "Depth theology seeks to meet the person in moments in which the whole person is involved, in moments which are affected by all a person thinks, feels, and acts.... Man must use a language which is compatible with his sense of the ineffable."[109]

Still Heschel acknowledges the necessary interplay between theology and depth theology, as if the evocative power and ecstasy — the enthusiasm — of depth theology, must be tempered by the stability of belief expressed through more conventional theological formulation. The interplay is similar to that which Heschel sheds light on in his analysis of the dialectical relationship in Judaism between the enthusiasm of Rabbi Israel, the Baal Shem Tov (ca. 1690–1760 C.E.), and the relative sobriety of Reb Menehem Mendl, the Kotzker (1787–1859 C.E.). The Baal Shem Tov, Heschel says, is the Song of Songs; the Kotzker is Ecclesiastes. The one focused on ecstasy and poetry, teaching the near presence of the Holy One, the other preached contrition and judgment.[110]

In the case of theology and depth theology, as in the case of the appreciative contrasting of the Baal Shem Tov and the Kotzker, it is clear where Heschel's greater sympathies lie. It is in the priority of depth theology that the humility of religions lies and under its influence that we avoid idolatry and exclusivism: "Theologies divide us; depth theology unites us.... Depth theology warns us against intellectual self-righteousness, against self-certainty and smugness. It insists upon the inadequacy of our faith."[111]

Finally, depth theology is religious expression that emerges from prayer: "You will not enter the gates of religion through the doors of speech. The way to God is through the depths of the soul.... There is only one legitimate form of religious expression: prayer."[112]

Theological language that flows from gentle but firm effort to practice holiness will never result in smug and violent universalism, absolutism, and exclusivism. The theologian, and all of us thinking and speaking theologically, whose expression arises from such purity of heart, must embrace radical religious pluralism and depth interreligious dialogue.

The Catholic Spirit and Interreligious Reverence

There is a dynamic force in historical Christianity that should serve as a great impetus for interreligious dialogue, honoring religious pluralism, and revering the "other" paths and those on them. This force, or spirit, is what Rosemary Haughton calls "the Catholic Thing."[113]

It must seem odd, if not contradictory, to link a Catholic influence to the growth of interreligious reverence. Anyone familiar with the history of the Catholic Church knows its association with intolerance, religious war, forced conversion, and ecclesiastical and political authoritarianism. Some of these patterns are being reenacted in the institutional life of the church even today. But the claim that the Catholic Thing embraces interreligious reverence is not primarily about the "Catholic Church" but about the "Catholic Thing," for Haughton's reference to the Catholic Thing, or Langdon Gilkey's to the Catholic spirit, are about a force that is not identical with the Catholic Church, or the sum of the lives of people baptized Catholics. Not only is this force or spirit not identical with the Catholic Church; though it is partially embodied in the Church, it is at the same time partially negated by the social reality of the historical Catholic Church. The Catholic Thing is not limited to Catholics or to their social institutions. The Catholic Thing is present as a deep current of inspiration and motivation in the lives and social institutions of many Protestant Christians as well (just as the "Protestant Principle" — the "prophetic principle," as Tillich says — is available in the individual and common lives of

Catholic Christians). Therefore, invoking this Catholic spirit is in no way anti-ecumenical.

The premise of the Catholic spirit is this: the divine and the human, the Holy One and all that is born of divine love, are utterly, inextricably, related. The Holy One is available to all creation; all that emanates from the Holy One is good, participating, however fragile and broken the emulation, in the "image and likeness" of the Holy One. The essence of the Catholic spirit is classically expressed in Saint Irenaeus's third-century treatise *Against Heresies:* "God created all things in such a way that they are not outside Himself, as ignorant people falsely imagine. Rather, all creatures flow outward, but nevertheless remain within God."[114] In the same work, Irenaeus exegetes from the Book of Genesis the phrase "image and likeness," providing the classic Catholic theological formulation of the divine-human interplay. Irenaeus insists that while the "likeness" (*simultudo*) of the divine in creation is broken by sin, the "image" (*imago*) remains. Despite sin, as Richard P. McBrien says, the enduring Catholic intuition is "the presence of God to the knowing subject.... Nature includes the radical capacity for grace."[115]

In contrast, there is the defining spirit of Reformation Protestantism: that the human realm is utterly corrupted by sin, the image dashed, everything in need of the saving work of Christ, nothing in its nature still good. Calvin writes: "I assert that the best of their [believers'] performances are tarnished and corrupted by some carnal impurity and debased by a mixture of some alloy. ... There is not a single action performed by the saints which, if judged according to its intrinsic merit, does not justly deserve to be rewarded with shame.... The finite has no part of the infinite."[116]

Compare Calvin's words to those of Saint Francis of Assisi two centuries earlier in Francis's ecstatic poem of joy for the Holy One suffusing all creation, available in all of life:

> All praise be yours my Lord through all that you have made, and first my Lord, Brother Sun, who brings the day; and light you give us through him. How beautiful is he, how radiant in all his splendor. Of you, most High, he bears the likeness. All praise be yours, My Lord, through Sister Moon and stars; in the heavens you have made them bright and precious and fair.[117]

Lutheran theologian Helmut Thielicke explains the difference between the spirit of Catholicism and that of the Reformation, saying that in the former instance it is believed that we continue justified in our nature (*justitia originalis*). We need the saving grace of the Holy One in Christ Jesus, but we are not utterly corrupted in our nature. Thielicke says that in the Reform Protestant view, justification or salvation is participation in the "alien righteousness of Christ" (*justia aliena*), something outside our totally corrupted natures.[118]

In addition to Catholic theologian Rosemary Haughton, the American Baptist Langdon Gilkey has written of this Catholic spirit. Of it he says, "Catholicism has a continued experience unequaled in other forms of Western Christianity of the presence of God and of grace mediated through symbols to the entire course of ordinary human life... of transcendent mystery impinging continually on human existence."[119] Haughton's own designation of the Catholic Thing is that it is life lived in devotion to Sophia — wisdom available throughout all life, working from within, giving marvelous parties: "Wisdom, it is clear, is not simply a personification of human wisdom, or an aspect of God, but is God, active and original, creating and teaching. Her job is a kind of cosmic home-making, creating from within rather than from without.... Wisdom dwells in a people... and here she gives splendid parties to which all are invited."[120]

Both authors insist that this spirit is not identical to the Catholic Church. For example, Gilkey writes that while "Catholic life itself... reflects a freedom from moralistic prohibitions and judgements,... the official and objective structure of Catholicism still reflects an anti-natural, anti-sensual, moralistic and even ascetic view of general human existence."[121] Rosemary Haughton contrasts the Catholic Thing, the spirit of Sophia, with "Mother Church": "That domineering, occasionally smothering, always self-assured old lady ... with her vast compassion and her low estimate of human moral worth... [and her] lunatic tidiness that tries to legislate creation into some humanly controllable pattern."[122]

The utility of this Catholic spirit as an adequate basis from which to promote religious pluralism and engage in interreligious dialogue lies, in the words of Michael Himes summing up the spirit, in this: "God and creation are not in competition. That, if anything, we [Catholics] should have learned from the doctrine of the Incarnation."[123] And if God and creation are not in conflict, there can be no justification for conflict between members of different religions for God's affection. To paraphrase Gilkey and Haughton, the presence of God is mediated through symbols to the entire course of *everyone's* ordinary human life; transcendent mystery is impinging on *all* human existence. Sophia is at home to *all*, creating from within *all*.

The corollary of Catholic incarnationalism — that the Divine is the presupposition of the human, inhering in all humans, available to all humans — is that the humans, *all* the humans together, work together with one another in companionship with the Holy One in divine work. And that work is "worldly" work. Ecclesiastical work, the intramural work of religious institutions, is instrumental, not central; supportive, not exhaustive. The one work of *all* the humans together with the Holy One, what Jewish and Christian Scriptures call the "reign of God," is our most important work, and it is interreligious. The great, contemporary mystic of the Catholic spirit Pierre Teilhard de Chardin captures this dimension; he prays to the Holy One: "I love irresistibly all that your continuous help enables me to bring each day to reality. A thought, a material improvement, a harmony, a unique nuance of human love, the enchanting complexity of a smile or a glance, all these new beauties that appear for the first time, in me and around me, in the human face of the earth — I cherish them like children and cannot believe that they will die entirely in their flesh."[124] And in the same spirit, Haughton says, "What I regard as the theological basis of the Catholic enterprise is the attempt to carry out that job of loving everything on earth to the point where earth becomes heaven."[125] Thus, the false work of so much religion, work that separates and generates suspicion, the work of building up idols of religious institutions, is repudiated. And the Holy One, who is in all of us, calls us all — together — to this authentic religious work.

Karl Rahner and the Theological Basis of Interreligious Reverence

The preeminent twentieth-century father of the Catholic spirit, or enterprise, is Karl Rahner. His thought supplies an inescapable and rigorous Catholic rationale and demand to embrace pluralism and dialogue, to repudiate sectarian exclusiveness. "God's offer," Rahner tells us, "of himself belongs to all men.... [It is] an element in man's transcendental constitution."[126]

Together with Bernard Lonergan, Rahner's great work was to retrieve and extend the genius of Aquinas, what McBrien calls "the original thomistic intuition" regarding the interplay of nature and grace, the divine and human. Like Aquinas, Rahner locates the experience of the Holy One in human experience, embracing the modern "turn to the subject," which Rahner scholar William Dych characterizes as "the absolute openness of the human subject in its unlimited transcendence."[127]

All women and men are created open to the Holy One, possessing possibilities of transcendence because the Holy One's "offer of Himself" takes the form of what Rahner calls a "pre-grasp" (*vorgriff*), "a pre-conceptual, pre-grasp of infinite being."[128] In our most concrete, most immediate, existential situation, we are already, *all* of us, flooded with the Holy One. For this idea Rahner employs the concept of the "Supernatural-Existential" — "a conception," Dych says, "used to explain how it belongs to concrete human existence to be called to what transcends our existence, to life in God."[129] Rahner speaks of this condition movingly:

> Whether he is consciously aware of it or not, whether he is opened to this truth or suppresses it, man's whole spiritual and intellectual existence is oriented towards a holy mystery which is the basis of his being. This mystery is the inexplicit and unexpressed horizon which always encircles and upholds the small area of our everyday experience of knowing and acting, our knowledge of reality and our free action. It is our most fundamental, our most *natural* [my emphasis] condition.... We call this God.... In its capacity as the very ground of the individual absorbed in knowing and acting, the holy mystery we call God is at once what is most internal to ourselves and also what is furthest from our manipulation.... However hard and unsatisfactory it may be to interpret the deepest and most fundamental experience at the very bottom of our being, man does experience in his innermost history that this silent, infinitely distant holy mystery, which continually recalls him to the limits of his finitude and lays bare his guilt yet *bids him approach* [Rahner's emphasis]; the mystery enfolds him in an ultimate and radical love which commends itself to him as his salvation and as the real meaning of his existence.[130]

Commenting on Rahner's metaphor of God as "horizon," Dych makes a point that extends the significance of Rahner's work for interreligious convergence. Already we see that God is the "holy mystery," not the captive of a sect. Further, all women and men are grasped in their existential constitution by the Holy One and open to the infinite. In the Holy One "as horizon which ever recedes as we move through the finite," Dych tells us there are further grounds for humility and reverence for those on many paths of holiness; for within the horizon "there is always 'more' to be known, to be loved, to be lived."[131]

A final element in Rahner's thought recommends convergence, embrace of pluralism, humility in relations with the other. It lies in his discussion of the historicity or temporality of being, that is, in the idea that time is a defining — constitutive — element of humanness. If fundamentalism is timeless and ahistorical, supposing a past golden age when a static truth — our truth, *the* truth — was deposited, Catholic historical consciousness insists that what we are is a becoming, necessarily and essentially effected by the "other." In Rahner's words, we are constituted in our being by "time, world and history": "As subject man has not entered accidentally into this material and temporal world as into something that is ultimately foreign to him and contrary to his spiritual nature. Rather, the subject's self-alienation in the world is precisely the way in which the subject discovers himself and affirms himself in a definitive way. Time, world and history mediate the subject to himself."[132]

Conclusion

We are challenged to lay aside religious absolutism, exclusivism, prejudice, and violence, and to cultivate interreligious reverence, even while devotedly attending to the clues to holiness in the life of our religious communities. This is a call to hold ourselves to the discipline of reality, the discipline of the truth of things. In his work on interreligious theological discourse, David Tracy cites Paul Ricoeur's idea of "truth-as-manifestation." "The truth of religion," Tracy says, "is not that of strict coherence or empirical verification or falsification, but "like its nearest cousin, art, [the truth of religion] primordially is the truth of manifestation."[133]

What is manifest, what demands acquiescence, and with acquiescence an end to religious xenophobia is that many religious paths produce saints: "If we mean by a saint a person who is much further advanced than most of us in the transformation from self-centeredness to reality-centeredness, then I venture the proposition that each of the great religious traditions seems, so far as we can tell, to promote this transformation in one form or another to about the same extent."[134]

All that is required to replace hatred with love and triumphalism with humility in interreligious relations is attentiveness to the saints among "them" and not only among "us." As Moran says, "If the language we speak is deeply rooted in the concrete realities of personal and communal experience, then we might be able to hear what others' uniqueness has to offer."[135] Then we will discover, as Paul Knitter writes, that "pluralism does not result simply from the limitations of the human mind to 'get it all together.' Rather, pluralism seems to be of the very stuff of reality, the way things are, the way they function.... Reality is essentially pluriform: complex, rich, intricate, mysterious."[136]

Having learned this, we will all be enriched. The beauty and power of religious particularity will not be lost, but celebrated across the lines of religion, confirming people on many paths of holiness and enriching all. For, as Walter Brueggemann says, "Reality is transactional.... Each receives life from our risk-evoking neighbor...."[137] In the absence of interreligious reverence, emerging from depth dialogue, all are diminished, for "when the transaction ceases to operate, when it dysfunctions or gives up on respect, dignity, and openness, both parties...are deeply diminished, placed under threat and driven to brutality."[138]

For Christians especially, heirs, as Rahner notes, to a tradition of absolutism, rooted in the doctrine of Christ which makes commitment to radical pluralism so problematic, the question becomes, to repeat Krister Stendahl's wonderful phrase, "how to sing my song to Jesus with abandon without telling negative stories about others."[139] It is to the doctrine of Christ, Christology, that we turn in chapter 3.

Chapter Three

Christology and Interreligious Reverence

A Personal Preface

David Tracy writes that "to hear again the story of Jesus, the Christ" is something that perhaps "we owe at least to the memories of our ancestors and perhaps even to the memories of our earliest — our childhood — selves who once heard it freshly."[1] If Jesus Christ is the preeminent symbol of the consoling, challenging, and immediate experience of the Holy One in a person's life, then they owe it, as well, to this man Jesus and the community of people within which he is present as Christ to "hear again" and "freshly."

This chapter is about theological language and catechetical proclamation of Jesus Christ that is both faithful to the experience of Christians and consistent with interreligious reverence. It is about christological language that is not exclusive or absolute, language that does not lead to religious prejudice. But it is not an exercise in easy intellectualizing, for the Holy One is especially present to me in Jesus Christ; I revere the man Jesus. I am a passionate participant in the community of people who are trying to be Christ and conform themselves to the Holy One in that way. My ancestors have bequeathed me a rich, joyful piety associated with the life, death, and resurrection of Jesus, and my childhood self is very much present to me and inextricably linked to Jesus Christ.

I remember "Lumen Christi," three times in the darkness at the Easter vigil in my home parish. I remember visiting churches with my "uncle-the-priest" to say the rosary. I remember benediction of the Most Blessed Sacrament and my favorite short prayer as a child: "Jesus meek and humble of heart, make my heart like unto thine." And I remember devotion to the Sacred Heart of Jesus. If much of the exclusively docetic[2] and highly metaphysical christo-

logical language I encountered unquestioningly through graduate
school (until I first heard it criticized by Gabriel Moran in 1968)
has fallen away, the good lives of parents and aunts and uncles,
parish priests, Dominican sisters and Franciscan brothers — people
so vivid in my imagination — and the indivisible link between the
quality of their lives and their faith in Jesus Christ ensure that this
exercise in christological language consistent with interreligious
convergence will not become an exercise in sculpting a "Jesus of
the gaps," the elimination of a "problem" for interreligious relations through reduction of Christian faith. To paraphrase Gerard
Manley Hopkins, Jesus Christ truly "Easters" in me when I let
him; he is a "day spring" to my "dimness." When I was a child
we simply called him "our Lord." And as John Macquarrie writes:
"Lord provides [an] existential element. . . . To call someone 'Lord'
is to assign a rank to him and thus to express an attitude toward him. . . . The word assign[s] a supreme rank, and therefore
express[es] an attitude of absolute commitment."[3]

The Christian reader will judge whether devotion to Jesus Christ
is served; other readers will judge whether the enterprise of constructing (really retrieving) a way of speaking about Jesus Christ
that does not lead back perennially to Christian triumphalism has
been achieved. For myself, I know I am not engaged in an act of
reductionism, that for me Jesus Christ is a unique expression of divine presence, that his death and resurrection are saving, that he
is present in the community — in its acts of charity and justice, in
the proclamation of the Word, and most intensely in the eucharistic celebration (though there is much to say about the meaning of
uniqueness, salvation, resurrection, and presence).

I am not constructing a Jesus Christ who is consistent with syncretistic impulses. I know I am "other," in the sense that my path
of holiness and that of my primary religious community is in irreducible ways "other" than Jewish and other than Buddhist. There
is here no flight from being other. In this vein, Krister Stendahl's
assessment of moments in Jewish-Christian relations is instructive.
Stendahl maintains that until recently, Christians involved in these
relations were concerned with similarity: the Jewishness of Jesus,
the Jewishness of the most primitive Christian communities, the
indebtedness of Christianity to its Jewish roots, both ethical and
religious. Now there is a need to focus on "otherness" but without
diminution of reverence and gratitude, without hint of resurgent
tribalism. Rather, the focus on otherness ensures reverence for the
unique richness of each path, allows for "holy envy," and forestalls

a process of conflating differences that is not actually motivated by tolerance, let alone reverence, but that is the result of a kind of group narcissism.[4]

Still, the prevailing language of Christology (especially within Catholic Christianity and despite real gains, whose continuance, however, cannot be assured) does not serve interreligious reverence or enhance religious meaning for people on many paths of holiness. Nor does the prevailing language serve as well as it might the catechetical needs of members of Christian communities.

The purpose of this chapter is to propose that there is other language, time honored and vivid in its effects on Christians through the centuries, that is more suitable, more faithful to the Christian experience of the near presence of the Holy One in Jesus Christ, and more intelligible in the contemporary setting. (Here we may be guided, however, by Karl Rahner's observation that "it is quite meaningless to want to be modern on purpose."[5]) Because if Jesus of Nazareth is simply and without qualification God, as the prevailing tradition of Christian piety has it, the best we can hope to offer people on paths of holiness other than Christianity (alienated as they are from God Godself by reason of not being Christian) is inclusion in Christ "anonymously." If salvation results from a successful struggle, the price for which is Jesus Christ's blood, what are we to make of the God who demands blood? And can there ever be an end to proselytizing? If the resurrection of Jesus Christ continues to be employed as a proof text about a resuscitated body, can the vision of human transcendence for which it is metaphor (but as David Power says, not "mere metaphor"[6]) prevail in the religious imaginations of human beings yearning for liberation and authentic existence? And if the presence of Jesus Christ in the Eucharist continues to be described in nearly magical language, can it ever take its place with sufficient power as a ritual that celebrates, in Rosemary Haughton's phrase, "the joy at the heart of reality"?

This chapter deals with better language about the interplay of divinity and humanity in Jesus, proclaimed the Christ by Christians; better language about salvation, death, and resurrection; better language about presence — better for interreligious reverence and better for Christians, but also better for people on paths of holiness other than Christianity. As David Tracy says, all religious traditions begin "with some moment or occasion of special religious insight," which, if the traditions are "not purely at the mercy of psychological or social forces," can have universal implications, provided "the special religious experience and language are sufficiently evocative of our common human experience to bear claims of universal meaningfulness."[7] In other words, it is possible for Jews and Muslims and Buddhists to experience "holy envy" of Christian symbolism, not wanting therefore to replace their own symbolic structures for making meaning and living well, but rather experiencing in Christian symbols parallel yearning to love the Holy One, revere what is good, and act compassionately. And when Jews and Muslims and Buddhists experience that these Christians too are on a genuine path of holiness, they may find that their own hope is bolstered, that the yearning of their hearts has a real referent.

The Language of Classical Christology

The reference to classical christological language directs our attention to the early centuries of the life of the church and to the formulas regarding the *being* of Jesus Christ that emerge from theological debate and from the two great christological councils of the early church, those at Nicaea in 325 C.E. and at Chalcedon in 451 C.E. From these sources Christians receive language about Jesus being "true God of true God, begotten not made, one in substance with the Father" and "like us in all things except sin." From these councils every Catholic school student prior to 1960 received the inexplicable teaching that Jesus Christ is of two natures (divine and human) but one person (divine). This preoccupation with answering metaphysical questions is consistent with the increasing influence of Greek thought in the early church, though such preoccupation with the ontological — with the nature of his being — seems not to have preoccupied Jesus himself. But as Paul Tillich writes: "We must not forget that when the Greek thinkers produced a confession or creed, it may seem like an abstract philosophy to us, but to them it was the mystical intuition of essences, of powers of being."[8] And in seeking to make the union of divine and human in Jesus Christ intelligible to their age, the theologians whose language has become defining through the ages, or at least until the Reformation, were very much caught up in ontological questions, in questions of essences. Tillich again says that for them "the question was: If the Son is of one substance with the Father, how can the historical Jesus be understood? . . . How can he who is of divine nature, without any restriction, be a real man at the same time?"[9] Though the Council of Chalcedon condemned the heresy called Monophysitism, "the teaching... that the human nature of Christ was totally absorbed by the divine nature,"[10] earlier at Nicaea Arius and his followers had been condemned for the teaching that Jesus Christ is only *similar* to God (the position characterized by the word *homoiousios,* from *ousia* or "essence"). Nicaea insists that Jesus Christ is the *same* as God (*homoousios*).

There is justification in Christian Scripture for at least two broad paths of interpretation of the meaning of the divine-human interplay in Jesus Christ. To these the general labels "high" and "low" christologies or, synonymously, "descending" and "ascending" christologies have been attached. Somewhat more expressively, these two strands have been named "kenotic" and "adoptionistic." The one, from the Greek word for emptying (*kenosis*), points to the preexisting divine being — God Godself — emptying the divine self to take on humanity. It is beautifully expressed in Paul's letter to the Philippians in the so-called kenotic hymn (Philippians 2:6ff.). Adoptionism places greater emphasis on the human person, Jesus, who is taken up into divine life by his loving "Papa," *Abba.* In the Acts of the Apostles, Peter speaks in an adoptionist tone when he confesses that "God has made both Lord and Christ, this Jesus whom you crucified" (Acts 2:36).

A great deal of vivid scholarship urges us, in the words of Joseph Fitzmyer, "to learn to respect the differences among the Pauline Christ Jesus [with the emphasis on the saving works of Christ], the Lucan Lord and Savior [in which there is neither incarnation nor preexistence] and the Johannine Word-made-flesh [in which Jesus Christ is *Shechinah*],... God seen among men."[11] There are, as Thomas Sheehan points out, three types of primitive Christian communities from which three interpretations of Jesus emerge. It is from the faith of these communities, expressed in the Scriptures that emerge from each community, that the classic formulations noted above derive, though the earliest list of the twenty-seven books of the canon of the Christian Scripture dates only to the year 367 C.E.[12] For the Aramaic-speaking Palestinian Jews, the Greek-speaking Jews of Palestine and Diaspora, and Greek-speaking Gentiles,[13] the image of Jesus Christ in his person and in his works varies.

Despite the plurality of scriptural emphases and the formal endeavor of authoritative church leadership in the early centuries, as now, to preserve a language that speaks of both humanity and divinity, and despite proliferation of images of Jesus Christ from the

Reformation to the present, a high Christology, indebted primarily to the images in Johannine Scripture, has come to dominate the religious imaginations of vast numbers of Christians, especially Catholics. In this emphasis, the humanity of Jesus is effectively eclipsed, and Jesus is understood as being identical to God. In effect, the "docetic heresy" prevails in a great deal of Christian life.[14] This is the belief that Jesus Christ only "seems to be" (*dokei*, "to seem to be") human but is actually and only God. And docetic Christology is also classical, not in the sense that it is ancient, time-honored, and capable of ever deepening interpretation, but in the sense Richard P. McBrien attaches to "classicism": "the world view which holds that reality (truth) is essentially static, unchanging, and unaffected by history. Such truth can readily be captured in propositions and statements whose meaning is fixed and clear from century to century."[15]

"Docetism," writes Paula Fredriksen, "was a coherent expression of Hellenism's deep-seated ambivalence toward material reality."[16] Gerald Sloyan associates its power then and now with the "attention given in the patristic age to resisting the Arians... [so that] while the humanity of Jesus was granted, it was done in such a way that the divine power of the Word was immediately proposed as the force behind it."[17] Sloyan notes with typical erudition mixed with humor a wonderful example from the late second century of how the docetic influence worked, and continues to work, concretely in the depiction of Jesus Christ. Noting the influence of Greek Stoicism in the writings of Clement of Alexandria (d. ca. 215 C.E.) and the glorification of the transcendence of all desire, passion, and impulse, Sloyan offers this quote from Clement's *Miscellanies:* "[Jesus] ate not because of bodily needs... but so that his companions might not entertain a false notion.... He himself was, and remained, untroubled by passion, no movement of the passions, either pleasure or pain, found its way to him."[18] Sloyan comments that such a picture of Jesus "would have left the Jews who knew him in his lifetime speechless" and then points to the implications of this docetic tone: "There is no need to spell out how influential this kind of thinking has been in the Church. It is defensibly Johannine, but is surely at odds with most of the other descriptions of Jesus found in the Christian scriptures."[19]

What is to be made of a situation in which classical language about Jesus Christ is preoccupied with ontological considerations that effectively, if not formally, deny the humanity of Jesus and incline traditional Christians to simply equate Jesus and God? And what of the accompanying tendency to see people in other religious paths as alienated from the Source itself? The answer is that this language, these emphases, must change. With Karl Rahner we must insist, "Let none say that nothing more is really possible in this field [Christology] any longer. Something is possible because something *must* [Rahner's emphasis] be possible, if it is a matter of the inexhaustible riches of God's presence with us."[20] We must be guided further by Rahner's compelling insistence on the provisional nature of inherited doctrinal formulas: "The clearest formulations, the most sanctified formulas, the classic condensations of the centuries — long work of the Church in prayer, reflexion and struggle concerning God's mysteries: all these derive their life from the fact that they are not an end but a beginning, not a goal but a means, truths which open the way to the — ever greater — Truth.... Every formula transcends itself... not because it is false but precisely because it is true.... This holds true for the Chalcedonian formulation of the mystery of Jesus too. For this formula is — a formula."[21]

The source of strength to revise ancient formulas rests, ultimately, in humility before God who is transcendent mystery. Dom Bede Griffiths writes: "This is true of the Christian God no less than any other. He — or It — remains the unfathomable mystery. The incarnation — the words, the actions, the 'history' of Christ — is an expression in human terms of this mystery, but the mystery remains."[22]

The language of classical Christology, "terms like substance, essence, being, nature (in its theological usage) and the like do appear to have an inert quality which can be devastating in its effects upon the biblical picture of the living God and his vital relationship with the world."[23] Speaking further of this language, Norman Pittenger says that language like "two natures and one person" "appears to many of us to be frankly and utterly incredible."[24] It seems to require a kind of *sacrificium intellectus*, consisting, as John Macquarrie writes, of flagrant contradiction, violation of natural reason, and "conflict with what we believe about the world on scientific or common sense grounds."[25] In place of such features of classical Christology, let us consider an existential approach that preserves much that is evocative in "high" Christology in general, one that nurtures devotion without triumphalism and that holds out clues, as Tracy says, of universal meaningfulness regarding common human experience.

An Existential Christology

To speak of Christology as existential is a bit of a conundrum. Christology is a body of theological expression. We try to give expression to experiences that move us to revere what is holy, to yearn for what is good, to practice compassion, and to be joyful. When a person experiences all that is holy, however fleetingly, as emanating from the One, the Holy One, the expression of the experience may be called "theology." Christology is a division of theology. So we may legitimately speak of an "existential Christology" resulting from one kind of human activity and experience, as well as one motive force. The activity and experience are those of study and conversation; the motive force, the desire, is clarity and understanding at the service of rhetoric, of persuasive language. Here the model for Christians is Paul, who said, "I believed, and so I spoke."

But what is hidden in the phrase "existential Christology" are other, equally profound human activities, experiences, and desires. For the people for whom Jesus Christ is the preeminent symbol of the presence of the Holy One not only want[26] to be clear with one another, to be persuasive in *conversation* with one another. The people who are Christian want God to be *present* to them in Christ; they want God present to them in Christ to *invade* and *pervade* their historical existence and experience; they want to experience the Holy One *personally* in and through Christ; they want God in Christ to suffuse their *deciding* and their *doing;* they want, in some sense, to be Christ, and this both individually and *communally.* So in discussing existential Christology and its effects on both Christians and on interreligious enrichment, we need to attend to each of these dimensions: to a theological conversation about an existential Christology but also to God in Christ actually present, invading human experience and therefore known personally. We need to consider God in Christ suffusing human action (deciding and doing) as well as our human community. Conversation and action, proclamation and example effect the near presence of God in Christ to those for whom he is preeminent symbol of that near presence. But I will propose later in this chapter that the most effective — the most vivid and intense — means of experiencing the near presence of the Holy One in Christ is eucharistic practice.

After considering the several dimensions of action, experience, and desire of an existential Christology, we must ask to what it points. And we must answer that it points to the universal possibilities of human transcendence. Existential Christology points to the reality, in Rahner's beautiful expression, "that man [the human person] is the event of God's absolute self-communication."[27] Existential Christology points to the human vocation to embody effectively one of the Holy One's infinity of purposes. Only existential Christology gives us a way of speaking about Jesus Christ that evokes this vocation for Christians, and a way of speaking that is not only consistent with interreligious reverence in the sense of not being offensive, but that is genuinely illuminating. First, however, let us consider the several dimensions of existential christological conversation.

To be existential, Christology must, in David Tracy's words, evoke a "mode of being-in-the-world" in which we confront what he calls "limit-experiences." Limit-experiences pertain to the properly "religious dimension" of life, to "those features of human existence...[that] bear on the human desire for liberation and authentic existence."[28] Such christological conversation will entail discussion of the man Jesus of Nazareth confronting the limits of his existence, his desire for transcendence, for genuine freedom. It will not be content with existentially meaningful analogues detached, in the manner of Rudolf Bultmann's theology, from the historical figure of Jesus. This figure confronts anxiety and despair, selfishness and fear, death and annihilation. And according to the faith of the people who follow Jesus of Nazareth, he becomes peaceful and compassionate. He dies to anxiety and despair, selfishness and fear. He dies to death, and he experiences resurrection.

But an existential Christology will necessarily go beyond these historical events and their continuing historical interpretation. It takes us beyond what Tillich called "the 'official' theology of the Church...[that] thinks of objective historical happenings on which faith can be based."[29] As properly existential, this approach, in the words of John Macquarrie, starts from the premise that "we can understand history only by overcoming the subject-object dichotomy, and by approaching it from within our own historical existence.... [And] as far as sacred history is concerned, faith can never be established by demonstrating that certain objective happenings took place in the past. Faith arises on the basis of an existential interpretation of the sacred history which lets us see it as the disclosure of our own historical existence."[30] I am confronted with anxiety and despair, selfishness and fear, death and annihilation. An existential Christology proposes to me that God is present in Christ in these experiences of mine as the possibility of resurrection, as liberation and authentic existence. Existential Christology insists that something that has happened can continue to happen. Such continually present events are called by Nietzsche "monumental events," by Heidegger "authentic repeatable possibilities." Macquarrie notes these descriptions and says of such continually present events that there is a "paradoxical character that belongs to any great creative event in history. In one sense, it is an event that happened at a given time in the past.... Yet in another sense, the more the event is genuinely creative, the more it is an event that is continually being made present again, so that it happens, not literally or factually,[31] but none the less truly over and over again in the experience of those who have made it part of their history."[32]

As present, as "disclosive of our own historical experience," (as Tracy says) Jesus as Christ, as symbol effecting the near presence of the Holy One, is experienced in a very personal way. And an existential Christology will not hold back from discussing the dimension of personal relationship with Jesus Christ for fear of sentimental and often highly individualistic "Jesusology." If the event of God's near presence for some in Christ Jesus is continuing, then the existential experience (immediate and concrete and vivid) of a relationship with Jesus Christ is the heart of the matter. Thus it was for Saint Paul, who says, "It is no longer I who live, but it is Christ who lives in me" (Galatians 2:20). Thus it was in the restless desire in Augustine's heart, for Francis of Assisi in the tenderness of his feeling for the Christ child, for Ignatius bringing the full power of religious imagination to re-presenting Christ in the Exercises, for Teresa of Avila with Christ in her heart, for Francis de Sales who cries out, "Live, Jesus!" And thus it was for Martin Luther: in the personal experience of Jesus Christ lies Luther's great work of diminishing the centrality of highly metaphysical Christology. Of Luther's Christology, Paul Tillich writes: "I would call it a real method of correlation; it correlates what Christ is for us with what we say about him. It is an approach from the point of view of the effects Christ has upon us.... All the formulas concerning his divine and human natures or his being the Son of God and the Son of Man, make sense [for Luther] only if they are existentially understood."[33]

An existential Christology will take as one of its themes a major theme of existential thought in general. This is that we become ourselves in deciding and doing. (All the themes of existential

Christology parallel existential thought in general. The idea of a mode of being-in-the-world that overcomes alienation, the idea of presence, and the importance of genuinely personal experience are central in the literature of existentialism, whether atheist, agnostic, or theistic.)

In this feature — becoming by deciding and doing — existential Christology will be in a sense what Alan Race calls an "action christology," one that emphasizes the internal interplay, of the deciding and doing of Jesus and my own — and our own — deciding and doing. Of such an emphasis, Race writes: "Jesus is 'important' not because he possesses extra divine quality which is absent from other human beings [though such quality need not be denied], but because he focuses in himself the purposes of God for the world and the human response which God is continually... working to elicit."[34] This feature of Christology is time honored; it is implicit in Saint Paul's speech about Christ living in his heart, for the heart is the self not simply being self-conscious but deciding and doing. Tillich associates the emphasis with Peter Abelard, the twelfth-century theologian and emblematic figure for existential Christology. Abelard expounds, and Tillich approves, Christology that focuses on interior action rather than cosmic struggle. Tillich says: "In christology, Abelard emphasized the human activity of Christ and denied in a radical way that Christ was a transformed God.... For him [Abelard] the personal activity of Christ is decisive, not his ontological origin in God."[35] The point here, however, does not depend on separating the action of God from the response of people, the ontological (Being Itself in beings) from the existential (what humans decide and do in creating themselves). As Macquarrie says, "God's ontological action is inseparable from man's existential relation to it."[36]

Finally, an existential Christology will promote and disclose a communal experience of the near presence of the Holy One in Christ. And this, too, is consistent with the general themes of existential literature and philosophy, even though some characterize it as narrowly individualistic, and some existential thinkers lapse into individualism. The social dimension can be seen especially in the work of Camus, in which existential heroes labor heroically with immense sympathy for battered humanity, even while they eschew pseudo-identity subsumed in what Whitehead called "mere sociability."

The idea of Christ as a community of people who experience the near presence of the Holy One in Jesus Christ and are moved to act in a communally responsible way is especially enshrined in Catholic Christianity. (That is to say, the theological *idea* is a special emphasis of Catholicism. In fact many expressions of Christian life, liberal Protestantism and progressive Evangelicalism for example, reveal extraordinarily edifying examples of common action rooted in human sympathy.) In the period of rich renaissance of Catholic theological thinking, at first suppressed but eventually brought to some fruition at Vatican Council II, Karl Adams spoke persuasively of the social dimension of Christ. He wrote: "A Jesus Christ disassociated from the Church of fellow humans that prayed in his name led to every sort of individualism and sentimentalism."[37] Now Gabriel Moran expresses the relationship between existential encounter with Christ and compassionate encounter with others in these words: "Christ is the name of a personal and communal relation, rather than the name of an event, person, or truth of the past.... The term Christ, without ceasing to be a title attributed to Jesus ... foreshadows the concrete realization of a world of persons in peace with other humans and nonhuman life."[38]

I noted at the beginning of this section that an existential Christology will finally rest on the proposal, at once exhilarating and awesome (like the awesome exhilaration of Meister Eckhart exclaiming that humans are all "aristocrats"!), that the human vocation is transcendence; the divine is in the human; Jesus Christ means that the "natural"[39] existential situation of human beings is that we are the "event of God's absolute self-communication." It is to this vision of humans as transcendent, a vision at the heart of an existential Christology, that we turn.

Existential Christology and Human Transcendence

John Macquarrie writes that "if we hold fast to the existential dimension in the understanding of christhood ... we see christology as a kind of transcendent anthropology ... with christhood as the goal toward which created existence moves."[40] By "transcendent anthropology" Macquarrie means the view, noted already, that the existential vocation of humans, as such, is to be transcendent. This vocation is expressed by Christians as participation in Christ. (And from the start let there be no ambiguity about the moral expression of real human transcendence: the human vocation of transcendence will manifest itself in charity and justice, in courage in pursuit of compassion.)

Another way of framing this, again following Macquarrie, is to say that all humans are destined to express in their own selves the "Expressive Being" of God Godself. The term is part of Macquarrie's cogent discussion in *Principles of Christian Theology* of a way of speaking about the Trinity that is consistent with an existential theology. In this schema God as creator is "Creative Being"; God manifested is "Expressive Being"; and God acting in and between and among all created entities is "Unitive Being." Macquarrie writes of Expressive Being: "It is through Expressive Being that Being goes out in creation into a world of beings"; and again, that as Expressive Being, "God emerges from his hiddenness and comes to light."[41]

What Macquarrie speaks of as "Expressive Being" is more traditionally called the "Logos" or "Word" of God, the "side of God," as Karl Rahner writes of the Greek doctrine, "which is reflected in creation, which touches the finite world."[42] Rahner characterizes the Logos doctrine of Philo: "Logos [is] God's instrument of self-revelation whereby the inaccessible God could make contact with the material world and man could be lifted into eternity."[43] Paul Tillich also notes of Philo's exposition that "the unapproachable mystery of God...demands a mediating principle between God and man and drives to his Logos doctrine." Tillich himself calls Logos or Word the "universal principle of divine self-manifestation."[44]

In the Christian symbolic structure of meaning and purpose, this power — the Holy One as manifest, as near, as self-revealing (which is grace) — is experienced in Jesus Christ. He is, in the words of Saint Paul, the possibility of "New Being" (Galatians 6:15). Tillich writes of the possibility of New Being, the divinely given human capacity for transcendence expressed in Jesus Christ: "To experience the New Being in Jesus as the Christ means to experience the power in him which has conquered existential estrangement in himself [and] in everyone who participates in him."[45] And Macquarrie says, "To claim that Jesus is the 'Word made flesh' is to assert that in and through this particular being, Being has found signal expression."[46] Finally, note how Rahner expresses the belief that Jesus is the divine Logos: "Insofar as in the concrete historicity of our existence one and the same God strictly as Himself is present *for us* [my emphasis] in Jesus Christ, ... we call him Logos."[47]

Jesus as the Christ is Logos "for us," but the Holy One is manifest and near, self-revealing and lifting to eternity all that divine love has brought into existence. Or else God is not God, and there is only blasphemy. As Bede Griffiths writes: "In his one

Word, God expresses an infinite multiplicity of thoughts; every created being is a thought of God, a word of God to which he gives expression.... Every creature is a capacity of God.... It is as though the one divine light were received into each of these 'capacities,' each reflecting in its own way and breaking it up into innumerable colors, each a unique reflection of the one light. The one Word reflects itself in each of these energies, giving to each its own proper being.... The Spirit fills each of these capacities with its infinite energy and pervades the whole creation to the furthest reaches of matter."[48]

What is to be made, however, of the perennial, orthodox[49] claims made about Jesus Christ, under the doctrinal heading "Incarnation," that Jesus is the (exclusively) unique, singular, decisive expression for all creation of the divine in the flesh? As Norman Pittenger notes, there is in much — not all — of Christianity the central idea of "incarnation" (with a small *i*) that "man's approach to God is through the physical world." What was said above implies this perspective. But, Pittenger points out, the orthodox interpretation of "Incarnation" (capital *I*) is that "God was personally and uniquely present in Jesus of Nazareth in a sense which cannot be said to be true of any other human being, or founder of a religion."[50]

D. M. Baillie's excellent study of Christology, *God Was in Christ,* speaks of the interplay of divine and human in Jesus of Nazareth under the heading "the paradox of grace." In John Knox's superb book *The Humanity of Jesus,* divinity in Jesus of Nazareth is Jesus' involvement in "God's supremely redemptive action."[51] Alan Race notes "the important shift which the newer christologies make...away from concentrating exclusively on the person of Christ and the puzzle posed by viewing him as both divine and human, and [toward] talk of what can broadly be termed the action of God in Christ."[52] Karl Rahner, as part of his enterprise of redeeming a truly humanistic Catholic theological understanding, speaks of the incarnation as shedding light "on what is meant by 'being human,'" the point of our discussion above. But none of these approaches fully accomplishes the twin purpose of speaking about Jesus Christ in a manner faithful to the historical Christian experience of the near presence of God in Christ and, at the same time, consistent with a radical commitment to interreligious reverence. Not even Rahner's emphasis on the paradigmatically human meaning of the Incarnation seems sufficient. He writes: "If human nature is conceived as an active transcendence towards the absolute being of God, a transcendence that is open and must be personally realized, then the Incarnation can be regarded as the (free, gratuitous, unique) supreme fulfillment of what is meant by 'being human.' "[53]

Pittenger, writing in the key of process theology with its distinctly evolutionary perspective, is quite stark in holding that one, absolute, singular, supreme, exclusively unique Incarnation invalidates incarnation: "If we attempt to confine Incarnation to that individual in his supposed discreetness we shall find ourselves in the end in a position where we are in effect denying genuine humanity and thus making the Incarnation a docetic exception to human conditions, circumstances and situations."[54]

Now Christians should certainly maintain that Jesus of Nazareth is unique. This is done precisely to render him meaningful not only for Christians but for people on other paths of holiness. It is only in the particular details of how universal human possibilities of authentic existence are expressed in Jesus of Nazareth that he has any meaning (and we might add, any interest). In maintaining the uniqueness of Jesus of Nazareth we may be guided by Gabriel Moran's important analysis of the quality of uniqueness discussed in chapter 2. But, as Moran notes, though "Jesus is unique and Christ is unique," because Jesus is a fact and Christ is a claim, "I would suggest that the statement 'Jesus Christ is unique' is unintelligible; it is neither a true nor a false statement."[55]

What, if anything, can be the final position of Christians who confess Jesus as their Lord and feel at the same time moved to reject all triumphalist claims made in his name? How to speak of Jesus Christ as Logos without denying Expressive Being pervading all being? The answer is that at a certain point, the final position should be silence!

Speaking about the importance of silence for both theology in general as well as for the work of interreligious reverence, Paul Van Buren writes: "In making its confession... the Church would do well to adopt a humility that the early witness ascribes to Jesus himself (cf. Phil 2:3). In speaking of what is known, it would do well to not speak of what it does not know.... Whether and how God has related himself to and allowed himself to be met and known by the rest of creation is something that simply has not been revealed to the Church."[56]

Speaking with specific reference to the doctrine of Jesus Christ, Edward Schillebeeckx writes: "Through his historical self-giving, accepted by the Father, Jesus has shown *us* [my emphasis] who

God is: a *Deus humanissimus.* How the man Jesus can be for us at the same time the form and aspect of a divine 'person,' the Son, . . . is . . . a mystery unfathomable beyond this point."[57]

Salvation, Death, Resurrection, and the Cross in Existential Christology

The history of Christian teaching about salvation in Jesus Christ is defined by these polarities: a thoroughly ontological and objective interpretation, and an existential and subjective interpretation that does not, however, diminish God's action in these events and experiences. In the former, the objective interpretation, the cross of Jesus Christ and the spilling of his blood are the price paid to God for salvation, the culmination of a vast, titanic cosmic struggle. The resurrection is understood as the resuscitation of a dead body, miraculous proof that only in Jesus Christ is salvation possible.

In the subjective or existential interpretation of salvation, all creation is understood as under a sentence of death (physical death as well as the possibility of alienated existence and lack of freedom), incapacity to achieve our transcendent vocation. Jesus of Nazareth accepts his death but not passively or masochistically. Rather, Jesus of Nazareth dies to anxiety and despair, selfishness and fear. In his physical death, he "dies" to hopelessness, to the feeling that annihilation is human fate. He responds to the near presence of the Holy One, "God's absolute self-communication. . . . " God "rescue[s] [Jesus] from the fate of utter absence from God (death) and . . . admits [him] to the saving presence of God."[58] And this is resurrection.

(It may be helpful to borrow here from Buddhism. There is a Zen gatha, or prayer, that goes, "In order to exist in the realm of Buddha nature, it is necessary to die as a small being moment by moment." As raised from the dead, Jesus of Nazareth has died to alienated being and exists as "New Being." In other words, he comes to exist in the realm of "Christ nature." He exists in eternity, but "eternity is not an incalculably long-lasting mode of pure time, but a mode of spirit and freedom which have been actualized in time."[59])

When Christians say that we are saved in Christ Jesus, we are saying that we experience in God's saving Jesus from death and raising him what Tillich (speaking of Abelard's idea of salvation) describes as "the subjective act of divine love which evokes in us a love for him [God]."[60]

Regarding the purely objectivist idea of salvation, John Macquarrie writes: "One model that, as it seems to me, has usually
been developed in such a way that it becomes sub-Christian in its
thought of God and its idea of reconciliation is the notion of substitutionary punishment, the thought that Christ was punished by
the father for the sins of men in the place of men."[61]

Rahner also rejects as inadequate at best a doctrine of salvation that focuses religious imaginations on the satisfaction of God
though substitutionary punishment, the bloody sacrifice of Jesus
Christ: "The death of Jesus is obviously regarded as a cause of our
salvation in a true sense, but in what precise sense? The causality
is presented among other ways as that of a sacrifice of his blood
which is offered to God, the blood which is poured out for us or
for 'the many....' We can say on the one hand that in the New Testament milieu such expressions were a help towards understanding
the salvific significance of the death of Jesus, because at that time
the idea of propitiating the divinity by means of sacrifice was a current notion which could be supposed to be valid. But...we have to
say...that this notion offers little help to us today."[62]

Both Macquarrie and Rahner, indeed all those who criticize the
prevailing classical theological interpretation of salvation, are rejecting the "sub-Christian" idea of God that is implied in it. It
should also be noted, regrettably in passing, that the social consequences of giving so prominent and positive a place to "sacred
sacrifice" have been destructive. For example, Delores Williams
asks, "Does the 'sacred sacrifice' achieved through the brutaliza-
tion of Jesus' body...encourage battered women to stay in their
situations...?"[63]

In contrast, an existential Christology affirms that salvation is
personal, that it is not the result of this cosmic "transaction" between an angry God and a bloody Jesus (though this is not to
say that it is a private, individualistic experience). The personal
nature of salvation is well expressed by those theologians whose
work we have sighted already. First Macquarrie: "Man is saved
only in so far as he responds to and appropriates into his existence
the saving activity that is directed toward him. So we must criticize any attempt to represent the atonement as a 'transaction' that
goes on outside of those who are at stake in the matter."[64] And
Tillich writes that salvation "is man's...personal...response to
the forgiving act of love....It is a doctrine of atonement in the personal center. The mechanism of atonement through substitutionary
suffering is ruled out."[65] And finally Rahner: "If...a person af-

firms his existence as permanently valid and redeemable, and does not fall into the misunderstanding of a platonic anthropological dualism, then he is affirming his resurrection in hope.... [But] in salvation all initiatives proceed from God Himself, and... all real salvation can only be understood as taking place in the exercise of each individual's freedom."[66]

A purely objective, what is sometimes called "physicalist," theological interpretation of the resurrection of Jesus Christ, and of one's own resurrection, must also be rejected in existential Christology. As Rahner writes: "We miss the meaning of 'Resurrection' in general and also of the resurrection of Jesus to begin with, if our original preconception is the notion of a resuscitation of a physical, material body. The resurrection which is referred to in the Resurrection of Jesus... means the final and definitive salvation of a concrete human existence by God and in the presence of God. The abiding and real validity of human history, which neither moves further and further into emptiness, nor perishes altogether."[67]

Each of us in principle can strive to overcome death and respond to the near presence of the Holy One, can respond with love from our "personal center" to the "subjective act of divine love." Each of us can hope that human history, including our own histories, "neither moves further and further into emptiness nor perishes altogether." As Rahner says, each of us can accept "his own self as it is disclosed and offered to him in the choice of transcendence in freedom."[68]

Classical Christology maintains that it is only in Jesus Christ that there is salvation. We saw in chapter 2 in the discussion of theology of religions that under the constraining influence of certain classical traditions and theological methods, the best that can be said of good people who are not Christians is that they may be *included* anonymously (the "anonymous Christians") in God's saving actions in Christ. This unfortunate expression from so revered a Catholic theologian as Rahner is given a cogent and gracious twist by Gabriel Moran, one that is consistent with the burden of the argument of this chapter. Moran says of "anonymous Christians": "The idea is simply a liberalizing of Christian theology as far as it can go.... Rahner did not intend to say (though the words may indeed say) that non-Christians are, despite themselves, members of the Christian Church. Rahner meant that they are followers of that universal ideal which Christians call Christ."[69]

Feminist Theological Contribution
to Existential Christology

As in chapter 2, when discussing the contribution of Christian feminist theologians to a theology of religions on which to base radical pluralism and depth dialogue, feminist thought is treated separately. I do not intend by this to suggest a marginal or idiosyncratic contribution but rather to emphasize the importance of the feminist theological contribution. This is especially important in the case of feminist christological critique and reconstruction, because it is sometimes accused of contributing to theological anti-Judaism. For example, Judith Plaskow writes that "the feminist struggle with patriarchal christologies leads back into traps of anti-Judaism," an "easy" disassociation of the real — read "feminist" — Jesus from his patriarchal fellow Jewish men.[70] It is important, therefore, for more than one reason to underline that feminist christological critique, directed primarily at unearthing cultural and gender bias in classical formulas, has the equally beneficial result of reconstructing Christology in ways that reject Docetism and salvation as bloody sacrifice, embrace an "action Christology" focused on Jesus' message of "connectedness" rather than exclusiveness, and speak of uniqueness in inclusive fashion.

Perhaps the first and most important contribution of feminist Christology to repudiating triumphalism is its incisive uncovering of the historical context and cultural biases of classical formulations. Elisabeth Schüssler Fiorenza writes: "Christological doctrines were shaped at a moment when those segments of the ancient Church that became hegemonic 'orthodox' Christianity pivoted into a place of prominence in the Constantinian imperial Roman Church."[71] The christological formulas of the fourth and fifth centuries, then, "exercise normalizing functions by which the increasingly imperialized Church establishes its rule, sanctions its violence and sacralizes its power."[72] And therefore, as Elizabeth Johnson points out, "the image of Christ ... assumed contours of the male head of the household or the imperial ruler. ... Christ was then viewed as the principle of headship and cosmic order, the ruling King of glory, the Pantocrator par excellence, whose heavenly reign sets up and sustains the earthly rule of the head of the family, empire and Church."[73]

In criticizing christological language framed by social interests associated with power in the empire, these theologians are also revealing the social interests that are the source of the ascendancy of docetic Christology. In contrast they offer a Jesus Christ understood by the actions of his life and the tenor of his message. This is a message of communality, relationship, and connectedness, of being one together. This is Jesus Christ speaking of the vine and the branches (John 15:1–11), of being where two or three are gathered in his name (Matthew 18:20). This is Christ whose body we all constitute (1 Corinthians 12:12–27), in whom we are all one (Galatians 3:28). Writing of the change from emphasis on the King of Glory to the Jesus Christ of communality, mutuality, and compassion, Carter Heyward says feminists "have sought to create a paradigmatic shift in feminist christological discourse from a 'heroic individualist' or 'heroic liberationist' Christology to a christological construction that privileges [sic] right relation, connectedness, mutuality and 'at-one-ment.' "[74]

Feminist Christology also rejects the prevailing classical interpretation of salvation. Johnson writes: "Feminist theology repudiates an interpretation of the death of Jesus as required by God in payment for sin. Such a view today is virtually inseparable from an underlying image of God as an angry, bloodthirsty, violent and sadistic father, reflecting the very worst kind of male behavior."[75] In place of struggle, blood, sacrifice, and propitiation of an angry God, feminists emphasize the paradigm of healing, wellness, and relationality. Schüssler Fiorenza writes: "The essentially communal nature of healing and human wellness through the relational power of the messianic Christian community, in all its cultural differences, makes clear that 'connectedness' constitutes a deeper and after all more redemptive reality than an ontology of struggle."[76]

Finally, feminist Christology is not as quick as prevailing classical Christology to embrace an exclusive meaning of the uniqueness of Jesus Christ. Speaking of "Sophia" (Divine Wisdom) in Jesus, Elizabeth Johnson says: "Jesus-Sophia personally incarnates her gracious care in one particular history, for the benefit of all, while she lays down a multiplicity of paths in diverse cultures by which all people may seek, and seeking find her."[77]

Fictions, Facts, and the Presence of Jesus Christ

Before concluding this section on an existential Christology, I want to return to the earlier discussion of David Tracy's idea that Christology is "limit language," language with a "properly religious dimension," the dimension of human existence that "bears on the human desire for liberation and authentic existence." In that same treatment, in the christological chapter of his work *Blessed*

Rage for Order, Tracy refers to the "Christian story, . . . the Christian proclamation of Jesus Christ," as a "supreme fiction" and as a "fact." By fiction he means a "more than conceptual analysis for understanding human existence, . . . [a] redescrib[ing] [of our] human reality in such disclosive terms that we return to the 'everyday' reoriented to life's real, if forgotten and sometimes not even imagined possibilities."[78] Tracy also calls the "proclamation of Jesus Christ" a "fact" and speaks about two meanings of the word "fact." A fact, Tracy says, may be a "possibility actualized," or a fact may be "a possibility re-presented." Fact as possibility re-presented is "making present anew, through symbolic expression, a human possibility which somehow had become threatened or forgotten."[79] If the near presence of the Holy One in Jesus Christ is made factual, if it becomes a possibility re-presented, then a Christian will say from the depth of her or his experience "the only God present to all humanity at every time and place . . . is present explicitly, actually and decisively as my God in my response to this Jesus as the Christ."[80]

But how is Jesus Christ as near presence of the Holy One rendered a "fact"? How does Jesus Christ become a possibility re-presented for me, for all Christians? Tracy answers: "A Christian sacrament is traditionally believed to be a fact as the re-presentation of a real possibility which God has made present to humanity in Christ Jesus."[81] We turn now to a consideration of what earlier was claimed to be the most effective — the most vivid and intense — means of experiencing the near presence of the Holy One in Christ; we turn to a consideration of eucharistic "practice."

The Priority of the Eucharist

David Power writes of the Eucharist that "the memorial of Christ's death and resurrection is today celebrated amid the ruins."[82] What is in ruins is the certainty of modernity, lost in the cognitive dissonance of an age labeled "postmodern." There is a less global sense in which the Eucharist may be said to be practiced amid the ruins, though it is by no means a narrow or marginal sense. The Eucharist celebrated by Catholic Christians takes place amid the ruins of conciliar and renewalist Catholicism, the revitalization of Catholic Christian life promised at the Second Vatican Council but now subject to the constraints imposed by conservative and ultraconservative reaction supported by and expressed in a "restorationist" papacy. One need not adopt an excessively negative appraisal of the situation, ignoring real progress in eucharistic practice or in Catholic life generally, to insist that much still needs to be done. The celebration of the Eucharist within Catholicism is still to a very large extent subject to ecclesiastical disciplines that render it less celebratory, less dramatic and intense, less flexible than it should be (bringing to mind Juan Segundo's observation in *The Sacraments Today* that one senses a problem in sacramental practice when Sunday Mass is conducted in precisely the same manner the day before and the day after the revolution!).

Not everyone feels welcome at the Eucharist: gay and lesbian Catholics experience strictures. People who are not canonically "regular" are rendered marginal. Intercommunion among the baptized is still to a large extent held ransom to triumphalist patterns in exercising juridical authority in the church. Catechetical formation of attitudes, feelings, and understandings of Catholic people of all ages about the reality of eucharistic practice, for all the gains, is still subject to some incredible ancient philosophical distinctions. Above all, women in the Catholic Church are excluded from serving the community as presiders at the Eucharist, a scandal of incalculable proportions.

There are two reasons for asserting that eucharistic practice should have a place of preeminence in our efforts to form a Christian people. First, the Eucharist is or can be direct, powerful, and deeply emotionally effective in re-presenting the possibilities of the divine life in us as symbolized in Jesus Christ. In this sense, quite simply, the Jesus Christ of eucharistic practice is more easily (not easily but *more* easily) shorn of ideology and bad theology and triumphalism. Therefore, giving priority to eucharistic formation is better for Christians than excessive emphasis on the doctrine of Christ. And second, for precisely the same reason, this strategy is best for the cultivation of interreligious reverence.

Power also writes that "the sacrament can take on new shape ...to the extent that the eucharistic memorial is alert to the human."[83] The Eucharist is a response to three great human needs: to experience presence, to cope with death, and to cultivate gratitude. It is to these dimensions of eucharistic practice and human need that we turn.

The opposite of presence is absence. Absence, in all its physical and psychological manifestations, is the great sickness — absence of meaning, absence of loved ones, absence of God. Absence is not solitude but loneliness. To assist a people to engage in sacramental practice, to cultivate sacramental imagination, is to attack absence in all its dimensions. John Macquarrie defines sacramental action as "objective form, visible and dramatic, conjoined with a form of words...focus[ing] the divine presence in the community of faith....In the word and sacrament, the divine presence is focused so as to communicate itself to us with a directness and intensity like that of incarnation itself."[84]

Kenan Osborne notes three theological theories that have evolved through the centuries to explain the redemptive work of Jesus Christ: the *victor,* the *victim*, and the *revealer* theories: "In the Revealer theory, Jesus is the occasion in which God reveals to us his saving love."[85] This is the function of remembering and celebrating the meal that Jesus ate with his friends, and his death and his resurrection. It reveals God's saving love as expressed in the gift of food, courage and self-giving in front of death, and the promise that human history, including my history, neither moves further and further into emptiness, nor perishes altogether (resurrection).

Eucharist is a remembering but not only a remembering. And, in any case, the memorial dimension serves presence. As David Power writes, the effect of the Eucharist as remembering is "not to make the past events present again, but to make ensuing generations of Christians present to the past event."[86]

The history of eucharistic theology has not, of course, been free of what Power calls "some naive realism" in speaking about the "real presence" of Jesus Christ as symbolic expression of the Holy One in this sacramental action. But this should not be a stumbling block for theology and catechesis of Eucharist. As Macquarrie points out, "Eucharistic presence...[is] a special case of what we have often spoken of...as the 'presence and manifestation' of Being in the beings."[87] The eucharistic practice, the ritual, in this sense "mediates" in a concrete, contemporaneous setting the pervasive availability of God as Presence itself. As Gabriel Moran has written of mediation: "In both Christian and Jewish thinking, everything in the universe represents divine creativity and creaturely response."[88] The Holy One, as love, yearns to be present, is available as Presence to all the loved creation. The presence is not a function of God overwhelming the creatures in such a manner as to rob their freedom. Nor is it simply a psychological state of the people engaged in eucharistic practice. Rather, "In all these cases in which Being becomes present and manifest, one cannot speak of a subjective or an objective happening, for since we ourselves participate in this very Being, the subject-object pattern is transcended."[89]

In addition to presence, eucharistic practice is integrally associated with death, the death of Jesus Christ. It will be clear from what has been said already, that the idea of the Eucharist as the reenactment of the bloody death on the cross of Jesus Christ, a death required to ransom us from sin, in this sense a sacrifice, will have no place in what is proposed and promoted, though this is, oddly, the overwhelming emphasis I remember from my own childhood. I say "oddly" because the general tenor of my early childhood religious formation was almost uniformly joyous. But the sapiential emphasis in dealing with Eucharist, that it is an occasion for remembering what my sins brought about, is a very vivid memory of an effective catechetical strategy. Though given the prominence of other elements, for me and I suspect for many raised in "those days," the sapiential emphasis did not result in a situation in which, to paraphrase Reinhold Niebuhr's criticism of Calvinism, the whole religious sentiment was dominated by the "act of contrition." But if not reenactment of bloody sacrifice to redeem us from sin, how shall we speak of death and sacrifice and Eucharist?

Religious literature from many traditions speaks of dying as human work to be about, as something to be achieved, an element not only of human "facticity" but also of human freedom, something, if you will, to be become good at.[90] The Qur'an, for example, counsels the faithful, "Die before you die." The tales of the rabbis contain anecdotes in which the rebbe enjoins the faithful to "repent the day before you die," make it your work to learn how to die to what is unrepentant in you. We have already noted the Zen saying that to exist in the realm of Buddha nature, "it is necessary to die as a small being moment by moment." And Jesus of Nazareth says that those who are willing to lose their lives will save them (John 12:26). The human work of dying takes two forms. There is cultivating courage to face one's physical death. And there is the related work of learning to die as a "small being," learning, Christians would say, to "put on Christ." This is dying to anxiety and despair, selfishness and fear, death and annihilation. For Christians, Jesus Christ is the paradigm of this human work. He succeeds (through his human courage but wholly by the grace of God — the "paradox of grace") in the human vocation of transcendence. And as we noted earlier, success here is observably concrete and moral. There is charity and justice and courage to act compassionately. Those who "die" in this sense (and for Christians, Jesus Christ is the preeminent exemplar) are available. They are a sacrifice, not in the sense of self-hatred and masochism but in the sense of self-giving. Utterly united with his *Abba,* Jesus Christ dies in the sense that he is self-giving. Of this meaning of the sacrifice of Jesus Christ, Macquarrie writes that it "is the very essence of God himself,..." and therefore "Christ is made 'like to God' which is indeed the destiny of the created being."[91] For the same reason, his relationship with God, Jesus of Nazareth dies his physical death without despair.

Bernard Cooke has a very powerful way of describing the relationship between Jesus Christ's self-giving, and food and body. It is that in the "Last Supper" Jesus combines two symbols effecting radical self-giving — those of parent and lover: "Jesus took the giving of food, which is the basic act of parents (beginning with a mother nursing her baby), manifest[ing] their concern for their children and he united its symbolism with that of a gift of the body in marital intercourse. Taking the bread, he said 'This is my body given for you.' "[92] And, because this transcendence is not private, "When Christians gather for that covenant meal they call 'eucharist,' they are pledging their 'being for' one another."[93] Or, in the words of Saint Augustine: "If you are the body of Christ and his members, it is your own mystery which has been placed on the altar of the Lord."[94] In place of bloody sacrifice, we have rich symbolism of death as transcendence, as self-giving.

Finally, consider the relationship between eucharistic practice and cultivating gratitude. It may be that "gratitude" is an adequate summary of what it means to succeed at the human vocation. Rabbi Heschel says, "It is gratefulness which makes the soul great."[95] And Brother David Stendahl-Rast asks, "Do we find it difficult to imagine that gratefulness could ever become our basic attitude toward life?"[96]

The sacramental ritual from which all of Catholic Christianity continually emerges is called by a word — "Eucharist" — that means thanksgiving. Saint Paul enjoins (and Kierkegaard insists this is the only refuge), "In all things give thanks." In the Eucharist we practice to become proficient at giving thanks for the presence of the Holy One whose life in us as in Jesus Christ is represented as a possibility. We also practice to give thanks for death. David Stendahl-Rast writes of the dual symbolism, the apparent ambiguity of the "message":

The very symbols of the Eucharistic meal are ambiguous symbols. Bread is a symbol of life. The breaking of the bread signifies sharing of life that grows in the sharing. And yet the breaking also signifies destruction; it is a reminder of the body broken in death. The cup of blood drained from the body signifies death. But it is also the cup passed around in a festive gathering of friends, in an hour of celebration. It takes courage to accept this double meaning. Only together can the two aspects stand for fullness.... When one approaches... to receive the eucharist... it is a gesture by which one says, "I trust that I can live by *every* [Stendahl-Rast's emphasis] word that comes from the mouth of God, yes, even the word that spells death...." This is done through gratefulness.... As we learn to give thanks for all of life and death... we find a deep joy.[97]

The prominence of food and of eating in this central ritual conveys the source of growing in gratefulness. Gratefulness arises from experiencing that the Holy One is present in everything, including a morsel of bread. This is why Rosemary Haughton says that the "party," the Eucharist, is the absolute center from which Catholic Christianity emerges, and that the purpose of the party is "to celebrate the joy at the heart of reality... with everyday food."[98]

We know that the dimension of meal is the most primitive and central feature of the Eucharist. Kenan Osborne writes: "The meal aspect of the Eucharist is rooted in the New Testament, and it would seem that this is the dominant or at least one of the dominant factors of Eucharistic celebration. Around the time of Theodore of Mopsuestia (d. 428) there seems to be a deemphasizing of the meal aspect of the Eucharist and a major emphasizing of the death/resurrection of Jesus. This led, of course, to the emphasis on the Eucharistic sacrifice. Still, it is the meal which contextualizes the New Testament data on the Lord's supper. As a result it is the ordinary human meal that offers a central phenomenon to understand the dynamisms of Eucharistic sacramentality."[99] There is, too, in support of keeping the focus on the meal that prompts gratitude for things simple and complex, ordinary and extraordinary, the fact that "when we search the Gospels for clues to how Jesus lived, we get the impression that in scarce two years of his mission, he spent an inordinate amount of time at the dinner table, and not always with the best of company."[100]

So this profound ritual, this most effective vehicle for re-
presenting the possibility of human transcendence ("christhood"
for Christians), speaks to us of presence and death and self-giving
and gratitude. It is so important that Bernard Cooke says that
the church is continuously emerging from it. And that "what the
eucharist is meant to provide for Christians is an opportunity to
decide what interpretation they wish to give their lives, how they
wish to understand themselves and their world, what values they
wish to espouse as the genuine goal of their life, what actions
they wish to undertake as part of the process of creating human
history."[101] In forming Christians deeply devoted to Jesus Christ
and at the same time deeply committed to interreligious reverencing, we can do no better than to focus energy and intelligence on
practice that is centered on the Eucharist.

On "Restoration" and Hopes for Existential Christology

The "restoration" of a certain kind of Catholic Christianity and
of a certain pattern of functional relationships within Catholic
Church structures of governance and pastoral life, and between the
church and other major structures of regional, national, and international society is the work of the papacy of Pope John Paul II.
This restoration is complex, immediate, and ongoing. It would be
naive as well as futile to attempt to fully define its reality and effects. One of the most salutary features of this effort at restoration
is Pope John Paul II's heroic repudiation of social and economic
injustice and its pervasively violent effects on poor people throughout the world and in every local venue. This pope has taken it upon
himself to recapitulate and to advance with prophetic denunciation, but with the prophets' comfort for the righteous, the political
and economic import of the teachings of Jesus Christ. This message
is that there can be no peace, no justification, no genuine religiousness without justice for the poor. And, further, he teaches that this
foundation of faithfulness is despoiled in the modern world by an
orgy of acquisitiveness expressing itself in the consumption of the
world's goods by the wealthy, an orgy justified by invoking the
rights of the individual.

One of the most destructive features[102] of restoration is the effort of the present pope and his supporters to excise from the life
of the church itself the healthiest features of modern freedom, individual rights, and reliance on the authority of experience. And this

program entails the effort to reinstate "classicism," which, as noted earlier, Richard P. McBrien defines as "the world view that holds that reality (truth) is essentially static, unchanging and unaffected by history. Such truths can readily be captured in propositions and statements whose meaning is fixed and clear from century to century."

There is today a national and international effort to restore to center stage as the very "stuff" of Christian religious education, the content of traditional doctrine. The effort is justified by reference to the supposed "religious illiteracy" of vast numbers of Catholic people. The signal indicator of this effort is the appearance of *The Catechism of the Catholic Church*. In the United States, the continuing struggle to restore doctrinal orthodoxy can be followed in the pages of the ultraconservative weekly Catholic newspaper *The Wanderer* and in books such as Michael Wrenn's *Catechisms and Controversies*.

The motives for restoring to center stage schooling in doctrinal language of the past seem to be twofold. On the one hand, there is, I think, a belief that the solidarity of Catholic Christian people in support of the message of the church and the teachings of Jesus Christ is diminished without a critical mass of Catholics who share a common propositional knowledge (knowledge that can be put into words, placed on paper — content, in this sense). And it seems beyond question that a feeling of affiliation is nourished by common language and beliefs. Restorationists also believe that instilling a vivid sense of belonging or affiliation is a legitimate goal of confessional religious education (catechesis or Christian religious education) within this or any religious community. In this they are correct, though it is important to recall the words of Heschel and Tillich and others mentioned in chapter 2 that such loyalty to the "religion" itself is not the ultimate goal.

The importance of schooling in the content of accumulated knowledge and formulas, texts and traditions of the church over the centuries was acknowledged in the 1930s by one of the most important Catholic figures in the change from a "classicist" to an existential approach to Christian religious education. This is Joseph Andreas Jungmann, who — even while proposing a shift in educational paradigm to a sacramental, narrative, affective, and experiential practice — could nevertheless write that "knowledge must furnish light for desire."[103]

Insofar as a common core of beliefs is necessary for achieving an appropriate level of affiliation, the point is almost well made.

But the problem of doctrinal illiteracy is not one of "religious illiteracy" because "religiousness" cannot legitimately be conflated with knowledge of doctrine. This brings us to the second motive for the vigor with which the restoration of "doctrinal initiation"[104] is pursued by restorationists. It is, I think, a belief that doctrinal probity — and acting out of doctrinal probity, which is to say, obeying — *is* faithfulness (or is a more prominent feature of faithfulness than in fact it is). It seems almost as if the *sacrificium intellectus* entailed in accepting the truth of certain propositions that may have little or no meaning for one effects a "humility" that is faithfulness.

The facts of the matter are entirely other than what the restorationist religious educators make them out to be. Holding up loyalty to the antique expression of beliefs of a religion as the ideal is the death knell of genuine religiousness. And the meaningfulness of propositional knowledge, inherited knowledge, lies in its relationship to my experience and to our experience now. In the restorationist diatribes against "the experiential approach" (Wrenn's are among the "best" examples), "experience" is always characterized as fleeting or vague, narrow, uncultivated, perhaps narcissistic. The appeal to experience is against the wisdom of the church down through the centuries, another manifestation of the worst of the "modern" spirit. But, of course, experience is what all "actual entities" actually are! And when the actual entity is a human person, endowed with consciousness and reflection, the entity, the person — all people — are experiencing-reflecting-assigning meanings-acting on purposes derived from those meanings. And they do this as members of an animal species that has "culture," that has clues about meaning and purpose derived from individuals and communities of people who have coded and left behind their "experiencing-reflecting-assigning of meaning-acting on purposes derived from those meanings." The goal of all forms of education properly called "schooling" is to assist people living now to *experience* what was vital in the experiencing-reflecting-meaning making-and acting of those people who have gone before and to experience what vital clues for my experiencing-reflecting-meaning making-and acting may be there. And therefore all education, including schooling, is experiential. Education in general and schooling in particular are what R. S. Peters calls "criteria words." If there is no link between what has gone before and my processes of experiencing-reflecting-meaning making-acting, then no education in the sense of schooling has occurred. This is what Alfred North

Whitehead meant when he wrote that all "education" (he meant "schooling") must possess the quality of "utility." This is what he meant when he said all "education" must be imaginative. Previous knowledge becomes "knowledge" for me only if it is vividly apprehended as useful, useful not in the narrow sense but useful to my experiencing-reflecting-meaning making-acting. This is what the ancient Greek Heraclitus the Obscure meant when thousands of years ago he wrote "to teach is not to tell, not to tell!" All of which has a great deal to do with nurturing an existential Christology, with embracing religious pluralism and depth dialogue, with an education of Christians that helps end Antisemitism.

The restorationist agenda in Christian religious education is inconsistent with vital, healthy, and effective formation of Christians. And it is inconsistent with interreligious reverence. The doctrinal orthodoxy that is promoted is to a large degree, though not entirely, obscure. It threatens to accelerate for some the process of deciding that Christianity should be consigned to the "dustbin of history." And the language was framed in an era in which historical cultural dynamics made almost inconceivable reverence for people on paths of holiness other than one's own. Page through *The Catechism of the Catholic Church* in the light of the discussion of classical and existential christological language contained in this chapter. It will become clear why the catechism slips back into a supersessionist treatment of Jews and Judaism vis à vis Jesus Christ and Christians.[105] The slippage arises from the fact that no effort to reconcile Jews and Christians is on firm ground, no gesture however moving is more than ephemeral, when at the same time Catholic Church authority seeks to restore the most universalistic, absolute, and triumphalist language about Jesus Christ and salvation. The language must change. The formulas, to cite again Karl Rahner, are formulas.

A Postscript on the Cross of Jesus Christ

Given its importance for Christians and for Jews, a note regarding the symbol of the cross deserves the place of eminence at the end of the chapter. Of the meaning of the cross for Christians, Mary Boys speaks eloquently: "The Cross is a symbol Christians have been given to image their hope that God is with them even in pain and tragedy and ambiguity. It is a symbol of the longing to give themselves over to a project larger than their own self-interest."[106] "Yet," she continues, "it is not a symbol that cannot be reappropriated without repentance."[107] And from Paul Van Buren: "A rule that would appear essential to govern our language in this area [the cross] is that the death of one Jew, no matter whom or what he was in God's purposes, should not be spoken of so as to lessen the significance and the pain of the death of any human being, least of all that of six million other Jews."[108]

Chapter Four

Gabriel Moran and
Religious Education for Reverence

We need to ask what human practice within religious communities offers the greatest hope of ending prejudice, absolutism, religious universalism. What characteristic activity of people in religious communities shows most promise for ending triumphalism, exclusive claims to the truth, exclusive claims to God? And we must ask whether, in choosing a means to this end, we are also choosing a mode of human practice in religious communities that evokes devotion to the particular clues the religious community has available to it for becoming holy and behaving compassionately. Otherwise, we might be left with real reverence for others but not ourselves!

All the available instruments peculiar to most religions are more often used at best to nurture religiousness through devotion to our own religions with little reference to the others. At worst, these same means are employed to instill loyalty to this one, exclusive way or path of holiness, right belief, exclusively unique congruence with God's plan. And there is, finally, the grey area in which formation in a religion includes some marginal element of toleration. But this is not the genuine feeling of religious pluralism for which some of us strive. Neither does it provide people on the many paths the enrichment of life that interreligious convergence promises.

The practices, the instruments, are at one level well known to us, though sometimes they are not what superficial assessment makes them out to be. We call them preaching and teaching, worshiping, and acting morally. With the exception of acting morally, any of these instruments can be used in ways that either advance or retard reverence for people on paths of religious life other than our own. And even in the case of acting morally, people can be persuaded to follow a route of xenophobia and violence in the name of morality. (I write these words within days, for example, of what has rightly been called the waking nightmare of the assassination of

Yitzak Rabin by someone apparently influenced by people whom he perceived as religious and moral leaders.)

So much of interreligious exchange — even encounter, if not yet reverence — occurs as conversation that it is quite natural to look to theology as the preeminent instrument for taking us from a position of exclusivism or tolerance alone to a position of genuine appreciation, perhaps reverence. And we have seen in previous chapters that theological discourse can be framed in ways that promote progress. We have also seen the limitations of theological expression. But, in any case, theological work, even when it is existential or revisionist or connected to the "depth," is simply too small a factor to bear the weight. Those who work for the end of religious exclusivism and the emergence of genuine interreligious reverence are working for catastrophic change: change that turns upside down the way things are. We work to replace oppositional and exclusive religious feelings and communities with a worldwide web of interrelated religious communities linked to one another with appreciation and reverence without loss of devotion. This requires individual and corporate change of heart. As typically practiced, theological reflection and conversation does not have the reach. As modeled in chapters 2 and 3 of this work, theology most certainly has a crucial part to play. But if we are to survey adequately the means and choose wisely how to strengthen both religious devotion within our communities and interreligious reverence, we will have to examine a complex pattern of human action within (and without) religious communities that is vastly more layered than theological work in a religious community and vastly more significant in its effects. The work is religious education and, parenthetically, theological work is a small but crucial part of religious education.

Some Reflections on the State of Religious Education

A few observations about a small sliver of religious education theory in the United States among Christians will help frame the analysis of Gabriel Moran's monumental work with which most of this chapter deals.

Education is action or practice that causes human faithfulness. Not all the action or practice is between and among human beings; some interaction between human and nonhuman beings promotes human faithfulness. Faithfulness is living in a way commensurate with the human vocation. The human vocation, in the words of my teacher Gabriel Moran, is "patient attentiveness and non-violent receptiveness to what is real."[1] The statement presupposes a religious way of life: fulfilling one's vocation as an occasion of "God's absolute self-communication." The Holy One is real. To work, as D. T. Suzuki has said, on my "masterpiece" is to practice expressing divine life. The human masterpiece is a human being who is grateful and peaceful, hopeful and joyous, reverent, courageous, and compassionate — in a word, holy.

Thus, religious education is education within but not limited to a religious community — a company of people at the same time solid and permeable who share a vision of the mystery of existence and a way of life commensurate with that vision: the vision of humans as divine self-communication. In other words, religious education is about *human development,* an idea, Moran notes, that "contains within itself a religious meaning and an educational meaning."[2] And "development means slowly becoming another person."[3] The idea of "slowly becoming another person" is not about feverish efforts at self-improvement or deficient self-regard. That the human vocation requires change is a genuine religious idea: *teshuvah,* "turning around," or "putting on Christ Jesus," or cultivating "buddha mind," and so on.

It follows from this understanding that tracing practice that deserves the name "religious education" is quite complex. The practice is not complex; the practice itself is simple. For example, Moran writes that religious education is helping one another "celebrate life's joys and bear with its sorrows."[4] Or again, "Anyone whose theory of education does not include a grandparent sitting quietly in the sunlight does not have an adequate theory."[5] Or a final example for now: "Part of religious education should be to resist what destroys sports: prize fighting, the violence of football and hockey, continuing discrimination against women, the domination by large corporate interests...."[6] But we encounter a great many trends and countertrends when we try to trace practice and make sense of the names people give this practice and the intentions and ideologies these names reveal. And just as some theologians in the orthodox model conceptualize their work in ways that do not serve convergence, many theorists of religious education think of it in ways that are neither religious nor educational in the sense noted above.

Like bookends near the beginning and end of this century, two distinguished thinkers, both Christian, both employing the term "religious education," help us trace this practice. In the 1920s, in the book *A Social Theory of Religious Education,* George Albert Coe asks rhetorically whether the purpose of religious education is to pass on a tradition or to change the world. In the 1980s, in the book *Educating in Faith,* Mary C. Boys says that religious education is giving access to tradition *and* to the transformative power of tradition. One might change the world a little, help people practice a bit more interreligious reverence, for example, but fail to pass on a religion. Coe thought the answer to his question was twofold, but he was accused of preferring to change the world. A few (or many more than a few) members of a religious community might assist one another to gain access to tradition and its transformative power yet still leave sports to corporate interests and ignore the roles of grandparents. Coe's signature statement of the intention of religious education is an adequate expression of its full breath. But his work (like Moran's) was rejected by many Protestant Christians as lacking Christian specificity or particularity. Reaction to it was part of the resurgence of "Christian education," message-driven practice by Protestant Christians in mid-twentieth-century United States. Boys's formulation is among the best available clues for defining theological education, but it does not attend to many layers of religious education work.

The intentions behind all the many names used to express what we should be doing when we call what we are doing "religious education" or use names that are related variations of "religious education" can be clarified by unearthing what the namers mean by "religious" and by "education." Many of the theorists who provide us with names for what we should be about believe that "religion" and "religiousness" are identical: that to be loyal to an institutional religion is the only way to be "religious." Such practice is properly called "Christian education" (or Jewish education, or Muslim education, and so on). One should not assume too quickly that one understands the stance of such thinkers or such communities of people with regard to interreligious relations. The fault here lies not in an inevitable separatism or exclusivism but in a failure to appreciate the dialectical relationship between "religion" and "religiousness." A crimped practice of religious education results. A term like "the faith" would be common parlance among those so predisposed. And though Christian (or Jewish or Muslim) education can be very vibrant, active, and life-giving (and can, as we shall see, be *part* of a broader religious education), conflating religion and religiousness diminishes a religion's ability to promote religiousness, faithfulness to the human vocation. In this regard, Moran writes: "In its most superficial meaning faith may not be religious at all. We sometimes say *faith* [Moran's emphasis] when all we mean is the holding of ideas as true."[7]

The other clue to what theorists mean by religious education, or variants, is what they mean by "education." Here at least three meanings can be identified. The first two are comparatively easy to identify; they are education (or "teaching-learning," in Moran's words) as schooling and as socialization. The third meaning is captured in the observation by Moran that "life teaches much if religious education can simply keep the door open on human development."[8] This is education understood as the whole matrix of relations through which we assist one another's development.

The meanings and practices the different words name need not be mutually exclusive, but they may be. For example, a religion may "school" its members in convictions and beliefs that are inconsistent with human development. In this context "human development" is synonymous with the "human vocation." Teaching people that God loves "our" people more than other people or that humans are utterly corrupt are two examples of such schooling. Or the pattern of loyalties and behaviors expressed in the common life of the followers of a religion (the socializational dynamics that form people in communities) might thwart human development or might be inconsistent with the explicit "school teaching" (what Moran calls "teaching with an end in view") that goes on in that religion. A good example of this is the systematic subordination of women in Catholic communities (actual socializational pattern) that coexists alongside various ecclesiastical documents (written expressions of school teaching) that speak eloquently but with hollow rhetoric about the importance of women in the Catholic Church.

As we move from schooling through socialization to education as "the complex patterns of relationship between persons and within communities of persons through which we strive to be faithful, to learn faithfulness from others and to instill faithfulness in others...,"[9] the practice becomes less "message-driven," less conscious, less intentional. Even if we rejoin the words and speak of religious education, the same holds true. In the first instance, religious education becomes instruction in this religion — preaching and explaining, conscious, intentional, message-driven. This practice will be called Christian education, Jewish education, and so forth. The same holds true for religious education as socialization

in a particular religion. Socializational theorists have a more sophisticated model of what forms people in a religion. In Moran's
words, they take account, as he does, of more than one "social
form" of education. (Moran notes four social forms of education: family, school, work, and leisure.) But again, the goal is the
enhancement and mutual enrichment of this people in this religion.

Whenever "religion-schooling" and "religion-socialization" do
not baldly undermine human development, they are all to the good,
of course, even if such practice is not sufficient to the ideals of
human development. In other words, Christian education, Jewish education, Muslim education, catechetical practice — as the
activity is often designated among Catholic Christians (from the
Greek for "to re-echo," "to pass down") — is the perpetuation
of the religious community. But something more — a more expan-
sive practice and a greater ideal — is needed. Christian, Jewish, and
Muslim education must form Christians, Jews, and Muslims. But it
must form Christians, Jews, and Muslims who are *religious!* This is
the challenge we have encountered throughout this book. In some
expressions, Christian education may "teach" that there is no salvation except by accepting Jesus Christ as one's personal Lord and
Savior. This may be "Christian" in some attenuated sense, but it is
not religious! (As Moran writes: "Christian as an adjective is not
a compliment or a virtue; it is a designation of a group of people
who have done some good things and some bad things in their
time."[10]) An ultraorthodox rabbi may teach that it is permissible
to murder an Israeli prime minister who seeks peace through the
ceding of land to Palestinians. This may be "Jewish" in some attenuated sense, but it is not religious! An imam may preach "holy
war." This may be in some attenuated sense "Muslim," but it is
not religious!

A broader practice and understanding of religious education is
required of people in all religious communities in order to nurture a deeper religiousness in each, so that "religion-socialization"
does not lead to idolatry and so that the enrichment of each by
interreligious convergence can occur. Such practice will inspire con-
fidence in the beliefs of my people but will not equate them with
"the truth." Such practice will inspire special loyalty to my people
but challenge xenophobia and insist that we are all one people,
God's people. For such a practice, we need a guide who, having
humbly and thoughtfully watched the practice of the people, can
provide clues for religious education in which truth is not equated
with beliefs, religious education with indoctrination in a religion,

my community exclusively with the people of God, teaching with telling, and morality with obedience to apodictic proclamations of hierarchs. That guide is Gabriel Moran.

The Thought of Gabriel Moran

Gabriel Moran is professor in the Department of Culture and Communications at New York University and director of that university's graduate program in religious education. His first published work, *Scripture and Tradition,* appeared in 1963; his sixteenth book, *A Grammar of Responsibility,* in 1996. Moran was studying for his doctorate in religious education at the Catholic University of America during the years the Second Vatican Council was meeting in Rome. That epic event in the history of Christianity, and of the Catholic Church in particular, was a watershed for the flowering of developments that were suppressed in previous decades — in some cases, since the so-called Catholic Counter Reformation begun at the Council of Trent in the mid-1500s. The Second Vatican Council ratified experiences of the Catholic people, what traditional Catholic theology calls the *sensus fidelium* (the beliefs of the people), and work of Catholic theologians that promised, as Edward Schillebeeckx wrote in *Catholic Theology, 1500 to 1970,* to end undue influence on Catholicism of post-Reformation defensiveness and Cartesian dualism. A strictly objectivist or classicist idea of truth was being replaced by a more vital and existential perspective. A static idea of tradition, with no account of historical development, was being replaced by the idea of revelation in both inherited traditions and also in the signs of the times. Such an understanding of the interplay of tradition and experience had been implied in Cardinal Newman's great essay, written at the end of the nineteenth century, "On the Development of Doctrine." Karl Rahner said the council was a beginning of a truly "World Church" and the end of a strictly "Eurocentric Catholicism." This, and the image of the Servant Church defined as the "People of God," promised the end of triumphalism and authoritarianism. The breakdown of old European prejudices led to a flowering of relations between Catholics and Jews as well as intramural ecumenical relations among Christians. In fact, all of the reforms of Vatican II are observable in Catholic life today in greater or lesser measure, despite the movement of restoration to which reference has already been made.

Finally, a strictly didactic approach to formal instruction in the

Catholic religion began to give way to a rich, narrative, liturgically driven approach to catechetics. At its very best, this is what is meant by the phrase "catechetical movement": placing "schooling" in being a Catholic in the larger context of "socialization" through many rich features of the life of the Catholic community and the enhancement of that life and its richness — as authoritarianism, absolutism about the truth, didactic instruction, and sectarian attitudes toward those who had come to be called non-Catholics diminished.

To be accurate it must be noted that Catholic life was rich in symbol and devotion, in social activities related to parishes, in the mysterious allure of the Latin liturgy of the Council of Trent and the special appeal of legions of priests, sisters and brothers in communities, or orders — of the church before the changes promulgated at the Second Vatican Council. I made reference at the beginning of chapter 3 to this experience in my own life. Conversely, despite what was urged at the council, there are in fact many venues in Catholic common life today that are quite vacuous, the result, though not inevitable or universal, of increasing affluence of Catholics in countries such as the United States. The affluence leads to consumerism and individualism, and these in turn blind people to the need for a rich, symbolic, common life.

The difference between the richness of Catholic life before and immediately after the changes of the council began to take effect is that in the former instance, no matter how vital the common life of Catholics was, it was nevertheless founded on a sectarian idea of being God's only true people, a triumphalist view of church authority, and the central importance of instruction in the absolute truth.

The most palpable influence of Moran's thought on large numbers of Catholic and other Christians can be discerned in the 1960s. His two best sellers in 1966, the works *Theology of Revelation* and *Catechesis of Revelation,* changed the practice and mind-set of legions of Catholic and other Christian men and women serving in professional pastoral and religious education roles.[11] Though both books contain more than a glimmer of the originality that will become a staple of Moran's thinking after 1970, the works are expert articulation and interpretation on the "New Theology" and the "scriptural-liturgical" theory of catechetics emerging over the previous decades from the most creative centers of Catholic thought in Western Europe. During this time, from 1965 to 1970, Moran directed a graduate theology program at Manhattan College in New York, which disseminated these ideas and began publishing what now amounts to approximately two hundred essays in the most progressive and influential journals in the English-speaking world. He also began serving as guest faculty at religious education institutes springing up worldwide to help professional church workers to make sense of and implement the changes of Vatican Council II. By the early 1990s, Moran had served as guest lecturer in twenty of these institutes.

In *Educating in Faith*, Mary Boys speaks of Moran's "challenge to conceptualize religious education in a way that is larger than what Church people do to hand on their faith to a younger generation."[12] The challenge has, as one might expect, been met with resistance. Since the early 1970s, Moran has urged professional religious educators in the church to embrace a more radical ecumenicity than they would wish. He embraces pluralism at a level that is only being hinted at in the theological conversation of the 1990s (which was surveyed in chapter 2). With the publication of *Religious Body* (1974), a book containing a fundamentally alternative picture of the church, Moran's critique of church triumphalism hit a stride quite beyond the purposes of professionals working in the structures of that very church. His critical view of the church is bolstered by his care for Jewish-Christian relations and his belief in many feminist ideas. In 1983, Moran wrote of dialogue between Christians and Jews: "Dialogue does not fit, at least not yet, the relation of Christians and Jews. The first step from the Christian side is a kind of repentance, not mainly in the form of breast-beating for history's persecutions, but in the form of intellectual conversion.... Christianity without an inherent relation to Pharisaic Judaism is dangerous or nonsensical."[13] In 1974, speaking of a church of real sisters and brothers rather than a highly clericalized monolith, Moran wrote: "Women are faced with the larger burden in this struggle because of their subordinate role in the past.... The critical balance for the future probably rests on the emergence of a religious sisterhood.... [But] sisterhood cannot swing the whole change. Women need help from men who have developed a sense of brotherhood.... There are undoubtedly some men throughout society who are looking for something other than hierarchy in their jobs, religion and lovemaking. The bureaucratic system can only disparage them for being worse than women.... But there may yet arise a group of men who by experiencing brotherhood in a deeply religious sense will join with women in the constituting of a religious body."[14]

At a time when professional religious educators of all stripes and variations in title were beginning to embrace developmental psychology, Moran began recording a body of work critical of the prevailing schools' implicit rational, masculine, and elite presuppositions that is, through today, an unparalleled literature of dissent. As we shall see, the ground of his criticism is the same ground of thought about revelation, education, community, and the true sources of the moral life from which what he has called his design for ecumenical education rises. One aspect of this facet of Moran's work is his serendipitous writing about "adulthood" in such works as *Education Toward Adulthood* (1977). Here adulthood is the goal of religious education, but it does not mean pornographic, older, no longer a child, now capable of "having a religion." The adult in Moran's theory, it turns out, is a *religious* person, centered in both the silence and irony of the inner self yet devoted to the community, motivated not by rational principles of right and wrong but by the example of the "lives of the saints," and encountering others as "thou," not as parties with whom to be in dispute about truth and falsehood but as companions on a nonviolent journey.

Moran moved from the 1970s through the 1990s from catechesis of revelation to religious education proper (though he has moved back again to appreciation of the catechetical element of religious education). An important source of this development is his search for a knowledge that is deeper than language, a nonobjectifying knowing. He has sought to bring us along with him, and this, too, has met with resistance. In this Moran has been influenced by Martin Buber and the idea that knowing is relational, and by pragmatic philosophical perspectives and the proposition that knowing is active (though in Moran's appropriation of the latter, the Transcendent, the Holy Mystery, remains). Moran stands with Karl Rahner, for whom a formula, however important, is still only a formula; with Bede Griffiths, for whom even after doctrinal teaching the "mystery remains"; with Abraham Heschel for whom there are theology's "permanent facts" but more important the "moments" of depth theology. In all this, Moran's counsel is never as "message-driven" as the perceived exigencies of religious organizations require (again the restorationist charge of "religious illiteracy"). But in this Moran provides clues to religious education practice that is far better than message-driven methods in its power to disclose the actual graces in the ordinary common life of people, and to promote catechetical activity. And Moran's ideas about religious education place interreligious reverence and depth dialogue at the center. We turn to his treatment of revelation, religious education (including his discussion of teaching), community, the sources of the moral life and holiness as the end of religious education.

Revelation

Gabriel Moran has said that revelation is the central theme of his work over thirty-plus years and that he is not fearful of being stuck in a "foolish consistency." His master's thesis, which became the 1963 book *Scripture and Tradition*, dealt with revelation. A paper delivered at the twenty-fifth annual meeting of the Association of Professors and Researchers in Religious Education on November 4, 1995, is a remarkable summary of his thinking to date.

In "Revelation in a Culture of Disbelief," Moran writes that revelation "express[es] the fundamental relation of divine and human that includes some degree of understanding."[15] The opposite meaning of revelation is that it is divinely revealed truths to be believed. Moran says of this view: "To make revelation into an object of believing has been a disaster." He goes further, observing, "I think there is a good deal of Christian belief...that could use a strong dose of disbelief." The idea will appear later in a discussion of patterns of religious education development. On the brink of young adulthood, Moran maintains, people often experience an impulse of disbelief that can be quite salutary. As I write, Peter Steinfels reports in *The New York Times* that the Vatican Congregation for the Doctrine of the Faith, with the pope's approval, has announced "that Roman Catholics must consider their church's doctrine that only men can be priests to be 'infallibly' taught."[16] A leader of the Catholic bishops in the United States is quoted: "I ask you now prayerfully to allow the Holy Spirit to fill you with the wisdom and understanding that will enable you to accept it."[17] This is a virtually blasphemous assertion that the Holy Spirit, God, actually wants women excluded from the possibility of being ordained Catholic priests (whereas, if we followed Micah, we might see God as wanting us to "do justice, love mercy, and walk humbly," with God leaving the strictly historical struggles of religion to us to work out). The most disastrous element of equating revelation with teachings of the hierarchs of religions is present in the bishop's plea, namely. equating human and divine will. And another element is also present: that "accepting revelation" is an endless series of acts of intellectual grovelling in which we try to muster "the wisdom and understanding that will enable [us] to accept it."

We could fruitfully juxtapose this most recent "disaster" in understanding revelation with earlier classics (classics of disaster): God
wills that the Jews wander forever without a homeland to educate
humanity in the results of faithlessness; or, the earth is the center
of the universe. Or even the very early tradition, dating to at least
the ninth century, that it is heretical to say that a pope cannot act
infallibly.[18]

Moran believes that the history of ideas about revelation is
a struggle between metaphors of sight and metaphors of speech
(speaking and listening). The unfortunate victory of the visual
metaphor is the result of both ancient Greek and eighteenth-
century, rational, Enlightenment influences. He notes that Philo (a
Jewish thinker influenced by Greek thought), for example, considers *theoria,* beholding an object, the most adequate means for
beings to relate to Being itself. The Enlightenment represents a victory, Moran tells us, of *ratio* over *narratio,* both elements of classic
Logos doctrine to which reference was made in chapter 2. Truth results from a rational process that constructs "visual objects in the
mind," and "language is reduced to factual statements." In contrast *narratio* as a means of knowledge is speaking and listening
employing language that is narrative, poetic, and even homiletic. In
the "clash of metaphors for expressing the truth...the supremacy
of the oral metaphor, [to speak and to listen] is clearly traceable to
Hebrew origins."

The prominence of the rational mode of expressing truth is the
basis for equating divine-human relation with beliefs, sometimes
including ignoble beliefs. Moran traces modern protest against this
rationalism from Nietzsche through Heidegger to Foucault, noting
that "the search for a 'non-objectifying' knowledge easily leads to
irrationality. But it can also be the opening to a relational kind of
knowing."

This is the heart of the matter: "The image of revelation refers
to what happens between persons at intimate levels of exchange";[19]
revelation is relations. Beliefs are but "the least inadequate expressions of a developmental process in which the divine and
the human are revealed together."[20] It follows, Moran says, that
because revelation is essentially relations, it is both present and responsive. He acknowledges the intentional redundancy in the title
of his 1972 study, *The Present Revelation,* because "revelation is
always present, and another word for presence is revelation." For
the actual state of relation to exist, there must be presence; the opposite of presence is absence. I am not relating to what is absent

from me. Regarding response as constitutive of revelation, Moran writes: "The beginning of a Jewish or a Christian or a Muslim life is not possession of secret knowledge but the activity of responding to others wherein the divine is revealed."

(It might be helpful to frame what has been said thus far of Moran's ideas on revelation in the context of the earlier discussion of the spirit of the Second Vatican Council. Of all the many, dramatic changes that occurred in Catholic life in the years after the council — such obvious developments as the vernacular liturgy, advances in ecumenism, ideological trends that led to what appeared to be unprecedented dissent, for example — the linchpin of the renewal of Catholic life in the church was, and remains, the retrieval of a rich, traditional idea of faithfulness. A signature essay of earlier years, closer to the time of the council, that dealt with this idea in theological language was written by Avery Dulles in 1977.[21] In the essay "The Meaning of Faith Considered in Relationship to Justice," Dulles — a thinker far more moderate in his view of appropriate reform and renewal than Moran — argued that the spirit of conciliar renewal was based on correcting a narrow view of faith, one that gave undue weight to "intellectual assent," to what tradition had come to call "assensus" [what the United States bishop quoted above was appealing for]. Renewed vitality, Dulles said, rests in granting equal measure of importance to the "performative" or moral dimension of genuine faithfulness and, especially noteworthy in our context, to the "fiducial" dimension: to faith[fulness] as trusting relation.)

The most misunderstood and volatile aspect of the discussion of revelation as present, responsive relation between the divine and human and between and among human and nonhuman beings is the treatment of experience. Moran wrote unself-consciously and without apology in *The Present Revelation* that experience is religious! He is fully aware that such an assertion is easily caricatured as the "faddish relevancy called Liberalism."[22] In fact, the idea has no relationship at all to naive liberal hope of "progressive lighting up of the morning...knowledge of G-d increas[ing] with the advance of modern science." Expressing his admiration for the treatment of revelation by Franz Rosenzweig — Rosenzweig's idea of the "continuing *availability* [my emphasis] of revelation" — Moran says, "What comes first is not intention, truths or events, but the relation of responding faithfully and lovingly to the deepest call in the human heart." The deepest call in the human heart! Moran's idea of revelation is not unreconstructed liberalism; it is traditional Catholicism! The human person is the event of "God's absolute self-communication." To understand revelation as relational, responsive, continually available and present in *all* experience is demanded not by liberalism nor even by the inter-religious convergence that such an idea makes possible (in contrast to apodictically expressed messages that make such convergence impossible). It is an understanding demanded by faith that God is! In *Design for Religion* in 1971, Moran wrote that "experience is not what the student comes with nor is it what the teacher supplies but it is what teacher and student take part in."[23] It is the "faith" of Catholic Christianity at least that the Holy One is available as Presence, loving, upholding, challenging in all creation (the "incar-nationalism" we encountered in the discussion of Anglo-Catholic theologian Norman Pittenger's thinking in chapter 2). "In God, we live and move and have our being." "Every place, every book, every person," Moran writes, "can be revelatory although none is guaranteed to be." In the 1995 essay, he cites an interview con-ducted by Victor Frankl with a survivor of the Nazi death camps. Frankl asks the woman how she bore the violence and cruelty, how she kept from despair, and the woman answers: " 'There was a tree I could see from my cell and it spoke to me.' 'What did the tree say?' asked Frankl. The woman's reply: 'It said life, life, life.' [Moran continues]: We might ask: Did the tree really speak? To a woman brought up on the Bible, it did. The revelatory relation requires a listener whose ear has been trained to hear all creation speak."

The history of any religion, including Christianity, demonstrates many blasphemous invocations of "God's revelation." Moran ac-knowledges a hierarchy of revelatory sources. "Some things," he writes, "some events, some writings hold more revelatory power than others. Personal love has been more revelatory than building bombs; the biblical story can reveal the divine in ways that *The Bridges of Madison County* cannot. But nothing, nothing at all, including the experience of nothingness, can be excluded."

Least of all would one dismiss as deficiently revelatory the divine-human relation expressed concretely in the lives and beliefs of many people on varying paths of holiness. In Moran's thought, revelation is not what the Christians (or the Jews or the Mus-lims or others) have; revelation *has* the Christians and the Jews and the Muslims and the Buddhists and the Hindus and so forth: "There is only one process of revelation within which Christians and Jews and Muslims are called to respond today." There is no one true faith, nor are there many faiths. There are many religions, particular expressions of a continuing, responsive relation of people and peoples to the divine and to one another under the influence of divine life in them and their communities. But there is one God self-communicating universally through these particular expressions: "There are faithful people and there are unfaithful people (only G-d knows who fits where). But there are no 'other faiths.' "

Religious Education

According to Gabriel Moran, *education* is a "process constituted by a set of *relations*"[24] rooted in *experience* and prompting *religiousness*. Education is a constant "reshaping of life's forms with end (meaning) but without end (termination)."[25] In no theory of which I am aware is the term "education" employed as a criterion word with such consistency as by Gabriel Moran. That is to say, the word is only employed to describe something good. (As R. S. Peters says in *Education and Ethics*, we speak, and rightly so, of being "schooled" in scandal or "learning" to pick pockets since neither is a criterion word, but not of "education" in these things). At the most universal and basic level, religiousness is "whatever keeps open the process of development."[26] It "refers to those attitudes and activities that challenge the limits of experience."[27] Education, occurring obviously in the matrix called experience (what we are in and what we are) is religious. And the "field" (experience itself) is religious. It must be said again that this is not liberalism; it is Catholicism! It is not a theory based on the denial of sin but on affirming the universality of grace! It is not a view based on blindness to the pervasive evil in human life and history, but on the Augustinian doctrine that only good has ontological status; evil is privation (*privatio*, "taking away") of good.

It is easy to see how a theory that begins with the idea of the universal availability of processes and activities (relations) that are educational (that promote human development, which is to say, that promote religiousness) can be mistaken for a doctrine asserting the existence of some kind of "religion in general" — how such a theory can be mistaken for the "homogenization" Moran himself eschews. Such an interpretation of Moran's work has been leveled as a charge many times over the years. Were it accurate, it would certainly render his thought useless for our purposes — useless as a vehicle for building up reverence for people on other paths precisely as *other* (as *particular* in their expressions of religiousness) and a vehicle for building up *us* in our particularity, in all our inclusive uniqueness. It is a charge whose frequency and rigor is proportionate to the zeal with which those leveling it are motivated by a radical and exclusive "christocentrism" or by triumphalist attitudes toward ecclesiastical structures and functionaries. It is, in fact, a complete misreading of Moran's work. Moran begins where he begins and asserts what he asserts first of all because of the deep resonance in his life and work of the "Catholic Spirit" of which we have spoken; because he is rooted in that particular, inclusively unique perspective. More specifically, this starting point is the result of following his own advice about the proper function of *professional* religious educators, indeed all professionals. This function is to *look* before we *preach*. (In a related insight, his colleague and wife, Maria Harris, says that the first act of teaching is contemplation.[28]) Moran writes that professional religious education practice "begins by naming the ways people live and then it attempts to give them a richer communal meaning for working out their lives."[29] There is real humility in this sequence; humility among professionals is not so common. Not starting with the message does not mean that the theory of religious education will inevitably lack specificity, the "Christian" or "Jewish" or "Muslim" dimension. It does not mean, in Catholic parlance, that the theory will lack a sufficient "catechetical" dimension. It means the theorist has *looked* and seen the universal availability of divine self-communication and human response embedded in the soil of the ordinary lives we live, in our joys and sorrows. The theorist has seen the working of grace embedded in the structures of "religious education development." Nothing in this theory prevents education in religion. What is rejected is the idolatrous idea that any religion exhausts religiousness.

Moran believes that in human life there is a movement of religious development through three moments. The earliest moment is being *"simply religious."* Insofar as religiousness is tied to awe and mystery and dependent in its origins and growth on gifts of love and nurture, the infant and child are "simply religious." The goal of all religious educators, including professionals, in every moment of their own and others' religious education development, is to "negate what negates." But at no moment are the relational processes and activities that negate what negates more important than when human beings are "simply religious."[30] It is for this reason that Moran highlights such religious education processes and activities as supporting mothers of infants, resisting the toy industry, advocating for nutritional programs for infants, fighting — to recall an earlier example — the despoliation of sports, and so on. The religiousness will grow if we can remove obstacles. Moran is fond of quoting G. K. Chesterton's aphorisms. One of the most effective of such citations is about the simple religiousness of young children. Chesterton writes: "A child of seven is excited by being told that Tommy opened a door and saw a dragon. But a child of three is excited by being told that Tommy opened a door."[31]

There follows the moment of *"acquiring a religion."* In discussing this extended moment in the lives of human beings, Moran employs such terms as the "visional/mythical" moment, the time of "narrative," the time to be "systematic" about a certain kind of teaching and content. Moran talks about this as a time of acquiring "our peoples' beliefs."[32] The charge that Moran's theory is insufficiently specific or particular, that it does not honor what is peculiar about "my people," breaks down here. But the interpretation is so common and resistant that it needs to be emphasized to the point of flirting with patronizing the reader: in discussing this moment Moran is accounting for the Christian or Jewish or Muslim educational practices and activities. And, as we shall see, he does so with more power and precision than those (the restorationists come to mind) for whom this is all religious education is. When Moran writes of this continuing moment of religious educational development, he is frankly, straightforwardly, and in a precisely appropriate spirit conservative!

However, "the situation of 'having a religion' [though] not bad . . . is also not good enough. . . . A further stage of development is demanded in adulthood. True, some people go around the rest of their lives 'having a religion' and professing that God is found only in that segment of reality. . . . [But] what hangs in the balance is the kind of unity that the world is coming to and the kind of integrity possible in individual lives."[33] For the good of the world and the integrity of individual people and their religious communities, we must assist one another to become *religiously Christian (Jewish, Muslim and so forth)*, though there is "no guarantee of an environment [through earlier movements and moments] that makes the third stage a genuine possibility."[34] Being Christian, or Jewish or Muslim, in a *religious* way is the fullness of faithfulness. It is setting aside the idolatry of religion but not the particularities of my religious community: "By many common standards the third stage of religious development can be called conservative.... It not only conserves the past but rediscovers it. It does not spend energies fighting free of doctrine; it reintegrates doctrines, rituals and codes of behavior with an openness of mind but *with passionate conviction* [my emphasis]."[35]

It must be clear that a short essay on Moran's work (or a long one, for that matter) does not require a section entitled "Interreligious Reverence and the Thought of Gabriel Moran." Such values are the foundation of his thought; they permeate it. He writes: "Religious education at this [adult] stage is not the building of one's case to score against one's adversaries. It is a journey of compassion for every human being who, no matter what his or her beliefs, is recognized, accepted and loved as a fellow traveler on this earth."[36]

It follows from his richly layered views on religiousness, education, and development that Moran's thought encompasses all the "social forms" of religious education development. Most attempts to describe religious education, regardless of the pains taken to be comprehensive or the sophistication of the model, belie a message-driven bias, as if the preponderance of educational practices and activities, educational relations, results from a certain kind of teaching — what Moran calls "teaching with an end in view." Virtually no theorist, even those in the "socialization" school of thought, is as consistent as Moran in naming family, job, and leisure as religious educational forms along with school. In these forms there may be an educational end in view, but as we shall examine below, intentionality is often muted in forms of education other than schooling. Moran's detailed schema of religious education development makes clear the importance he attaches to the other social forms, as well as to schooling. This picture of development is summarized below.

Stage One: Simply Religious — Simply Religious Education

Moment One: Physical. The infant is born and as a young child experiences, or is deprived of appropriate experiences of, love and gift and nurture in a community. Religious education is to "destroy the destroyers" of infant and childhood religiousness.

Moment Two: Visional or Visional/Mythical. Children are wrapped in brilliant imagery and told powerful stories: "Resisting whatever smothers the child's imagination or obstructs its involvement in story listening is religious."[37]

Stage Two: Acquiring a Religion — Christian (Jewish, Muslim) Education

Moment One: Our Peoples' Beliefs or Narrative and Systematic Religious Education. This is the practice to which "most educational resources" are directed. It is genuinely, unself-consciously "tribal" and later "ideological." Done well, such formal religious educational practice will frame and sustain very deep communal loyalties; the young child will develop a sense of belonging to "a people with a past shaping our future."[38] Done badly, such influences result at best in a sense that we "hold membership" in a "denomination." At worst, this Christian, Jewish, or Muslim moment (for Catholics, the sustained "catechetical" moment) will block forever the possibility of being *religiously* Christian, Jewish, Muslim, and so forth.

It is in his discussion of this moment that Moran's advocacy of schooling in the religion of my people is most straightforward. In discussing the "systematic" dimension of formal — one might say, professional — religious education, Moran names the "teaching-learning" in which we are engaged "theological education." Though he is uncomfortable with the term "theology" (for the reasons discussed in chapters 2 and 3), Moran is explicit in calling for very precise intellectual and ideological exchanges between teenagers and young adults. This is precisely the kind of teaching in which *school* teachers engage. In his discussion of this moment in chapter 9 of *Religious Education Development,* he suggests that a healthy element of development at this time of life may be "disbelief." This is not unbelief but disbelief "directed at the . . . external, verbal side of faith."[39] It is a state of mind and heart, Moran tells us, that is actually induced by religious tradition. The goal of conventional religion is to "provid[e] a coherent picture of the universe."[40] But "even if that system has the most beautiful ideas the world has ever heard of," most healthy, developing people come to appreciate that no rational, self-enclosed system of ideas accounts for the mystery of a single life path, its joys and sorrows, exaltations and tragedies.[41] Conventional religion, Moran notes, participates in the general societal deficiencies in responding to the young in a period of disbelief. Like society, it "provides little space for individuals to rebel against their religious upbringings and yet hold onto their underlying love of family and friends."[42]

It is also in the extended discussion of this broad catechetical and theological stage that Moran speaks most persuasively about liturgical engagement as religiously educational. This is a theme that corresponds to the emphasis recommended at the end of chapter 3 in the discussion of the eucharistic Christ.

Stage Three: Religiously Christian (Jewish, Muslim, and So Forth) Education

Moment Five: Journeying/Inquiry or Parable. In contrast to the young and to young adults, many people in their middle years come to know that no set of right principles, no single system simply answers the mysteries of life. Speaking of the parabolic qualities to be nurtured in one another over the expanse of this moment, Moran notes that "the religious adult does not possess a complete plan."[43] Much of adult life involves dealing with ambiguity, with limitation, with cultivating an ironic cast of heart and mind, with "living the tension of opposites."[44] If our catechetical practice has provided us with a people, a foundation, a set of noble loyalties, with patience in the face of disbelief, we may move into the period of prolonged "journeying/inquiry," knowing that "even the best theological system finally fails to provide . . . the answers, that is, whom to love, what to choose as a life's work, and how to live with a sense of wholeness."[45] But with all these resources (the community, the loyalties, the foundation) available to us, we try to become genuinely religious through our lives as lovers and workers and parents and friends. Moran believes that the single, signature quality of character that gives evidence a human being is navigating this moment with some success is the progressive cultivation of nonviolence.[46]

Moment Six: Detachment or Centering. The discussion of the final moment of religious education development reveals that for Moran, its culmination and end (meaning) is holiness, a topic discussed below. At this point, a consideration of his writings on teaching will conclude the discussion of religious education.

In a remarkable book on teaching entitled *Showing How: The Act of Teaching,* Moran expresses a view of teaching, or "teaching-learning," that, as one would expect, corresponds to the elemental values in his work. These include a deep, authentic Catholic conviction about the universality of grace and the continuing availability of divine self-communication and human response. For him, the universal possibility of graciousness is wrought in the fabric of ordinary common life, lived in family and school, at work and at leisure. To Moran, as we have seen, religion is not bad (an ironic way of putting it) but it is not good enough. The end, in the sense of meaning, of human life is religiousness. As a result of these core values, Moran insists the meaning of "to teach" can never be exhausted by "to explain." To teach is to show how, and at its most profound, it is "to show someone how to live (and die)."[47] What is eliminated from the beginning is any idea that equates teaching with didactic indoctrinational practice, and any idea that religious education ends with "education in a religion," because its end is much more profound: how to live and how to die. This idea is advanced by Moran's penetrating discussion of "intention" in teaching. He holds that "the emphasis on intention is an extraordinary deficiency and naivete in literature on teaching."[48] He writes, as only one convinced that grace abounds can, that "we all depend on human teaching every day, people doing things in our presence which inspire us to believe that there is goodness in the world, that one can say yes to living another day. And most of the time, the smile, the gesture of politeness or care, is all the more powerful as teaching because it is not intended as teaching."[49] Moran invokes the power in Malcolm X's life of the simple kindness he was shown by a white man in his pilgrimage to Mecca. He also sites Sherwin Nuland's book *How We Die*, noting how much that is profound in teaching-learning how to live and die results from the example of those who die with courage, nobility, and hope. Moran says: "There is a kind of teaching that arises in the human community.... The patterns may have a degree of consciousness and intention. Nevertheless this kind of teaching occurs without any one individual intending to teach."[50]

The general framework of this theory of teaching demands that messages (including messages of exclusive "revelation") be subordinated to a process of cultivating attentiveness and gratitude for gifts that surround us. And it demands that we acknowledge that more people show us how to live and how to die than are numbered in our own religious community. As the elaboration of five modes of teaching makes clear, Moran's view gives full weight to "acquiring a religion." But as we shall see, there is no room in the theory for teaching as manipulation or indoctrination, or for teaching a religion in a way that can lead to xenophobia.

Moran distinguishes five kinds of teaching, of showing how to live: (1) teaching by example, (2) teaching by design, (3) teaching with an end in view, (4) teaching to remove obstacles, and (5) teaching the conversation. Teaching by example is *being* an example, not setting up examples. It is, as Moran has written elsewhere, the chief instrument in acquiring a healthy religion.[51] It also leads members of religious communities beyond the boundaries of any religion. Teaching by design does not mean what it might at first seem to mean in an era intoxicated with "learning technologies." Moran uses the example of a batting teacher. In this mode of exchange, it is not "teacher gives, student receives... [but] student acts, teacher studies design, teacher proposes redesign, student acts differently."[52] (Once again, humility is required in a professional.) The teacher, with an end in view, employs the language of rhetoric: whether the form is story, lecture, or sermon, the goal is to persuade to believe. It is teaching to win loyalty (as Moran says, citing Gadamer) to "justified prejudice." But even here, in the mode of teaching most associated with inducting people into a religion, there is no room for indoctrination or absolutism. Indoctrination, Moran says, "results in a person so attached to one version of reality that multiple perspectives, ambiguity in language and the ability to stand at a difference from one's own beliefs, have been eliminated."[53] Even as rhetorician, and even with children, Moran makes plain that the "teacher has to convey two viewpoints: the truth that the teacher is convinced of and the acknowledgement that another truthful view is possible."[54]

Teaching to remove obstacles is not teaching with an end in view, except the end of removing obstacles. The teaching cannot be direct, saying things like "pull yourself together." Much of this practice entails employing therapeutic language — language that calms, soothes, heals, praises, welcomes, and thanks. This is a process of "removing whatever object starts acting as endpoint."[55]

Finally, there is teaching the conversation. Here Moran's ethos of intellectual humility repudiating triumphalism, his deep commitment to what in earlier chapters was designated "depth dialogue," is clearly on display. He articulates a mode of teaching that is essentially that of academic discourse (though it is by no means limited to academies). Authentically employed rhetorical and therapeutic language having served their function, conversation partners having been exposed to good example and expert design, we may now be able "to speak so that greater understanding is possible," Moran's wonderfully simple designation of the purpose of such teaching.[56] No such genuine conversation (speaking and listening and asking "what does it mean to ask the meaning of a text...") is possible "if we are obsessed with the realization of some future project,... [if] we do not have the mental space to attend to the present." But in discourse with a good teacher of conversation, it may be possible (for Christian and Jew,

Hindu and Muslim) to have a conversation that "has no end, no predetermined endpoint that concludes the conversation."[57]

Community, Interiority, and the Sources of the Moral Life

It must be clear that in Moran's work, the idea of the community is given the central place. We experience the graces of ordinary life — including the grace of sustaining life and hope amid terrible tragedy — in religious and educational communities. It is the "saints in our midst" who are examples of religious and moral life. The social forms of common life are the vehicles through which we engage in a journey to faithfulness; they are where the absolute self-communication of the Holy One reaches us. Moran says these forms (family, school, job, and leisure) represent and promote universal values, partially embodied. Family especially exemplifies community and gives promise of experiencing real *communion*. School especially promotes knowledge and gives hope of true *vision*. Job affords the possibility, however fragile, of experiencing authentic work and gives hope that we may experience our *vocation*. Leisure especially promotes healthy experiences of recreation and gives hope that we can grow *contemplative*.[58] "Community," Moran writes, "refers to the specifically human way of relating."[59] It is "a small group of people getting on with life; birth, feeding, thinking, talking, planning, aging, dying."[60]

In Moran's thought there is no dichotomy between religious and moral life. One of the most powerfully expressed and frequent themes of his writings is the critique of this dualism; he ascribes it to the modern, rationalist, Enlightenment mentality. Under the influence of such an ideology, it may be well and good for those who need them to have their silly communal religious stories and superstitious rituals. But moral life will have to be governed by reason! For Moran, however, the true community (the religious and educational community) is the only venue for the cultivation of persons of "virtue/care/character." The underlying ideal of what Moran calls "adulthood" in the modern, rationalist mentality is one that "glorifies rational, independent, secure men." In what he calls the "ethics" of "virtue/care/character/community," adulthood entails the "evolving integrity of rational/non-rational, dependent/independent, living/dying in lives of men and women."[61] This is maturity; for the mature, only religiously educational communities will do: "Mature men and women are governed by a discipline of life within a community that shapes our character through visions, stories, rituals and innumerable gifts."[62] But "where there is not community, there are no persons [in this sense of "adulthood"]; there are individuals who do not recognize a universal humanity within themselves."[63]

Moran writes that "we become virtuous beings by participating in the life, story and vision of moral communities."[64] Here virtue is not understood as the end product of fearsome battles with the will, or as successful judgments about relevant principles of reason for deciding, impartially, what it is just to do or to refrain from doing. Virtue pertains not only to doing but to not doing, not only to one's behaviors, in the sense of social gestures, but to the strength of one's soul (to the "care of souls," to use the ancient phrase repopularized by the contemporary writer Thomas More). The faithful life, the religious life, is one fabric: social practice and interior practice. The stories, visions, and rituals of religious communities teach moral behavior: recognizing universal humanity in ourselves and acting with empathy and compassion. But "the morality of mature people...must include an element of the mystical."[65] The often atrophied mystical "muscle" is the human capacity to practice to learn to be still, to be silent, to be present, to let go, and to let be. The traditions of meditative or contemplative prayer of the religious educational communities are an indispensable source of moral maturity, for "to be morally adult is to know that the world does not divide into good and bad things, right and wrong choices. Every choice we make is contaminated by side effects that we cannot escape. If we let the choices flow *from the center of our receptiveness to being and in resonance with fellow travelers on earth, our actions will have a gentleness that lessens the violence of the world*" [my emphasis].[66] For all the heroism of many modern, secular people, secularism (the modern, rational mentality) cannot get us from individualism to a deeper, more inclusive personhood or from action to a deeper, more inclusive nonaction. For this, we need the religious educating community.

But the capacity of the community to teach us both contemplation and justice is imperiled not only by secularism but also by the triumphalism of the church. First among the criteria Moran articulates for changing religious *organizations* is that the "form of organization...[be] appropriate for religious activities."[67] Remember that Moran's operative definition of a community is a "specifically human way of relating," a way of relating leading toward (but never fully achieving) communion, vision, vocation, and contemplation. To a very great extent, the church is organized bureaucratically; it makes use of (1) concentration of control and supervision, (2) differentiation of function, (3) qualifications for office, (4) objectivity, (5) precision and consistency. Moran says this is "the metaphor of the machine imposed on human relationships."[68] He adds: "It is not the institutionalized action but the monopoly of institutions that is undesirable."[69] There is, to say the least, some tension between religious educational communities and the way religions are organized. So when Moran says that "every religious community by the fact of its existence is a threat to the rulers that be,"[70] he is referring to both secular rulers and the rulers of religions.

The tension between bureaucratic organization and religious educational community is also a subject of Karl Rahner's brilliant little 1976 book, *The Shape of the Church to Come*. There Rahner juxtaposes and contrasts "the Church of real spirituality" with that of "boring administration." Into this mix, we cast the issue of professionalism. It is a complex idea with which Moran deals at length in many of his books. Professionalism has positive and negative connotations. It can point to the elite and detached cadres of people within religion who wittingly or unwittingly alienate the members of the community from the gifts and revelations of ordinary common life, gifts of silence and of just action. Or the professional may bring special competence to the community. Or "professional" may simply mean that some peoples' practice is paid for. The function of the professional is inexplicable apart from some rendition of what "amateur" status in the community means. Are amateurs less competent than professionals, or are they the members of the community who "love to do something"? For Moran, these questions are crucial in determining whether the action of the community is dominated by the imperative of "teaching a religion" or it expands to take in "teaching to be religious."[71] Moran considers the hope well founded that religious communities might achieve a truly postmodern understanding of professionalism: "Here the single dividing line between a class of experts and an uneducated laity would be missing. There would be recognized a great variety of skills. Everyone could become competent to some degree in the most important areas of life. At the same time, it would be readily acknowledged that everyone has something to learn from the others. A professional would, therefore, be someone who works in a team of knowledgeable men and women, someone who invites people into participating in knowledge. This notion of professional involves recognition that we live in a dying and re-birthing universe; technique will not save us from dying. Acting professionally is based upon a wisdom born of confronting mortality."[72] Note, again, all insight culminates in an act of humility. The means to preserve the gracious function of religious community are modesty and honesty, willingness to let go of some measure of control, to let some things die so that other things can arise. In this lies the intrinsic relationship between Moran's idea of a genuine religious education community and that of interreligious reverence. He writes that "the very limitations of a community's existence create a tension with the greater world outside the community; the bond with a few human beings conveys the sense of what the human bond is."[73] And "to accept life in a community is implicitly an affirmation of life itself. It is a recognition that this people that I call my people is an embodiment of the universal human community."[74]

Holiness

I have said throughout this chapter that the end of religious education is faithfulness — faithful people, faithful communities. Faithfulness entails cultivating divine life in us and in our relations. Peoples and communities that are in thrall to the absolute self-communication of the Holy One are steadily, if undramatically, cultivating gratefulness and joy, silence and peace, reverence, courage, and compassion. This is holiness: practicing *presence* to the Holy One. For this, contemplation, from which just action arises, is necessary. The religious educating community is where holiness arises: "a place for contemplative prayer, rhythmically related to intense social action."[75] This is the purpose of religious education, though as Moran says, "The question is whether religious educators themselves see contemplation as a practical concern at the heart of religious education."[76] When holiness, "teaching to be religious" (rather than only "teaching religion"), is clearly named as the purpose of the community, interreligious reverence is assured. For though religion often divides, genuine religiousness — contemplative being — unites. And reverence must follow: "As imagination expands and the mind is quieted, we come to see the similarities among all things. Simultaneously we become detached from superficial perceptions of the self and from the apotheosis of any object. The journey [is] to the One beyond all names."[77]

Conclusion

The kind of religious education practice that Moran inspires is difficult. I have suggested that there is something intrinsically oppositional about religion, and it is a great art to balance "teaching religion" with "teaching to be religious." The art includes the religious critique of religion itself. But "Christianity [and most other religions] traditionally frowned upon a person partaking of its life while retaining the personal autonomy to compare Christianity and other possible forms of religious life."[78] Moran's career is instructive in this regard. Not a few frowns have been and continue to be directed at him. Many of his nuanced distinctions are misunderstood. The enterprise in which he is engaged, so intimately related to the Catholic religious ethos and to the prophetic condemnation of idolatry, is sometimes unheeded. And yet the message is so compelling: God is bigger than religion; education is more than school; teaching is more than explaining; the community is greater than organizations; morality is more a matter of response than solving rational puzzles. All people are God's people. Moran is no romantic, but his work has a quixotic quality.

Moran's life and work are instructive for all those who hunger (hunger gently) to purify their own religious communities and embrace persons in other religious communities. The instruction is this: Gabriel Moran is humble. The humility is founded on the virtue of irony. It is a strength of soul that is very important to pay attention to, to practice cultivating. "Irony with respect to the human condition is the capacity to hold simultaneously two seemingly contradictory views of the human being: greatest thing in creation/absurdly small and fragile creature."[79] In the true work of religious education, "by staying at our life's work even as we become aware of its limitations, we make our jobs an education in irony."[80]

Chapter Five

The Genius of Judaism

On the Advisability of Assessing the "Other"

Jacob Neusner writes: "While these days Christians and Judaists undertake religious dialogue, there is not now and there never has been a dialogue between the religions, Judaism and Christianity. The conception of a Judeo-Christian tradition that Judaism and Christianity share is simply a myth in the bad old sense: a lie."[1] Elsewhere Neusner explains why no such dialogue has ever or will ever occur: "How can two religious communities understand each other when one raises the issue of the sanctification of Israel and the other the salvation of the world?"[2]

Neusner's objectives, if I understand them correctly, are supported to a point by assertions in this book. There is no real reverence in the presumption that one understands or empathizes fully — the presumption that one knows the "full fact" of another individual or another community of people. Such presumption discloses what was earlier called a "group narcissism," not inter-religious sensitivity. The inevitable results of such illusory understanding are either syncretism or the triumphalism embedded in the term "Judeo-Christian."

But Neusner's thesis, while it functions as a very important caution, is ultimately antithetical to much of what has been claimed thus far and to the hope that gives rise to these claims, because Neusner calls into question whether people in any religious community could ever adopt a broadly inclusive view of their uniqueness. His is a challenge to Panikkar's idea that a gracious religious common life requires both concreteness and transcendence. More specifically, with reference to relations between Jews and Christians, Neusner's view is a challenge, and a valuable one, to whether Jews in significant numbers could ever, or should ever, experience "holy envy" of some feature of Christianity. Implicitly, he questions whether Christians could ever, or should ever, let go of universalistic claims, whether in doing so Christians would, in fact, cease to be Christians.

Neusner's ideas about the non-event of dialogue between Judaism and Christianity provide a stark backdrop for this chapter, because its purpose is to articulate an appreciative view of select elements of Judaism. The selection and the appreciation are the work of a Christian, and the potential pitfalls are real and obvious. The purpose of the chapter is to evoke admiration and to promote reverence in the light of persistent *stereotype*. But the outcome might be a subtle or not-so-subtle triumphalism. What is seen, selected, and expressed in this chapter is refracted through a perspective largely indebted to Catholic Christian categories of mind. The result might simply be "Christianized" Judaism. In trying to present a "partial fact" about Judaism, the Jewishness of Jews may become more remote to the reader. When a Christian assesses Judaism, however positive the motive, the result might be a subtle or not-so-subtle form of Christian "self-improvement." Joseph Bernardin has written that the separation of Christianity from Judaism "had the effect of deadening an important dimension of the church's soul."[3] And David Tracy, writing about Christian liberation theology, speaks of it as a "necessary re-Judaizing" of Christianity.[4] Stendahl says that when one sees something beautiful in the path of holiness of members of another religious community, concretely in the lives of the members of that community, one appreciates it but does not try to possess it. Here, although the primary intention is to highlight features of Judaism for which all should be grateful and to promote reverence and overcome stereotype, I also have in mind a "re-Judaizing" of Christianity. So what follows is much indebted to Neusner's critique insofar as it reminds one to tread cautiously.

Given the caveats, why proceed? The answer is the importance attached to debunking stereotypes. Some of this has already been attempted in the discussion, for example, of first-century Palestinian Judaism in chapter 1. The determination to proceed is bolstered by my own experience as a teacher of mostly Christian, traditional-aged collegians. As noted earlier, my experience is that when Christians allow themselves to be open to study and conversation about all that is prejudicial theologically in the orthodox Christian assessment of Judaism, when they allow themselves to acknowledge the brutality of the ages of the "teaching of contempt," there is sometimes genuine change. The change enhances Jewish-Christian relations, promotes the insight that there are many paths of holy life exhibiting rough parity to one another, and functions to vitalize Christianity.

What follows is organized under two headings: (1) the Jewish religious worldview, which is subdivided into discussions of God, the divine-human relationship, human relations, human knowledge and suffering, moral life/spirituality, chosenness, and land; and (2) further thoughts on the life and work of Abraham Joshua Heschel, for this author a deeply affecting embodiment of the genius of Judaism.

No chapter, no book, no library is sufficient to adequately render the diversity, complexity, and richness of Judaism. What follows is that small sliver of knowledge, insight, and understanding of some features of Judaism that have lodged appreciatively in my consciousness and imagination as a result of study and personal encounter.

Jewish Religious Worldview

From Judaism we receive a foundation for a worldview. It is that God is, and that God is one! Even those in the West who seek meaning and purpose without reference to a personal god inherit the yearning for a unitive and meaningful view of their lives from Jewish radical monotheism. Thus, Milton Steinberg writes that in proclaiming the one God, the prophets of Israel "were bent on establishing the principle that reality is an order not an anarchy; that mankind is a unity not a hodge-podge; and that one universal law of righteousness holds sway over men, transcending borders, surmounting all class lines."[5] As implied by the reference to righteousness, every rich element of a classical Jewish religious worldview flows from this affirmation of Jewish faithfulness: God is one! The most profound Jewish prayer, the *Sh'ma,* which continues with an injunction to love God, is an act of worship and at the same time a supreme act of hope: hope against anarchy, hope for humanity. *Sh'ma Yisrael Adonai Elohayno Adonai Echad:* "Hear, O Israel, the Holy One, our God, the Holy One is one!"

It is not possible to meditate too much on the implications of the Jewish affirmation that God is one. All religions labor, as James D. G. Dunn has written, with the "fundamental problem of how to conceptualize both the unknowable transcendence of God, and at one and the same time, God's self-manifestation in the world."[6] We have seen that the deepest cause of xenophobia caused by religion is precisely the genius of religion: its particularity, its categorical nature, the specific ways in which members of religions experience and express God's manifestation in their midst. We have seen how the mere expression of "categorical revelation" usually diminishes a sense of common "transcendental revelation": the universal "event of God's absolute self-communication" to all human beings. It would be the crassest philosemitism (attributing everything good and nothing bad to historical Judaism) to imply that Jews have not been and are not capable of being xenophobic. But what Dunn calls "the apparently simple clarity of Jewish...monotheism"[7] is a reliable basis on which to found reverence among peoples in different religions. It is from the depths of his meditation on God's oneness that Rabbi Heschel exclaimed: "God is either the Father of all men or of no men."[8]

God, who is one, is experienced as both utterly transcendent and mysterious and also near to us, upholding us like a loving parent. This most fruitful paradox of religious imagination is bequeathed to Western consciousness in the Jewish imagery of God's transcendence and immanence. (Contrary to ignorant stereotype, this paradox is also present in Eastern religious traditions, for example, in the interplay of Brahman and lesser divine embodiments in Hinduism, or of Buddha — deicized — and Buddha mind.) Thus, we have the Kabbalist's characterization of the Godhead as *En Sof,* "the Infinite." But also in Kabbala, as well as other classic sources, God is experienced and spoken of as *Shechinah,* as near presence. The Christian stereotype of Jewish God-imagery asserts that Jews understand God in only one way: as the "wholly other," sitting in judgment. But the medieval Jewish poet Solomon ibn Gabirol, speaking of the manifestation of God through the heavens and the earth, says that above all else, the Holy One is experienced in "the stirring of my heart when I look inwards."[9] The theological idea of God as both immanent and transcendent, as both mysterious and intimately related, is the linchpin of healthy religions, enabling them both to comfort and to challenge, to encourage hope in a meaningful worldview and to evoke prayer.

God, according to classical Jewish religious consciousness, is good. Indeed, God is loving! When Christians read and pray the moving lines from John's Gospel, "God is love," they are encountering a basic tenet of Judaism, not a "Christian" novelty or innovation. The most elemental pattern of Christian stereotype has been to contrast the supposed harshness of the Jewish God and the legalism "he" inspires with the mercy and love of the "Christian God" and the freedom and joy that derive from Christian life.

In fact, a frequently recurring characterization of the Holy One in Hebrew Scripture is of God as *compassionate* and *forgiving*. And compassion and forgiveness are the universal, functional expressions not only of what theologians call *agape*, god-like, gratuitous love, but also *eros*, or romantic love, and *philisthia*, the love of friendship.

Christian stereotype has rested for centuries on teaching a "reduced essence" (as Sanders calls it) of Judaism. Well, says the traditionally trained Christian, what of all the punishment meted out in Hebrew Scripture? What of the warrior god, *Shaddai*, Lord of the Mountains, and *Adonai*, Lord of the Universe? It serves the purposes of replacement theology to ignore, or underplay, the Jewish religious genius from which we receive the teaching that the Holy One is *Yahweh*. A common interpretation of Moses' exchange with God (Exodus 3:13) is that the Holy One tells Moses to tell Pharaoh "I AM" has sent you. There is also exegetical support, however, for translating this name of the Holy One, which derives from the Hebrew verb *hayah* ("to be"): "I AM present with you," or even "the Present One." (For example, in his recently published and highly acclaimed translation of *The Five Books of Moses* [1995], Everett Fox translates the verse "I will be-there howsoever I will be-there.") In the discussion of revelation and presence in chapter 4, the relationship between presence and love was noted. When there is loss of presence, there is loss of love. It is an experience to which Emily Dickinson gives poetic expression, writing that loss of presence is like "cobwebs of the soul" leading imperceptibly but inevitably to love's demise. As she says, "Slide is crashes law."[10]

A characteristic often ascribed to the Holy One in Hebrew Scripture is compassion (the noun is *rahamim*). Leo Baeck notes that the word is best understood as the "love of a mother toward a child."[11] The specification is justified by the derivation of the word from another: *rehem*, the Hebrew word for "womb" (a point that feminist theologians, Jewish and Christian, have rightly focused on in criticizing classical god-talk). The compassion and the forgiveness are of one fabric: it is because one is compassionate that one forgives. (And here we may note Rabbi Heschel's dismissal in a number of writings, including *The Prophets*, of the idea that imputing compassion to God is wholly anthropomorphic, when what is most obvious through human history is that the ideal of compassion cannot possibly derive from human behavior.) Where Christians are taught to see a "Jewish" God who is perennially punishing the Hebrew people for transgressions, what is in fact in the text is forgiveness and the renewal of covenant. So we read of the Holy One in Hebrew Scripture: "The love of the Lord never ceases, his compassion fails not. They are new every morning. Great is thy faithfulness" (Lamentations 3:22–23). And: "When my father and mother forsake me, then will the Lord take me up" (Psalm 27:10). The device of juxtaposing parental rejection with the sustained compassion and forgiveness, the love, of the Holy One is extraordinarily powerful. It is evidence that this "God-intoxicated people" (not a people intoxicated with rules) have had — and that many, even in the face of the Holocaust, sustain — the most profound experience of God as love. This religio-poetic device reaches its most sublime expression after the exile in Babylon not only in Lamentations, as noted, but in Second Isaiah, where it is written: "Can a woman forget her suckling child, that she should have no compassion on the son of her womb? Even these may forget, but I will never forget you" (Isaiah 49:15).

If one is to account for the recurrence of punishment, "divine wrath," in Hebrew Scripture, it must be in the spirit of biblical *interpretation* and not under the influence of fundamentalist attitudes. Ascribing "punishment" to the Holy One in the texts and lives of people in any religion, it this language is to avoid blasphemy, must be understood literarily as dealing with human freedom and responsibility. If humans are "the event of God's absolute self-communication," if the human vocation is to return to the Holy One and to live the divine life in compassion and peace, courage and hope, then deviation from this vocation brings suffering and pain. This is a meaning of Moses' speech in Deuteronomy when he enjoins the people to "choose life." It is also expressed in the extracanonical (but Jewish) text of Sirach: "He has placed before you fire and water; stretch out your hand for whichever you wish. Before a man are life and death, and which ever he chooses will be given him" (Sirach 15:15–17).

Because God is one and God is good, and everything emanates from this one, good source, it follows that everything that the Holy One creates (which is everything) is good! Historical, biblical, and contemporary Judaism is in large measure a resounding rejection of *dualism*. In Genesis we are told that the Holy One looked upon all that the divine love brought into being and declared it "good."

There is dualism of a sort in Jewish insistence that the Holy One is "other." Yahweh says of creation, "It is good." It is Brahman, having created everything in the word *om,* who looks upon it and says, "This I am." The dualism Judaism rejects is that which divides creation into the realm of light and the realm of darkness. Of ancient Judaism's encounter with Zoroastrian dualism, Steinberg writes: "Some time in the sixth century before the Common Era, Judaism met Zoroastrianism.... Distinctive of this faith was its doctrine of dualism. Behind the world it discerned not one but two creative beings, the first the force of light and goodness, the other the power of darkness and evil."[12] He goes on to say of this dualistic view of reality: "Dualism despairs in advance of half of reality and half of human nature. Judaism holds that there is nothing which cannot be retrieved for the good."[13]

Judaism's rejection of dualism honors God. It is the foundation of a moral view in which care for material reality is taken with absolute seriousness (the ethic of *tikkun olam*, the healing of the world). This in turn helps frame the modest theological view in Jewish eschatology, which is to say the Jewish view of the end times or afterlife, what an overdeveloped Christian eschatology defined as the study of death, judgment, heaven, and hell. (I have heard a very distinguished Christian Hebrew Scripture scholar express sympathy for Jews because of their "underdeveloped" theology of the next life. A more accurate assessment, and the final word on the matter, belongs to Rabbi Heschel, who said: "We believe in an after life, but it's God's business what to do with us."[14]) Jewish rejection of dualism is very much at the heart of its attention to *sanctifying* life on earth, an orientation, it was suggested earlier, that authentic Catholicism has preserved. Thus, while there are many things to be said in appreciation of Christian ascetic practice, seeking discipline of bodily appetites in support of "purity of heart," the unhealthy spiritualism to which it often leads throughout the history of Christianity is virtually absent from most Jewish life and practice. Judaism stands as a rejection of the theological anthropology of Reform Protestantism that humans are "utterly depraved." Also rejected is any notion of personal *salvation* by flight from the world. It is not from Jewish interpretation of the story of Adam and Eve that a doctrine of the pervasiveness of sin, carried by carnal desire, emerges in Western history. Rather, as Elaine Pagels argues persuasively in *Adam, Eve and the Serpent*, this is a distinctly Christian interpretation attributable in large measure to Saint Augustine under the influence of Christian dualism (Manichaeism).

Jewish rejection of dualism is the foundation of a joyous religious psychology to which the salutation and toast *L'Chaim* ("To life!") gives vigorous testimony. Thus, the Jewish sages write: "He who sees a legitimate pleasure and does not avail himself of it is an ingrate against God who made it possible."[15] The sentiment is still present in the "Catholic spirit" that has been spoken of. One can glimpse it, for example, in Aquinas's observation in the *Summa* that one could sin by *abstaining* from wine. Nevertheless, much of Christianity is pockmarked by the influence of a dualistic association of deprivation and suffering with holiness.

The worldview that emanates from "And God looked upon all that God had made and said 'It is good' " is one that embraces *ordinary things in ordinary time*. Actually, for Judaism, no person, event, human exchange or activity, or place is "ordinary" in the pejorative sense. The events of ordinary life — which is to say, all times — are sacred. Ordinary life in ordinary time constitutes the events and times for our sanctification. The separation of holy from secular time at the end of the Sabbath in the *Havdala* ("separation") ritual should not be understood literally. The ritual focusing of the Sabbath is a device helping bodies and minds and imaginations to practice reverence. But as Rabbi Heschel makes clear in his beautiful work *The Sabbath,* the remainder of the week is also available for holiness. Because in the Genesis story the first thing the Holy One calls "holy" (*qadosh*) is time (Sabbath time), Judaism bequeaths to all a reverence for ordinary activities of family life, for eating and drinking, for study and recreation, for all the activities, including resting, with which we fill up our time. The Holy One is encountered in these times and activities. One engages in both ritual and ethical works (*mitzvoth*) but not with fearful feverishness before a wrathful God, even though the rabbis enjoin the faithful to *dikuk b'mitzvot,* that is, exactitude in performing all our human works — whether ritual, moral, or everyday tasks — with care. Still we completely misunderstand Jewish observance if we either limit it to ritual *halakhic* activity or view observance as nothing more than what has been called "ritual fussiness" (though, of course, all observance can deteriorate into fussiness). The attitude in which the Jew engages in *mitzvoth* is *simcha shel mitzvah,* doing our human work with joy, with "a sense of being linked, through Torah, to the joyful Source of all being."[16]

Of this extraordinary bequest, Gabriel Moran writes: "Central to the Jewish understanding of covenant is the belief that God is found in the midst of ordinary time. The daily events of ordinary life — being born, eating, studying, laboring, loving, suffering, dying — are the revelatory occasions of a divine presence."[17] Because of this, the tales of the Jewish sages are filled with wonderful stories of people experiencing religious inspiration through such ordinary occurrences as seeing the back of their rebbe's neck or observing him put on his gloves! The insight is analogous to Zen Buddhist stories about experiencing enlightenment while cleaning the lettuce. It is preserved in the medieval Catholic mystical tradition of the "practice of the presence of God." Without the richness of this Jewish worldview, Annie Dillard might never have written: "Every day is a God, and holiness holds forth in time. I worship each God, I praise each day splintered down, splintered down and wrapped in time like a husk, a husk of many colors, spreading at dawn fast over the mountain split.... I wake in a god...."[18]

The Divine-Human Relation

Emmanuel Rackman recounts an early rabbinic discourse over which is the most important sentence in the Bible. Rabbi Akiba maintained that the most important sentence is: "Thou shalt love thy neighbor as thyself." But Ben Azai held that the most important sentence in the Bible is: "These are the generations of Man. In God's image did God create Man." Rackman continues:

> How does one improve on the command to love your neighbor as yourself by saying that God created Man in His image? The answer is beautiful. Ben Azai won the day. Ben Azai said that there are people who might say to themselves: I want to demean myself. Let my neighbor also be demeaned. I don't mind living in a hovel. Let my neighbor also live in a hovel. To this Ben Azai says: You have no right to denigrate yourself. You must understand that you are created in the divine image and you certainly cannot permit yourself to denigrate the next man who is also created in the divine image. That is why it is not enough to say thou shalt love thy neighbor as thyself. You may hate yourself, but that doesn't give you permission to hate someone else. This is an example of the great sensitivity of the Jewish tradition to the uniqueness of Man, and with it Ben Azai won his argument with Rabbi Akiba.[19]

For Judaism, the divine-human relationship can be one of utter intimacy, though other images, such as "ruler," while lacking intimacy, still communicate the experience of God caring. The intimacy is seen in the teaching that the Holy One created humans in the divine image; male and female, they are created in the divine image. Thus, while even Rabbi Heschel approves the value of a "little fear and trembling" before God, *Emunah* ("faithfulness" or "trustworthiness") is the quality that typifies the divine human relationship. Heschel has said facetiously that if Moses had asked him, he would have said not to write "Let us make man in our image and likeness," because it is an impossible saying, contradicting the Second Commandment of the law given to Moses. "And yet," Heschel writes, "there is something in the world that the Bible does regard as a symbol of God. It is not a temple or a tree, it is not a statue or a star. The symbol of God is *man, every man* [Heschel's emphasis]. God created man in His image, in His likeness."[20]

Heschel maintains that the intimacy of the relationship between God and humans is so great that God should be understood as confronted with the challenge to trust humans just as humans are challenged to trust God. In one of the most moving expressions of the Jewish understanding of the divine-human relation, Heschel speaks of humans as a "divine need" (as *zorech gavoha*): "Man is man because something divine is at stake in his existence. He is not an innocent bystander in the cosmic drama. There is in us more kinship with the divine than we are able to believe. The souls of men are candles of the Lord, lit on the cosmic way . . . and every soul is indispensable to Him. Man is needed, he is *a need of God*."[21]

It follows from this teaching that the dignity and reverence due every human being is an inviolate right. In his study *The Prophets,* Rabbi Heschel asserts that it is from ancient Israel, not from Greece or China or anywhere else in the ancient world, that humankind first receives this teaching. He says that the first time the sanctity and inviolability of every human person is articulated is when the prophet Nathan holds even a monarch, King David, accountable for the unjustified death of a human being, Uri'ah the Hittite, for whose wife, Bathsheba, David lusts (2 Samuel 11–12). Bathsheba and David have conceived a child, and David is unable to induce Uri'ah to sleep with his wife before going into battle, so the king arranges for the death of the Hittite. Nathan comes to court and tells the king a story of a rich man who kills the only lamb of his poor neighbor rather than slaughter one of his vast flock for guests. Hearing this, "David's anger was greatly kindled against the man; and he said to Nathan: 'As the Lord lives, the man who has done this deserves to die, and he shall restore the lamb fourfold, because he did this thing, and he has no pity'" (12:5, 6). Then "Nathan said to David: 'You are this man'" (v. 7). Made in

God's image, no human being may be treated as a means, not even
by a king.

Human Relations

The normative ideal for human relations follows from the divine
human-relation and from the teaching that we are made in the
image and likeness of the Holy One. In biblical anthropology, as
Richard McBrien has said, "to exist is to co-exist." Those views of
human social life in the West that proceed from a *relational* rather
than an *individual* starting point are founded on biblical perspectives. This loyalty is alive and well in Jewish common life down to
our own times; it stands in contradiction to every form of group
narcissism and social Darwinism. The first humans are depicted
as transparent to one another, as "naked ... [but] not ashamed"
(Genesis 2:25). The word for "naked," *a'rum*, constitutes a bit of
word play; it also connotes "wisdom," sometimes with an element
of cleverness attached. There is, as well, in this depiction the seed
of a much more positive view of bodiliness and human sexuality
in Judaism than in religious traditions in which dualism has had a
major impact. If the rabbis have from time to time shown themselves as uncomfortable with the plain meaning of the love poetry
of the Song of Songs as was Saint Bernard of Clairvaux, still the
most beautiful and sensuous poetic expression appears in the Hebrew Scripture and "the tension between body and soul which so
harrowed first the pagan world and then the Christian is relaxed
in Judaism."[22]

Human Knowing and Human Suffering

We have seen that there is an intimate relationship between human
claims to certain knowledge — above all, knowledge of divine
matters — and prejudice, xenophobia, and violence. Here again,
biblical, historical, and contemporary Judaism has a great deal to
teach us about true knowledge and its sources, the ambiguities of
knowledge and the limits of dogma.

Leonard Bialles calls the "myth of Adam and Eve," especially the association of human finitude with eating of a "tree of
knowledge," a "masterpiece of symbolic compression."[23] In his
discussion of revelation, Gabriel Moran speaks of a longing for
knowledge that is deeper and less violent than "objectified knowing" but that does not end in irrationality. Earlier, in chapter 2,
Langdon Gilkey was cited speaking of religious convergence that
seems impossible in theological discourse but that is achieved in

the *praxis* of interreligious relations. It is to biblical, historical, and contemporary Judaism that we look for wisdom about the limits of knowledge, the unreliability of objectified knowledge, caution about the efficacy of dogma (which has been called Jewish "canonizing of dissent") and, despite the passion of Talmudic disquisition, humility in claiming to speak for God. Judaism also bequeaths to humankind an idea of relational knowing of which contemporary feminist thinkers, among others, speak.

Recognition of finiteness in the area of human knowing is not limited to Judaism. The Sufi story of the blind men trying to identify an elephant; the Zen saying, "Those who know don't say, and those who say don't know"; the Taoist distinction between "great knowledge" (which "sees all in one") and "small knowledge" (which "breaks down into many") all speak of the limitations of human knowing. More contemporary commentary includes George Bernard Shaw's appraisal of the human capacity for embracing illusions when he said that there are always two games being played: the one you are playing and the one that is being played.

But it is the biblical idea of knowledge resulting from intimate engagement rather than abstraction and detachment that most influences Western culture. Many are now familiar with the interchangeable use of the Hebrew verb *yada* ("to know") for both sexual intimacy and true knowledge. This is the basis of praxeological philosophies that have had such a profound influence on modern life. It is also the foundation of the Jewish idea of moral life as response, an idea that stands as a perennial caution against equating morality with ideas: "Judaism,...[as] highly as it rates the life of reason,...rates the good life even higher. For all its heavy intellectualism, it sets morality above logic, the pursuit of justice and mercy over the possession of correct ideas. This is why the Talmud lists among those who may 'acquire eternity in an instant' heathens who lack the true faith and the ignorant and simple [sic] incapable of grasping it."[24]

That we will not be saved by right knowledge, by "orthodoxy" in that sense, but rather by doing justice, loving mercy, and walking humbly with God is especially exemplified in the well-known story of the disputations of the followers of Hillel and of Rabbi Shammai. At odds over every feature of interpretation, the followers of each sage hear a voice from the heavens that says that the words of both are God's words. But, and here is a telling counterpoint to the passion of Jewish argumentation, the voice says that the teachings of Hillel are to be preferred. For when Hillel teaches, he always begins by setting out the alternative interpretation of Shammai. And he seeks to do so with the greatest sensitivity to the merits of Shammai's view. Only then does Hillel set out his own interpretation.

As he so often does, Rabbi Heschel captures the essence of Jewish genius regarding human knowing: "In our passion for knowledge, our minds prey upon the wealth of an unresisting world and, seizing our limited spoils, we quickly leave the ground to lose ourselves in the mist produced by fads and phases. We refuse to take notice of what is beyond our sight, content with converting realities into opinions, mysteries into dogmas and ideas into a multitude of words.... But time and again we awake. In the midst of walking in the never-ending procession of days and nights, we are suddenly filled with a solemn terror, with a feeling of our wisdom being inferior to dust. We cannot endure the heartbreaking splendor of sunsets. Of what avail, then, are opinions, words and dogmas?"[25]

It is above all in striving for an explanation of innocent human suffering (indeed, all innocent suffering) that human knowledge is seen as less than dust. Here, again, Judaism is not without a body of speculation. But when "dealing with evil Judaism is true to character. It makes no effort to attain conformity on points of theory, but is crisp and clear on what it expects by way of behavior. It expects a man, no matter what else he may think about evil, to recognize it as something to be fought and to go out and fight it. It expects he will care for its victims, comforting the mourners, feeding the hungry, clothing the naked, healing the sick.... It expects him to root out its causes from the world of nature, from his own soul and from society. And as for the uncorrectable evils of the human lot, those which can not be fought off or remedied by any means whatsoever, Judaism expects him to endure these with dignity and courage, mitigating their bitterness and hurt with the medicaments of faith, utilizing them to the purification and refinement of his soul."[26]

With regard to that masterpiece of drama about innocent suffering, the Book of Job, there is a rabbinic tradition according to which its moral is: "It is not in our power to explain either the tranquility of the wicked or the sufferings of the upright."[27] But a more adequate and inspiring interpretation is provided by the contemporary Jewish philosopher, theologian, and spiritual writer, Carol Ochs. Her view is also more consistent with a strain of Jewish religious experience that Einstein was tapping when he said God does not play dice with the universe. In Ochs's interpretation, God and Job are partners — within the context of human finitude and necessity — in Job's transformation. Transformation entails "stripping away...surface levels of wealth, status, relationships, even bodily integrity....In the Book of Job the essential action is not tearing down Job's self but opening it up to a new vision of reality....What Job gains...[is] the transformation of the self, as portrayed in the theophany."[28] God is Job's companion in human development (as Moran uses the term), at once the thundering monologist who asks where Job was when the pillars of the heavens and the earth were set but also Job's *go'el*, his advocate and support: "God invites Job — and us — to see ourselves from God's perspective, allowing us at last to feel God's joy in creation and to experience true self-acceptance....The Book of Job does not end with justice, which Job originally seeks, but rather with love, which satisfies him beyond his original quest."[29] (Ochs's reference to the ending of the Book of Job acknowledges exegetical evidence that chapter 42, the "happy ending," is a much later redaction of the text.)

It is more than a little suggestive and encouraging that, with no apparent reference to him, Ochs's interpretation is strikingly similar in message and evocative power to that of my teacher Gustavo Gutiérrez in *On Job: God Talk and the Suffering of the Innocent*.[30] For Gutiérrez a central question of the Book of Job is whether it is possible to love God *for nothing*, which is to say, gratuitously — as God loves us. Is it possible, loving God for nothing, to overcome *sorrow* even while still *suffering?* Life strips Job of all the contractual reasons for "loving" God, all the reasons, as Gutiérrez says, that are part of "capitalist Christian [or Jewish] ideology," all those that have the character of a profit-and-loss quid pro quo. Further, and Ochs emphasizes this as well, Job comes to associate himself compassionately with others who suffer innocently. When in 42:5, Job says to God, "I had heard of thee by the hearing of the ear," Job is on the brink of rejecting rational cause-effect thinking about the Holy Mystery, God. He is on the brink of realizing that the language of orthodox theology had until this time made him a victim of secondhandedness, William James's term for doctrinal language that squeezes the life from religious experience. "But now," verse 5 continues, "my eyes see thee." Job *contemplates* the Holy One. He is fully developed! As to verse 6, in which Job is portrayed as apologizing for nothing and promising to repent (even though God says in chapter 42 that Job has nothing for which to repent), Gutiérrez maintains that it is a mistranslation. It should read: "I repent *of* dust and ashes," which means "I will turn around and no longer be sorrowful, even though I still suffer, because now I see you with my eyes."

Moral Life/Spiritual Life

The Jewish idea of the moral life is implicit in everything that has been written thus far. It is wholly derivative of the Jewish sense of God. As Norman Solomon writes: "Our perception of God, *through Torah* [his emphasis] is thickly intertwined with our sense of right and wrong."[31] God is compassionate and forgiving; we must be compassionate and forgiving. God reveres us, made in the divine image as we are; we must revere ourselves. (As the rabbis say, "A man is his own next of kin.") God creates only what is good; we must cherish and enjoy all legitimate pleasures. God requires righteousness of peoples and of nations and is not content with *private* virtue; we must frame just social structures.

Like most religious people, Jews possess both supreme ideals of the moral life and a great body of principled but conventional accommodations to what David Hollenbach calls "claims in conflict." It is not a coincidence that the great Christian moral theologian Reinhold Niebuhr, whose thought is sometimes summarized by the term "ethical realism," so prized Judaism and the Jewish roots of Christianity.

One of the multitude of anomalies in Christian stereotypes of Judaism is the notion of Jewish moral rigidity. In fact, no religion rivals Judaism (the Catholicism of canon law may come close) in ongoing development of moral accommodations, under the judgment of moral ideals, for resolving conflicts between traditional devotion and contemporary needs as well as conflict between and among people. This extends from air travel on the Sabbath to hiring a "shabbas goy" to perform "servile" work. Jewish law seeks to deal well with an imperfect and complex world. As Milton Steinberg notes: "Judaism does not expect perfection from man.... In this respect Judaism is mellower [than some religions], more realistic. It thinks too well of God to portray Him as exacting impeccability from flesh and blood. He made us frail. He is too responsible to ask that man walk but never slip."[32]

Still the "calculating ethics" of Judaism (or Catholicism) are subject to "routinization"[33] and are easily co-opted by human selfishness if they are not inspired at every turn by a profound moral ideal. Niebuhr spoke of this as the interplay — really the grinding conflict — between "rough justice" and the "necessary illusion" of a world of "perfect justice," a world of love (an utterly Jewish idea). He writes in *Moral Man and Immoral Society:* "But justice cannot be approximated unless the hope of its perfect realization creates a sublime madness in the soul."[34] The most profound vision of the moral life, the most "sublime madness," the most efficacious foundation for moral realism is the moral ideal of the prophets of Israel.

Heschel writes of the prophets' religious experience: "The typical prophetic state of mind is one of being taken up into the heart of divine *pathos....* Prophetic sympathy is a response to transcendent sensibilities."[35] The prophet is a woman or man who demands that both our personal and social lives be characterized by the compassion and forgiveness of God!

The depth of the moral ideal of the prophets can be gauged by contrasting it with modern moral liberalism, by which I mean the ideal of the moral life that has been emerging in Western culture since the Renaissance. This modern moral ideal begins with the individual rather than the community, places greater emphasis on individual rights than responsibility to a community of people, and is founded on the effort to discern rational principles for balancing rights rather than customary wisdom about responsible common life. The fundamental ways in which the modern moral ideal differs from the prophetic ideal can be seen by contrasting five features of each.

1. The basic principle of the modern moral ideal is the Aristotelian notion of *suum cuique,* rendering to each person what is his or her due. For the prophets, each person is due compassion and forgiveness because each is made in the divine image and likeness. Though the prophetic ideal is unattainable broadly, it functions as a contradiction of the prejudice, hierarchy, and masking of self-interest that infest modern notions of who is due what!

2. A major goal of modern morality is *fairness,* the effort to balance competing claims. The prophetic ideal is *compassion* and *forgiveness. Prudence* (for Aristotle, "the mean between excess and defect," between too much and too little) characterizes the modern approach. *Compassion,* literally "feeling suffering" (*cum,* "with" + *pati,* "to bear, suffer"), characterizes the prophetic ideal. Modern notions of fairness mask self-interested illusions. For example, we say that this is "my property" and fairness dictates that I not

be compelled to share it with you. In fact, most property at one time belonged to someone else and was stolen from them. And in any case, Scripture tells us, "The earth is the Lord's and all that is in it." Or, in meting out forgiveness in modern cultures, we strike the stance Cornel West calls the "conservative-behaviorist" view of social policy.[36] In this view, a prudent and balanced societal distribution of forgiveness is linked to an illusory ideal (applied to others) of people's capacity to "pull themselves up by their bootstraps," regardless of brutalizing social conditions that affect even consciousness of an ideal of moral comportment. The person, or the people, who are forgiven are forgiven perhaps once. This contrasts with the prophetic message of God's constant willingness to forgive.

3. Because of the individualism at the heart of the modern moral ideal, the *poor,* provided one is not oneself poor, can hope for nothing more than *philanthropy* from people of means who subscribe to the modern ideal. In the prophetic ideal, because God is compassionate, there can be no justice if we do not, in the words of Isaiah, "correct oppression, defend the fatherless, plead for the widows" (Isaiah 1:17). Modern philanthropy is voluntary, but in Judaism and Christianity love and service to the poor are divine commands.

4. The modern moral ideal is *conventional* rather than *radical.* The distinction pertains to what Rabbi Heschel calls levels of "sensitivity to evil." He writes: "To us injustice is injurious to the welfare of the people; to the prophets it is a death blow to existence; to us, an episode; to them a catastrophe, a threat to the world. . . . We ourselves witness continuously acts of injustice, manifestations of hypocrisy, falsehood, outrage, misery, but we rarely grow indignant or overly excited, . . . [but the] prophet . . . feels fiercely. . . . God is raging in the prophet's words."[37]

5. In the modern mentality there is a certain naivete about *power,* or comfort with its ambiguities, because dominant powers favor the modern person of means. The prophetic ideal demands *suspicion* of power and of those who wield it, whether they are political, religious, or economic figures. Heschel writes that "history is first of all what man does with power, . . . "[38] and a great deal of what humankind does with power through the centuries is kill! But peace, the ideal of *Shalom,* is the heart of the prophetic message.

The radical distinction between moral and spiritual life is virtually unknown in Judaism. This is not, as the Christian stereotype maintains, because Judaism is solely a rigorous set of rules of devotion and ethical behavior devoid of mystical experience. The distinction is absent because in general, as already noted, Judaism eschews any purely *private* or *individualistic* idea of sanctification or salvation, any idea that a purely *interior* feeling of connectedness to the divine is a sufficient expression of righteousness before God. It is only in what Leo Baeck calls "romantic religion" that such an experience is considered sufficient: "Feeling is supposed to mean everything: this is the quintessence of romanticism.... Its danger, however, which it cannot escape is this: the all important feeling culminates eventually in vacuity or in substitutes, or it freezes and becomes rigid. And before this happens it follows a course which takes it either into sentimentality or into the fantastic; it dodges all reality, particularly that of the Commandments, and it takes refuge in passivity when confronted with the ethical task of the day. Empathy makes up for much and gives a freedom which is really a freedom from decision and independence from inner obligation."[39]

This is a devastating criticism of the nineteenth-century liberal Protestant Romanticism associated with Schleiermacher. Apart from the obvious silence about Christ, it could have been leveled by Barth. Baeck meant it as a critique of Christianity in general, and there are legitimate grounds for these strictures. The very dualism that was spoken of above makes Christianity in every era a roll of the dice about whether the effort to cultivate a genuinely *contemplative interior life* feeds deep moral concern and action, or it exhausts itself in a spiritual narcissism, mistaking the voice of ego for the voice of God within. We noted in chapter 4 Gabriel Moran's association of moral and mystical dimensions of human life. And Schleiermacher's program — locating the essence of the religious experience in an inner "feeling" (*gefuhl*) of utter dependence on and relatedness to the Holy One — is not so different from that of Solomon ibn Gabirol experiencing the Holy One in "the stirrings of my heart when I look within." Also, it is to Schleiermacher that we are indebted for the genuinely liberal Christian impulse that is the gateway to interreligious reverence. Catholic Christianity, in particular, preserves a very rich tradition of meditative prayer and methods for cultivating a peaceful, calm interior life. Such a life is not to be confused with withdrawal from the world or a merely aesthetic religiosity. The maxim of Catholic contemplative or meditative tradition is that of the fourteenth-century mystic, Meister Eckhart: "What a person receives in contemplation they must give back in love."

Still, the dice roll many different ways. And much of what has concerned Catholic Christians in the period after the Second Vatican Council, the period of "conciliar renewal," has had to do with rejecting a merely private religiosity without losing the richness of traditions of prayer, contemplation, and spiritual direction. The postconciliar understanding of "spirituality" is deeply indebted to Judaism; it seeks to balance elements of moral rigor with attention to the inner life. Both together constitute one's spirituality. And this, as Gutiérrez says, is "death to the alleged *ways* [his emphasis] that individualism of one kind or another creates."[40]

So when Sherry Blumberg writes eloquently of "Forms of Jewish Spirituality,"[41] she points to patterns of action as well as interior disposition. There is no purely interioristic connotation. Her typology is instructive for the creativity and diversity of approaches to principled Jewish life that it reveals. The diversity extends to forms of Jewish spirituality that are "secular," a challenging position for Christians. The forms are: (1) the "spirituality of deeds," focused on sincere performance of a variety of ritual and ethical *mitzvoth;* (2) "spirituality of study," focused on reverent reflection on Torah, Talmud, and other sacred texts; (3) "spirituality of the pursuit of justice and social action" (*tikkun olam*), which admits of a wholly secular expression and which, as the reader might imply from the quote above, was for Leo Baeck the essence of Judaism; (4) "spirituality of Jewish peoplehood" (Zionism), also admitting of a purely secular devotion; and (5) "mystical paths," including the highly esoteric and the highly ecstatic (as in Hasidic life).[42]

Law

To misunderstand the Jewish idea of observance of ritual law is to miss the significance of what has been called "sacramental imagination": ritual focusing of attention and devotion in order, as Tracy says, to re-present possibilities. For centuries Christian stereotype has masked the real intent of *halakha* and halakhic observance, as well as the covenantal relationship with God that is the framework of the halakhic action. It is the work of sanctifying ordinary activity and ordinary time by reminding themselves that God is. In her essay on the treatment of law in *The Catechism of the Catholic Church*, Carol Deutsch says the essence of misunderstanding the Jewish ideal and practice of law, before Jesus, during his time, and in Judaism since, is believing "Jewish observance was [and is] indeed 'legalistic' rather than being a matter of heart and spirit."[43] Leon Klenicki maintains that *halakha* should not be translated as "law" at all. The word is a noun derived from the verb *halak,* which means "to go." "Halakha is a way of being and going, a manifestation of the covenant with God, a manner of living and reliving God's commands and partnership. To be *halakhic* is to make God's presence a reality in all aspects of life: at the moment of waking up in the morning, thanking God for restoring the soul; at meals, thanking God for the goodness of food; at prayer and at study, thanking God for God's presence. Halakha is the joy guiding and shaping life by the experience of covenant, guided by tradition. Halakha is the discipline of being religious and living a religious existence, a way of being with God, for God."[44] The stereotype of Jewish law masks the example of a joyous sanctifying of everyday life from those, Catholic Christians for example, who profess a similar way of going.

It is the same with ethical law. A stereotype prevails, and clues are lost. The body of ethical law is erroneously characterized as unyielding in its rigor and therefore unforgiving in its application. In fact, the elemental principle of Jewish ethical law preserves it from atrophy and apodictic application. The principle is revealed in the use of the word for "law" — *mishpat* — in the Bible and in virtually all sacred texts developed since biblical times. *Mishpat* hardly ever appears by itself. "It is usually part of a compound noun — *mishpat-tzedaka* — law and charity."[45]

It is the same with the idea of an unforgiving application of law; the false stereotype hides a treasure. Forgiveness, Leon Klenicki maintains, is the heart of Jewish spirituality. Over and over again, in biblical and post-biblical texts and Jewish life, one who "returns" or "turns around" (*teshuvah,* "repentance," from *shuv,* "return") is always forgiven. Thus Maimonides writes: "Even if a man has sinned his whole life and repents on the day of his death, all sin is forgiven him."[46] And the Talmud says: "The unforgiving man is not of the seed of Abraham."[47]

Chosenness

We have already seen, in the discussion of uniqueness in chapter 2, that the claim to an experience of being chosen is not an arrogant assertion that puts an end to dialogue. It is rather an expression of humility that is the necessary starting point for interreligious reverence. The experience of call or vocation, as Moran says, necessarily entails a feeling of being chosen. Yet even Leon Klenicki can write: "The very expression 'Chosen People' makes me tremble. It brings back an impression of triumphalism, of arrogance of the heart which I associate with fanaticism and a lack of respect for other people."[48] But, Klenicki points out, the "unmistakable intent" of the Hebrew word *bahar* ("to choose") is to be chosen for a *particular* role; it "does not imply special privileges, but imposes extra obligations and responsibilities."[49] God's covenant with all of humanity is expressed in the covenant with Noah. The particular vocation of the Jews is expressed in the covenant on Sinai. Heschel reminds us that the prophets were ceaselessly pointing out to the people "that chosenness must not be mistaken as divine favoritism or immunity from chastisement...."[50] Noting that in the ancient world, Ethiopians were often sold as slaves, Philistines were the archenemies of Israel, and Syrians were a menace to the Northern Kingdom, Heschel quotes the prophet Amos: "Are you not like the Ethiopians to Me, O people of Israel? says the Lord. Did I not bring up Israel from the land of Egypt, and the Philistines from Caphtor and the Syrians from Kir?" (Amos 9:7).

There is an unhappy irony in the fact that the very people whose belief in their chosenness is subject to so much misunderstanding and condemnation are alone among the three monotheistic religions of the West in holding a theological interpretation of chosenness that honors the working of God in the lives and religious communities of others. They are the only ones whose experience of uniqueness is not universalistic.

Land

The purpose of this chapter is not that of chapter 1. Earlier, the intent was to unmask the "teaching of contempt" and the long history of violence to which that teaching gives rise. This chapter expresses an appreciation of the richness of Judaism for the purpose of overcoming stereotype and for discovering what can be learned from Jews and Judaism. Still, it is probably not amiss to note again the extraordinary history of cruelty, of pogrom and expulsion, to which Jews were subjected — expulsions justified by the theological status afforded acts that perpetuated the misery of the *wandering* Jew. The importance John Pawlikowski attaches to Vatican repudiation of a theology of providential wandering, signaled by its formal (de jure) recognition of the State of Israel, was noted in chapter 1. It is difficult to conceive of any serious effort to repair Jewish-Christian relations in which Zionism is not embraced. The same holds true for efforts to appreciate the distinctive place of the land (*Eretz Israel*) for most Jews: "In dialogue with Christians, Jews have explained that they do not consider themselves a church, a sect or a denomination . . . but rather as a peoplehood that is not solely racial, ethnic or religious, but in a sense a composite of all these. It is for such reasons that an overwhelming majority of Jews see themselves bound in one way or another to the land of Israel. Most Jews see this tie to the land as essential to their Jewishness."[51] In Jewish mystical traditions the land is symbolic of a marriage contract (*ketubah*) between God and the Jewish people.[52]

Christian theological reflection about what can be learned from Jewish rootedness in the land is underdeveloped. One of the better efforts to express what this might mean for Christians, without displacing the primary meaning of the land for Jews, is Walter Brueggemann's *The Land*. In his treatment, Jewish "landedness" becomes a metaphor (not a "mere metaphor") and lesson about all that is concrete, ordinary, and communal in healthy religion. He says the problem for people in religion, including Christianity, "is not emancipation but rootage, not meaning but belonging, not separation from community but location in it."[53]

Abraham Joshua Heschel

We have already seen the range and richness of Rabbi Heschel's life and work. This has included reference to his critique of prejudicial religion, his discussion of depth theology, his ecumenical and interreligious commitments, his deeply moving writing about a loving God for whom the loved creatures are a "divine need." We also noted Heschel's study of the dialectic of ecstasy and obligation in healthy religion (in his discussion of the Baal Shem Tov and the Kotzker rebbe), his moving study of the Sabbath, and his powerful work on the prophets. Other features of his remarkable life and work, not touched upon thus far, include his rigorous social action against racism and war, his steadfast engagement in the academic "wars" against reductionism in the treatment of the spiritual nature of humankind, his moving studies of Eastern European Hasidic piety, his creative and voluminous writings on classical texts, and his deep concern for youth and education.

The reason for invoking Rabbi Heschel at the end of this chapter is not, however, to try to fill these gaps; this is not, after all, a treatise on his life and work. Rather, it is because he is perhaps the most adequate embodiment in our time of utter commitment to reverence and respect across religious and other differences that usually divide people that this chapter concludes with further consideration of Rabbi Heschel. He is for me the paradigmatic figure in whose life and work we encounter a holy person and a brilliant thinker who shows us the way.

Rabbi Heschel serves as our exemplar of interreligious reverence because in his life and work, *holiness* (or piety) is always the purpose of religious people. *Praying* is what we learn to do. *Awe* is our "natural" condition; *gratitude*, its fruit. And all this because God is *love*. This view of the human condition, of the divine human exchange, of the proper end of religiousness is pursued with unflagging zeal. There is in it no place for absolutism, universalism, xenophobia, or violence. Because of this life and work, "particularly extraordinary is the diversity of those who regard him as their teacher: Catholics, Jews and Protestants, whites and blacks, liberals and conservatives, pious and secular, Americans, Europeans, Israelis. His life changed our conventional expectations."[54]

To let Rabbi Heschel teach us, we must frame his extraordinary commitment to reverence in the context of his life experience and that of Jews in this century: the destruction of European Jews, the Holocaust, his own experience of "abandonment...[by] Christian colleagues, who did not speak up on behalf of Jews" in Germany in the 1930s.[55] We must know that his sister Esther was killed by Nazi bombing during the invasion of Poland; that his mother was murdered in Warsaw; his sister Gittel, most probably in Treblinka; his sister Devorah, at Auschwitz; that he, in his own words, was "a brand plucked from the fire of Europe" at the last moment.[56] We must know that Rabbi Heschel never returned to Germany, Austria, or Poland, and that he wrote: "If I should go to Poland or Germany, every stone, every tree would remind me of contempt, hatred, murder, of children killed, of mothers burned alive, of human beings asphyxiated."[57]

Such a man wrote of reverence, of God being either the Father of all or of none, of God not being a monopolist, of God's tender love and *pathos*. Rabbi Heschel persevered in cultivating the elemental religious attitude of *awe*: "a sense and taste for the transcendent, for the reference everywhere to mystery beyond all things. It enables us to perceive in the world intimations of the divine;...to sense the ultimate in the common and simple; to feel in the rush of the passing the stillness of the eternal...."[58] He wrote of *prayer* as "our humble answer to the inconceivable surprise of living"; of *gratitude*: "Who is worthy to be present at the constant unfolding of time?...Suddenly we feel ashamed of our clashes and complaints in the face of the tacit glory of nature. It is so embarrassing to live! How strange we are in the world and how presumptuous our doings! Only one response can maintain us: gratefulness for witnessing the wonder, for the gift of our un-earned right to serve, to adore, to fulfill. It is gratefulness which makes the soul great."[59]

His daughter Suzannah Heschel's characterization of him is a fitting conclusion to this appreciation of Judaism. She writes: "Like the Baal Shem Tov, he brought heaven to earth, and in his writings we have a revelation of the holiness of Jewish life."[60]

Chapter Six

Practice for Reverence

Life, finally, is practice. This proposition transcends pragmatic philosophies or Marxist analysis, though these are certainly rich resources for the insight that thought is at the service of action, not a sublime refuge from action. As Parker Palmer writes: "You don't think your way into a new kind of living. You live your way into a new kind of thinking."[1]

The priority of practice is implied in Ignatius of Loyola's dictum to "do what you are doing," in the Zen Buddhist injunction to do what one is doing with the *mindfulness* one would bring to bathing baby Buddha, in Amos's injunction to "do justice, love mercy and walk humbly with God." Jesus of Nazareth points to the priority of practice telling his disciples he *is* the way, the truth and the life. We come, therefore, to a consideration of practice: practice promoting interreligious reverence, practice directed at ending Antisemitism.

Paradigm (Shifts)

The term "paradigm" is trendy and the claim may seem pretentious, but what has been set forth in this book thus far requires that those who practice religious education — in all its professional and amateur expressions, with varying degrees of intention, across all the social forms of religious educational development — submit their hearts and minds to the discipline of living out paradigm shifts. The word "paradigm" came into general use with Thomas Kuhn's study in the late 1950s, *The Structure of Scientific Revolutions*. It means that a fundamental and inclusive set of assumptions about the nature of things — the reigning, previously unquestioned ideology of a whole, complex culture and the people who constitute it — is giving way to a new, different, and in many ways antithetical set of assumptions. A paradigm shift is a seemingly slow and steady but ultimately catastrophic change in the perspectival base of a people. My friend and colleague Robert Ludwig has recently written a challenging book dealing with paradigm shift, entitled, suggestively enough, *Reconstructing Catholicism.*[2]

Those who yearn for the end of xenophobic religion and the beginning of the era of interreligious reverence, and those who yearn specifically for a way to educate Christians free of anti-Judaism and Antisemitism, are part of a sevenfold paradigm shift. It entails re-envisioning (1) who God is, (2) paths of holiness, (3) interreligious encounter, (4) what religious education is for, (5) the "critical" function of religious education, (6) relations between Jews and Christians, and (7) what to be silent about. The content of this book thus far has elucidated the substance of this shift. The elements are briefly rehearsed here for the sake of clarity and because they are the presuppositions of the principles and programs with which the rest of the chapter deals.

1. God. God, quite simply, "is greater than religion." It is, as Rabbi Abraham Heschel never tired of pointing out, "an inherent weakness of religion not to take offense at the segregation of God." Religious educators of the future must practice Christian (and Jewish and Muslim and so forth) education in front of the prophets, those who decry idolatry and idolatrous violence. The challenge is to "teach-learn" our experience of the Holy One without limiting God's presence to our people alone.

2. Paths of holiness. The Holy One "speaks" and people "listen" in many ways, in many times, among all peoples in all cultures. "From God's perspective we are all minorities." The religious educators of the future must practice Christian (and Jewish and Muslim and so forth) education in front of the concrete reality of the holiness of people on many paths. The challenge for Christians is to "teach-learn" the near presence of God in Jesus Christ without lapsing into christological triumphalism.

3. Encounter. Interreligious encounter and reverence is the will of God. "To understand is to understand differently." "To be is to be in communion." "Reality is transactional." The religious educators of the future must practice Christian (and Jewish and Muslim and so forth) education that prompts reverence for others even while forming a *peculiar* people. That, obviously, is the challenge.

4. Religious education. The purpose of religious education is to help people and communities to become holy. Religion is not an end but an instrument. The religious educators of the future must practice Christian (and Jewish and Muslim and so forth) education

in a way that manifests their loyalty to "teaching religiousness" over "teaching religion." The challenge is to form people who are, as Raymundo Panikkar says, concrete yet transcendent.

5. Being critical. It is religious educators themselves, even while they strive for Christian (and Jewish and Muslim and so forth) education, who must sponsor critical thinking about religion in general and Christianity, Judaism, Islam, and so on, in particular. If the members of religious communities do not develop self-renewing generations of loyal but critical members, secularism will out! The challenge is to encourage healthy "disbelief" without inducing cynicism.

6. Jews and Christians. Relations between Jews and Christians are central to Christian authenticity and identity. These relations are not marginal or dispensable but central! It is a moral imperative for Christians to be engaged in continuing reparation of relations with Jews and Judaism. And Christians cannot fully understand their own self-renewing work apart from Jewish-Christian reconciliation. As Edward Flannery says, ignorance of its relations with Jews and Judaism "blocks the way to Christian self understanding... [and] denies [Christians] an opportunity to confront a capital sin of the Christians... and to undertake the *metanoia* this requires."

Christianity, as Gabriel Moran says, is "unintelligible" apart from Judaism. And as David Tracy says, a certain "re-Judaizing" of Christianity is essential for Christianity. The Christian religious educators of the future must practice with Jewish-Christian relations at the center, not the periphery, of their work. The challenge is to convince large numbers of Christians that this work is not the result of being suborned by an alleged Jewish special pleading.

7. Silence. Maria Harris writes that teaching begins with silence and ends with release, or letting go, itself a kind of metaphor for silence. This idea about silence, trying to discern what to be silent about for the sake of interreligious reverence but without abandoning catechetical work, was introduced in chapter 3. It pertained to advocating a eucharistic focus in Christian formation. You remember the challenging words cited there of Paul van Buren and Edward Schillebeeckx about humility and the necessity to be silent. Actually, the shift is more radical than that implied in chapter 3. It is a call to end Christian proselytizing. It is a call to refound Christian missiology on the example of the holiness of people in the church, not on claims about the superiority or exclusivity of that holiness. This aspect of the paradigm shift is

corollary to the first and second features noted above. It is something of a problem for prevailing Jewish theology of Christianity (and of course, an enormous problem in Christian orthodoxy). If there is a positive orthodox Jewish theology of Christianity, it is that expressed in contemporary times by Franz Rosenzweig (1886–1929). The Christians, being the children of the Noahide covenant with all humans, have the mission to "preach" the God of Israel, Yahweh, to the heathens. Rosenzweig says that "Christianity must proselytize."[3] But Christian religious educators of the future must reject this role, for there are no "religious" heathens. The challenge is to cease proselytizing those who are *faithful* at the same time as we strengthen the mission and message to those seeking faithfulness. But there is no mission, as such, to the "faithful."

Principles

I propose seven principles that arise from religious education practice that promotes interreligious reverence and sunders what has seemed until recent time the inextricable link between Christian formation and, at best, Jewish subordination.

1. *Knowledge Furnishes Light for Desire*

This principle is paraphrased from Joseph Andreas Jungmann's observation noted earlier. I have in mind, specifically, knowledge of the "teaching of contempt" and knowledge of the genius of Judaism illuminating Christian consciousness and revealing anti-Judaism for what it is. Chapters 1, 2, and 5 in this text hint at the vast literature available to help redress misunderstanding and distortion. At the developmentally appropriate time for teaching in a schooling context "with an end in view," the corollary study of the *ambiguities of religion* should also be introduced. More attention will be paid to this "teaching-learning" enterprise below, under principle 5.

2. *All Teaching-Learning Has a Profound and Deep Emotional Content*

Knowledge (perhaps at the beginning it is better called information) most certainly must be made available to "furnish light for desire." But there exists no detached human capacity to take in information and transform it into usable knowledge (knowledge available for understanding and action); there is no knowing that transcends emotional commitment. In this vein, the philosopher John MacMurray argued that there is no reason as such but rather a human capacity for "emotional rationality."[4] In *The Activity of Teaching,* Thomas Green writes that "teaching is that activity of education aimed not simply at transmitting reasonable beliefs, but at transmitting them *in such a way* [my emphasis] that they become believable."[5] I think that Green means teaching with passion, with controlled but nevertheless pronounced emotion. When John Shea writes that "effective communication...is always a matter of one generation holding another generation to its heart,..."[6] he means, I think, not only that one generation cherishes the other, but that one generation exposes the other to the commitments of its heart, which is to say, that about which it feels passionately. In this regard all teachers should be examining the research on emotional intelligence (so-called "EQ") being conducted at Yale University.[7]

Acknowledging the emotional basis of teaching-learning brings us into the realm of images and of imagination. In teaching-learning for interreligious reverence, as in all teaching with an end in view, we should not fear engaging imagination through striking symbol, powerful narrative, song, poetry, and visual imagery. As William Dych writes: "Our images of the real differ from our concepts of the real not because the one is 'subjective' and the other 'objective,' but because images contain the real, objective concreteness and particularity of the objective world and concepts do not."[8] A commitment to engage those with whom we work in emotional "knowing" (as well as conversational clarification) employing powerful symbols and other catalysts of imaginative intelligence such as narrative is especially important in the realm of education for interreligious reverence. As we have seen throughout, repudiating religiously inspired xenophobia in general and Christian induced anti-Judaism and Antisemitism in particular, is a catastrophic act. It requires genuine conversion. Paul Ricoeur, the great philosopher of symbolism, writes that "every real conversion is first of all a revolution at the level of our directive images. By changing their imagination, human beings alter their existence."[9]

We may take as a case in point the use of powerful visual imagery about the Holocaust. Apart from developmental consideration (which images are appropriate to which human beings at what ages), the larger controversy over whether the powerful images of horrific human suffering, immeasurable human cruelty, and unconquerable human courage and hope should even be employed (given their "emotional content") is entirely suspect.

Consider what is left unchallenged in the absence of these images: a tranquil and unexamined attitude toward nationalism and a naive idea about the goodness of religion (rather than its ambiguity). No, "the world of symbols," Ricoeur writes, "is not a tranquil and reconciled world. Every symbol is iconoclastic in comparison with some other symbol just as every symbol left to itself tends to thicken, to become solidified in an idolatry."[10] With reference to the best means of employing such volatile imagery, the work of Jan Darsa on use of media in Holocaust education and specifically the testimony of survivors is most instructive.[11]

3. Eucharistic Practice Should Occupy a Central Place in Religious Education

This principle calls to mind the discussion of the "priority of the Eucharist" in chapter 3, a chapter given over to examining whether the purposes of Christian education can be achieved without promoting christological triumphalism. The idea is that the greater portion of our educational effort should be directed to evoking the near presence of the divine in Jesus Christ in eucharist practice rather than giving the most time and energy to doctrinal instruction about christological claims. The latter emphasis, apart from its tendency to result in inert and didactic instruction, almost inevitably promotes exclusive claims about Christ and salvation. The idea in that section of chapter 3 was twofold: first, that the eucharistic Christ is more existentially personally affecting than the Christ of doctrinal instruction, and second, that emphasis on Eucharist — in principle — is less prone to result in ideological assertions.

However, this principle goes beyond what was previously said. Though it may seem paradoxical (because the Eucharist is unavoidably, though not exclusively, about Jesus Christ), I mean in this principle to claim that the Eucharist is a profound ritual for evoking interreligious reverence, as well. The ritual begins with a powerful prayer of reconciliation, proceeds to what should be a rhetorically influential moment of preaching about the meaning of sacred texts, and concludes with an awesome realization of the holiness of ordinary things and expressions of gratitude for them. Interspersed are words and other images of compassion, of welcome, of peace and unity, of utter dependence on the love of the Holy One for everything, including "our daily bread." How is it possible to "run" millions (scores or hundreds of millions?) of Catholics and other liturgically oriented Christians through such a potentially transforming ritual — again and again, all over the world — and not undermine pride and hatred and exclusivism? We know it is possible. It is possible to ignore the reconciliation ritual at the beginning of the eucharistic ritual and to insist that a single (no pun intended) individual better represents the community's capacity for forgiveness than the community itself in ritual assembled. It is possible when preaching badly — or even when preaching well, which is more problematic — to wholly misconstrue the sacred texts and their timeless, if *particular,* expression of universal (inclusive) religious values. It is possible to deal with the eucharistic bread and wine themselves, and with eating and drinking the bread and wine, as a magical act rather than a celebration of the "joy at the heart of reality," the celebration of presence, dying to delusional and small self, and being grateful. It is possible; it happens every day! But it need not be so. I myself know inspired communities of people who celebrate the Eucharist with inspired presiders. And every immersion in this ritual results in deepened commitment to compassion, to gentleness, to peace and broadened definition of "my people." As Bernard Cooke says, "When Christians gather for that covenant meal they call 'eucharist,' they are pledging their 'being for' one another."

4. A Decision Should Be Made about Doctrine

"Doctrinal education" pertains primarily to the moment of religious education development that Moran designates "narrative/systematic" especially to the second, systematic phase (elsewhere called the "philosophical" time, the time of striving for a stated worldview). This roughly parallels teenage and young adult life. Prior to this time, the convictions of the community are wrapped almost exclusively in story and ritual, and these should never cease being prominent as means of growth in faithfulness. But doctrinal education very much pertains to what Moran calls "teaching the conversation." This is speaking and listening "so that greater understanding is possible." The phrase — so that greater understanding is possible — seems innocuous and obvious enough. In fact, much doctrinal education in the church today, even when it is initiated at a developmentally appropriate moment, is carried on as if its purpose were the *sacrificium intellectus,* which has been mentioned. Thirty years ago, a few years after the close of the Second Vatican Council, Avery Dulles contributed an essay to a collection on conscience in which he noted that in Catholicism dominated by an obsessive need for everyone to be able to repeat doctrinal formulas word for word (Dulles stated the case more moderately), the acceptance of the "truth" *in* doctrinal propositions becomes itself a kind of moral test.[12] Langdon Gilkey, in his appreciative appraisal of the "Catholic spirit," makes a similar observation: that alongside Catholic intellectual tradition there is a tradition of accepting the most fantastic beliefs. The point is made with hilarity in a movie of the early nineties, *Nuns on the Run,* in which the Catholic figure (Robbie Coletrane) dressed as a nun to escape danger tries to explain to the Protestant (Michael Palin) that the "Trinity is a lot like a shamrock," all with great comic effect but utter incomprehension of whether the doctrine *could* mean *anything* at all. (We have seen, citing John Macquarrie's existential doctrinal interpretation, that it could indeed mean something; it could be a way of expressing the modes of experiencing the Holy One.)

The point is: doctrinal statements are supposed to mean something! Recall Green's reference to teaching beliefs "in such a way that they become believable." And Tillich's encomium to Luther, who according to Tillich insisted that what we *say* about Christ should correlate with who he is for us.

Apart from the basic insight that at a certain moment — but not before that moment — doctrinal education should be a focus in religious education development, two other benefits arise when we think carefully about how doctrine fits into religious education. First, as stated, doctrine must mean something; it must be believable — but not believable *in general.* A doctrine must be capable of being believed by this or that concrete, experiencing subject. Thus, as I have tried to show in earlier discussion of Moran's thought (as well as in the discussion of the confusion of "restorationist catechesis" among ultraconservative Catholics) doctrinal assertions must be correlated (shown to be related) with human experience. They must be perceived as *metaphors for concrete human experience.* This, of course, drives fundamentalist Christian (Jewish, Muslim, and so forth) educators crazy. Metaphor becomes the antithesis of "real." "Christ," to use an example cited earlier from Moran, cannot simultaneously be a claim about the man Jesus of Nazareth *and* a metaphor pointing to hope for a certain quality of communality among people. For the fundamentalist, if the resurrection is a metaphor for the end (purpose) of life, then it cannot at the same time be real in the life of Jesus of Nazareth, the Christ. (To return to the meaning, or a meaning, of the doctrine of the Trinity, imagine the reaction of fundamentalist Christian educators to the great Bede Griffiths saying the Trinity is the divine "Saccidananda," the divine being, knowing, bliss.) When religious educators assist those who

are searching for a "philosophy of life" to understand that statements of their religion dealing with convictions about the "nature
of things" (doctrines and dogmas) can *mean* something, they save
religion from absurdity! That's the first benefit of thinking carefully
about how doctrine fits into religious education.

The second benefit pertains to interreligious reverence. It is simply this: when it slowly but definitively dawns on people who are
examining a religious worldview and searching for the meanings
available in communities of common conviction that the point of
doctrine is its meaning, the kind of vision and hope and purpose
that it implies, when it dawns on people that doctrinal statements are not meaningful simply because they are stated, then the
apologetic use of doctrine and dogma will recede. (It was, in fact,
receding in the postconciliar church.) And the eclipse of an apologetic use of doctrine is the beginning of the end of prejudicial,
exclusivist religion!

5. School-Based Education with Youth and Young Adults Should Include Critical Inquiry

Catholic Christians are not alone in possessing an impressive resource of schools for young children, teenagers, and collegians. The
resources for "teaching the conversation," for what is essentially
academic discourse with youth and young adults in educational
institutions of the church, are more then ample for sponsoring,
within the religious community itself, critical inquiry about religion, including the religion with which the school is affiliated. This
is a resource that is to a large extent squandered. I spoke above,
under elements of a paradigm shift, of the formation of "self-
renewing generations of loyal but critical members" of religious
communities. This presupposes that in secondary and collegiate
educational institutions of the church, efforts to enhance loyalty
by engaging in conversation about the meaningfulness of religious
symbols, rituals, and convictions are joined to an effort to help students appraise the limitations of all religion, the mistakes that are
made, the historical "track record" that must not be defended at
any cost. By and large, this conversation does not take place. Fear
of inducing cynicism, fear of hierarchs (scholastic or ecclesiastic),
lack of a critical spirit on the part of some teachers, fear of what
was called in old-time Catholicism "giving scandal" interfere with
this crucial function. As a result, the first time a traditionally reared
young Catholic man or women, for example, hears about the history of religious wars, the teaching of contempt, the slaughter of

so-called witches, the carnage of the crusades, or the lifestyles of some popes may well be in an environment hostile to religion itself.

I am familiar with Catholic secondary schools, an ample resource with hundreds of institutions in the United States and highly professionalized faculties in most instances. By and large, the mood of religious education in these schools is neoorthodox. The teaching is often not "systematic," in the sense Moran uses the word, but is catechetical in a way more suited to local "pastoral" communities or parishes than to schools. (Perhaps the best and clearest writing about the blur between "academic" and "pastoral" in Catholic secondary schools has been done by the Australian religious education theorist Graham Rossiter.[13]) In the former, systematic approach, genuine intellectual wrestling is encouraged. In more pastoral educational approaches, invoking religious feeling is predominant. There is, frankly, too little sponsorship in these schools of what Moran calls "disbelief... directed at the external verbal side of belief."

By itself, of course, sponsoring critical inquiry without an equally systematic encouragement of appreciation for the students' religious traditions is a disaster. The fault that is most often perpetrated, however, is dispensing with this critical educational focus.

6. Dialogue Should Begin Early

Those who accept Moran's view of the moments of religious education development will see clearly that nothing but confusion can result if well-intentioned religious educators of every kind, in every social form begin too early to overlay education for interreligious reverence on top of the many, varied, and creative educational activities initiating children into *their* religious communities. These are the times and the practices Moran refers to as "visional," "mythical," and "narrative." And the focus must be on "my people." But even in the earliest years, children of the religious community should be impressed with the fact that there are many communities of God's people. And certainly young members of religious communities who progress much beyond early adolescence without substantial, appreciative, firsthand exposure to the authenticity and richness of religious paths other than the path of the community into which they were born are unlikely to develop appreciation later on. Or, being denied even the barest exposure to other religious paths through young adulthood, they may, depending upon the degree and healthiness of formation within their religious communities, find other paths so attractive that they "convert." This is not a problem on the face of it (recall, for example, Panikkar's rule about openness to conversion here). But many such "conversions" are to what is exotic in the unfamiliar rather than to what is life-giving in another community's path of holiness. It need hardly be said that this principle, while challenging to people firmly rooted in all the religious communities, is especially problematic for Jews in places such as the United States where intermarriage with people who are not Jewish happens often, and assimilation and loss of religious identity and practice are commonplace. Still, as Rabbi Everett Gendler has said, Jewish and Christian youth and young adults are not studying their religions together to any great extent, yet intermarriage and assimilation continue. Bringing Jewish and Christian youth together to study the richness of their respective traditions may help youth of both communities appreciate their heritages.[14]

7. Christians Who Can Should Embrace the "Catholic Spirit"

The reader will recall from the exposition of the "Catholic Thing" or spirit in chapter 2 as well as the discussion of Rahner's theology in chapter 3 that its essential feature is emphasis on the universal predisposition of all creation toward the Holy One, that, again in Rahner's words, humans especially are "the event of God's absolute self-communication." *All* human beings are this event. This leads to a positive theological anthropology; it is also the essential theological presupposition for interreligious reverence, for accepting the first and second elements of the paradigm shift to which reference has been made: that "God is greater than religion" and the Holy One is available to all through paths of holiness possessing "rough parity." The reader will also recall that the "Catholic spirit" is not coterminous with Catholicism or the Catholic Church. I myself count as friend and noble exemplar a Southern Baptist Christian educator who is a courageous incarnation of this elemental feature of the Catholic spirit. We must be grateful for the genuine insight of Reform Protestantism regarding human frailty and predisposition to illusion and hubris. But there can be no religious education for interreligious reverence and no end to anti-Jewish Christian religious education if humans are, as depicted in Reform theology, utterly corrupt and all in need of the "alien justification" (Helmut Thielicke) available only through Jesus Christ. The Catholic ideas of the universality of grace and the goodness of even fallen human nature are the theological foundations of interreligious reverence.

Programs

As one might suspect, there are no programs under Christian auspices that systematically set out precisely to convince Christians that there is "rough parity" among the many paths of holiness religious people follow. There is, however, a great deal within formal religious education in the church that seeks to develop appreciation and respect for religions other than Christianity. Public and private education in schools also presents us with some models of teaching for critical thinking that serve the general purpose of enhancing and expanding such attitudes. It is to these that we turn.

Texts and Programs

Philip Cunningham's *Education for Shalom: Religion Textbooks and the Enhancement of the Catholic and Jewish Relationship* has been mentioned earlier. Though it is not a large book, it is a work of prodigious scope and precision and an indispensable guide especially to Catholic religious educators in choosing textbook series that are relatively free of anti-Jewish bias.

Cunningham's book contains excellent profiles of historical anti-Judaism, Catholic documents constituting what he calls "the modern Church's renunciation of anti-Judaism," and a fine assessment of the treatment of Jews and Judaism in *The Catechism of the Catholic Church*. In his detailed and scientific study of the treatment of Jews and Judaism in Catholic textbook series, Cunningham studies seven "period categories" and nine "theme categories." The "period categories" are: (1) Hebrew Scripture, (2) the New Testament, (3) Rabbinic Judaism, (4) the Middle Ages, (5) the Reformation to the twentieth century, (6) the twentieth century, and (7) general or today. The "theme categories" are" (1) Jesus as a Jew, (2) Jesus and the Jews, (3) the Pharisees, (4) the crucifixion, (5) divine retribution, (6) the Shoah, (7) modern Israel, (8) relationship of covenants, (9) the Crusades/Inquisition. He analyzes fourteen primary and secondary educational texts series from twelve Catholic religious education curriculum textbook publishers.[15] Those familiar with the multidimensional texts put out by major publishing houses know that most series contain not only books to be placed in students' hands, these often tailored to whether the setting for study is school or a parish religious education program, but also materials to guide catechists and sometimes parents as well. Thus, the texts series that score well in Cunningham's analysis (and his report is generally hopeful) contain materials that can be used to influence reform of attitudes and adjustment of understandings of adults as well as children. It is probable that the series that show the most positive, and accurate, assessment of Jews and Judaism in themselves and in relationship to Christians and Christianity will also contain more rather than less adequate materials on such crucial areas of Christian life as the Eucharist. Thus Cunningham's survey may also be of assistance in selecting texts to help children in Catholic parishes prepare to participate in the Eucharist. This work cannot be recommended too highly.[16]

Many programs of study and appreciation of one another's religious traditions and values exist for adults. These programs usually arise from areas in which Jews and Catholics (as well as Jews and Protestants) live side by side in significant numbers and strive for greater understanding. Two examples will suffice to make the point and suggest possible resources. In 1995 the Catholic Archdiocese of Boston in collaboration with the Anti-Defamation League initiated a program entitled "Catholic and Jews Together." It is essentially a teacher-training program. The other program, "A Journey of Discovery: A Resource Manual for Jewish-Catholic Dialogue," was undertaken in 1989 by the Catholic Archdiocese of Los Angeles and Tabor Publishing Company. It consists of the published results of a sustained conversation between Jewish and Catholic leaders. There are a number of equally worthy programs like these. Readers who wish to survey what works in these and similar models should contact the national interreligious affairs directors of the ADL (Rabbi Leon Klenicki) and the American Jewish Committee (Rabbi A. James Rudin). Both people, significant scholars who are indefatigable in promoting Jewish-Christian relations, are located in New York City.

Content and Educational Method

"Facing History and Ourselves" is a program of "critical thinking skills" focusing on "themes of racism, anti-semitism and violence," with special attention to "events that led to the Holocaust," designed to "encourage...[students] to reflect on their role in society." In the words of its leaders:

> Facing History and Ourselves is a national educational organization [headquartered in Boston, with offices in Chicago,

Memphis, New York, and Los Angeles] devoted to teaching about the dangers of indifference and the value of civility by helping students and teachers confront the complexities of history. It provides a powerful and thought-provoking course of studies for middle and high school students [and collegians] on the events that led to the Holocaust and the results of the policies of genocide. It directly links these histories to issues of individual choice and social justice in the day to day experiences of young people. It is a dynamic, long-term educational approach that provides an ongoing system of services to help improve the overall quality of instruction to a school system, encourages professional development of teachers and helps to link the school and the community to the latest scholarship.[17]

"Facing History and Ourselves" is a multidimensional "system of services," including written resources, teacher education, classroom education, and media resources. It embodies "teaching the conversation" at its most informed, passionate, and analytic. Its director, Margot Stern Strom, considers that it treats youth as "moral philosophers." The spirit of "Facing History and Ourselves" is prophetic in the sense Rabbi Heschel meant when speaking of the difference between a contented conventional moral view and the rage of the prophet. It is critical in the sense noted earlier in this chapter. (For a discussion of how one Catholic high school, Georgetown Prep, implemented the "Facing History" program, see Julie Collins, "The Holocaust: An Icon for Religious Education," *Professional Approaches for Christian Educators* [PACE] 21 [November 1991].)

Like Cunningham's survey of Catholic religion texts, "Facing History" is indispensable in helping students see the palpable horrors of hate and the need to treat all other human beings as subjects.[18]

Interreligious Theological Education

"Theological education" is the result of "teaching the conversation" about what we mean by the verbal and written expressions of our experiences of faithfulness (and failure to be faithful). Theological education is a humble but crucial element within the rich pattern of relations and multiple modes of teaching-learning that constitute religious education. Theological education for interreligious reverence will assist members of different religious communities to *approach* the "full fact" of the religious experience of the "others," and at the same time to convince members that they cannot fully know and understand the full fact of the religious experience of the other. Such theological education will correct the mistakes of "reduced essence," E. P. Sanders's term for the reductionistic appraisal of the meaning and importance of the traditions of other religious communities. It will correct error, embellish appreciation, and even induce some "holy envy" without the slightest taint of intention to convert. It will, above all, confirm the conversation partners in the meaning of their respective ways and will never lapse into syncretism.

A model of such practice is available. In 1994 with a grant from the Lilly Endowment, two distinguished religious education theorists — Mary C. Boys, whose work was sighted earlier, and Sara Lee — began experimental implementation of a model of interreligious theological education, what they call the Catholic-Jewish Colloquium. Boys is Skinner and McAlpin Professor of Practical Theology at Union Theological Seminary in New York City. Lee is Director of the Rhea Hirsch School of Education, Hebrew Union College, University of Judaism in Los Angeles. Over the course of two years, Boys and Lee brought twenty Catholic and twenty Jewish religious educators together for sustained theological conversation. Participants came to know one another well. They ate together and prayed together, and they studied the classic texts of one another's traditions with the greatest care, with the assistance of two outstanding teachers (people capable of showing how to have "conversation"). The goal as I discern it has been to establish such conversation at a level of clarity, empathy, and precision previously unattained for a sustained period of time. Boys and Lee are committed to the crucial issue of genuine interreligious convergence through depth dialogue with which this text has been concerned: that we not understand one another too quickly, and that genuine understanding, which can never exhaust the experience and meanings of the other and which does not remake the other in one's own image, emerges from such conversation. (The project directors will be reporting on this model in book form in the future. Further information is available from the Center for Jewish Christian Study in Baltimore, Maryland.)

Prayer

It was noted earlier in this book, in Langdon Gilkey's words, that genuine convergence that seems impossible in theological conversation occurs in the *"praxis* of dialogue." David Tracy was cited saying that such dialogue is a genuine religious experience. In his work *Paths of Spirituality,* John Macquarrie speaks of a boundary crossed from thinking to prayer. For all the difficulties attached to praying together across differences of religion (and here Joseph Soloveitchik's message and spirit is prominent), there must be a way for Jews and Christians (and others) to be together acknowledging the presence of the Holy One. While much is written in interreligious theological discourse about the worship and prayer of the respective communities, little is available about praying *together.*[19]

The key to interreligious prayer by Jews and Christians lies is the traditions in each community of meditative or contemplative prayer or prayer of silence. The contemplative traditions of Catholic Christianity are relatively well known. Less well known, by Jews and Christians, is the rich and ancient practice within Judaism of prayer of silence, solitude, and meditation. Rabbi Heschel speaks of such prayer as "common practice among mystically inclined Jews...of the Middle Ages," noting from a later period, for example, these words about a follower of the Baal Shem Tov: "According to the great-grandson of the Baal Shem Tov, Rabbi Nahman of Bratzlav, solitude is an indispensable perquisite for spiritual living. He called upon his disciples to set aside an hour or more every day for seclusion and meditation."[20]

Heschel himself writes: "Is not listening to the pulse of wonder worth silence and abstinence from self-assertion? Why do we not set apart an hour of living for devotion to God by surrendering to stillness?"[21]

Rabbi Leon Klenicki has pioneered in developing interreligious prayer, not meditative prayer properly so called, but prayer rituals with a deeply meditative spirit. His outstanding interreligious Holocaust memorial prayer as well as the recent "A Dialogue Service About Prayer" are two examples.[22] Many of the guided meditations that appear in my most recent books (*The Way of Faithfulness: Contemplation and Formation in the Church* [1993] and *Busy Life Peaceful Center: A Book of Meditating* [1995]) are suitable, some with slight adaption, for Jews and Christians who wish to sit quietly, still the clamoring, and listen to the voice of God in one another's presence. Those who practice meditative prayer gently but earnestly will recognize the accuracy of the assertion that it *matters* with whom you sit in quiet meditative prayer, even though no words are exchanged between those so engaged. Such people know, in the words of Abbot Thomas Keating, "The contemplative dimension of life, present in all the great religions, is the common heart of the world. There the human family is already one."[23]

The Insufficiency of Programs

In the end, no "program" is sufficient for the purpose of becoming holy. I hope to have secured this understanding with the analysis of Gabriel Moran's work in chapter 4. The teaching is by example and design, with an end in view, to remove obstacles and to show how to engage in conversation. It employs speech and silence. It is sometimes highly intentional and at other times inadvertent but habitual. Relationships that are religiously educational are available to everyone from everyone, in programmatic settings and ordinary time. When the intent is "to teach religion," message is prominent. Deeper and more important is "to teach religiousness." Here, as Moran says, the practice is "cultivating attentiveness and gratitude for gifts that surround us." This is an adequate description of prayer. Those who strive to "become prayer" are grateful for the gift of Jews and Christians and all the "others" around them, now seen clearly as God's children.

Afterword

Can Jews Revere Christians?

As assertive and assured as this book is, it ends on a genuine note of perplexity. The question is not really, of course, whether any Jew or many Jews can revere some Christians or many Christians. Friends, by definition, have some reverence, affection, and respect for friends. And there are Jews and Christians who are friends!

Nor does the question imply the hope for a more rigorous or more effectively broadcast Jewish theology of Christianity. This theologizing has gone on from ancient times, is prominent in the work of Maimonides, was taken up by Baeck and Rosenzweig, and today is pursued by such authors as David Novak and Michael Wyschogrod.[1]

Nor am I referring to justification of the theological legitimacy of the other (Christian) path by Jewish thinkers such as this observation by Irving Greenberg: "We should measure religion by the criterion of how people act after they hear the word in community. If the Incarnation and Resurrection of Jesus leads to Christian triumphalism, to persecution and idolatry then Christianity proves itself to be false. If it leads to deeper compassion and understanding and a grasp of human realities and human needs and motivated covenantal action, then it validates itself as a channel of the divine."[2]

What I mean is captured when Leon Klenicki asks: "Can I overcome two millennia of memories," in the sense of "perceiv[ing] the other's faith as a call from God?"[3] And when David Hartman asks: "Can I happily see Christians in their passionate love for what mediates the spiritual life for them? Can I celebrate their joy and yet not feel that my joy of mitzvah is weakened?"[4] The quality of mutual reverence of which I speak is captured in what is for me one of the most moving testaments to such an attitude I have ever read.

In the March 31, 1996, issue of the *New York Times Magazine*, Stephen J. Dubner writes of "Choosing My Religion." It is an essay about the pain and confusion, but finally the exaltation, of retrieving his Jewishness after being raised a Catholic by Jewish parents, both of whom converted to Catholicism during World War II. At the end of the article, Dubner relates his intention to drive to his father's grave and pray Kaddish over it. He writes, "Just before Christmas, I drove upstate to my father's cemetery. I was ready to carry out my act of spiritual subterfuge: I had a yarmulke and the Mourner's Kaddish in my pocket. It took me a while to find his marker. I scraped off the snow, saw the cross and then his name. I never reached for the yarmulke. Would I want some son of mine saying the rosary when I'm lying in a Jewish cemetery? Painful as it has been to accept my father's choice, it was *his* choice, just as I've been free to make mine. I ended up having a conversation with him; it cleared up a lot of things. I did leave a little stone at the corner of his plot."

On Christmas Eve Dubner's mother calls him; December 24 is the 53rd anniversary of her baptism. She ruminates at the other end of the line about his father and how happy he must be " ... because he's got it all, face to face with God." Dubner concludes the article: "In the past I would have shut out a comment like that — it's too far removed from what I believe. Now I just listened to the serenity in her voice. There was a long silence on the line; it was the sound of forgiveness, I'm sure, and it was traveling in both directions."

I have assumed, throughout this book, that the end of Christian inspired anti-Judaism and Antisemitism requires of Christians reparation of relations, cessation of stereotype, embrace of deep Judaic religious values, and growth in reverence. And this, of course, is true. But only now does it dawn on me that for the fullness of interreligious reverence to be achieved, the greater work, the more poignant work, may be that to which Jews are challenged. It is monumental spiritual work to be of the seed of Abraham and Sarah — to be forgiving.

Notes

Chapter One

1. Edward Flannery, *The Anguish of the Jews* (New York: Macmillan, 1985), 4.

2. Benzion Netanyahu, *The Origins of the Inquisition in 15th-Century Spain* (New York: Random House, 1995), 24.

3. Rosemary Radford Ruether, *Faith and Fratricide* (Minneapolis: Winston Press, 1985), 3.

4. Mary C. Boys, "A More Faithful Portrait of Judaism: An Imperative for Christian Education," in David P. Efroymson, Eugene J. Fisher, Leon Klenicki, eds., *Within Context: Essays on Jews and Judaism in the New Testament* (Collegeville, Minn.: Liturgical Press, 1993), 4.

5. Ibid., 5.

6. Clark M. Williamson and Ronald J. Allen, *Interpreting Difficult Texts: Anti-Judaism and Christian Preaching* (Philadelphia: Trinity Press International, 1989), 3–6.

7. Most of what Isaac designates "anti-Semitism" falls under the definition of anti-Judaism in this work.

8. Jules Isaac, *Has Anti-Semitism Christian Roots?* (New York: National Conference of Christians and Jews, 1962), 77–85.

9. Christopher Leighton, cited in Norman A. Beck, introduction to *Mature Christianity in the 21st Century* (New York: Crossroad, 1994), 24.

10. Ibid., 24f.

11. E. Roy Eckhart, cited in James Charlesworth, ed., *Jews and Christians Exploring the Past, Present and Future* (New York: Crossroad, 1990), 164.

12. Bernhard Olsen, cited in Isaac, introduction to *Has Anti-Semitism Christian Roots?*, 11ff.

13. Eliezar Berkovits, cited in Beck, *Mature Christianity*, 30.

14. Eckhart, cited in Charlesworth, *Jews and Christians*, 163.

15. Olsen, cited in Isaac, *Has Anti-Semitism Christian Roots?*, 23.

16. Gustavo Gutiérrez, *The Theology of Liberation* (Maryknoll, N.Y.: Orbis Books, 1973), 101.

17. Normon Solomon, cited in Leon Klenicki, ed., *Toward a Theological Encounter: Jewish Understandings of Christianity* (New York: Paulist Press, 1991), 32.

18. Johannes B. Metz, *The Emergent Church* (New York: Crossroad, 1981), 24.

19. Emil Fackenheim, cited in Klenicki, *Theological Encounter*, 30.

20. Flannery, *The Anguish of the Jews,* 2.

21. The reference to "strenuous effort" should not obscure the insight that it is also in gentle effort that much is accomplished.

22. Abraham Heschel, cited in Samuel Dresner, ed., *I Asked for Wonder* (New York: Schocken Books, 1991), 40f.

23. For an expert discussion of the "classic," see David Tracy, *Blessed Rage for Order* (New York: Seabury Press, 1975), chapters 1 and 2.

24. See Sandra Schneiders, *Women and the Word: The Gender of God in the New Testament* (New York: Paulist, 1984), 38.

25. For a clear discussion of the evolution of belief regarding Jesus Christ in first- and second-century Christianity, see Richard P. McBrien, *Catholicism* (San Francisco: Harper, 1981), 373–75.

26. Charlesworth, *Jews and Christians,* 37.

27. Philip Cunningham, cited in Efroymson, Fisher, and Klenicki, *Within Context,* 64.

28. Daniel J. Harrington, "The Problem of 'the Jews' in John's Gospel," *Exploration* 8, no. 1 (1994): 2.

29. Ibid., 3.

30. Charlesworth, *Jews and Christians,* 50.

31. Harrington, "The Problem," 3f.

32. Ibid., 3.

33. Krister Stendahl, *Paul Among Jews and Gentiles* (Philadelphia: Fortress Press, 1976), 4.

34. Ibid., 7.

35. Ibid.

36. Harrington, "The Problem," 3.

37. Charlesworth, *Jews and Christians,* 37.

38. Eugene Borowitz, *Contemporary Christologies: A Jewish Response* (New York: Paulist Press, 1980), 179.

39. James Charlesworth, "Philo: the Jewish Genius of Alexandria," *Explorations* 8, no. 1 (1994): 2.

40. Eugene Fisher, "The Passion and Death of Jesus of Nazareth: Catechetical Approaches," in Efroymson, Fisher, and Klenicki, *Within Context,* 114.

41. Leon Klenicki and Eugene J. Fisher, *Roots and Branches: Biblical Judaism, Rabbinic Judaism and Early Christianity* (Winona, Minn.: St. Mary's Press, 1987), 18.

42. Ibid., 15.

43. Fisher, "The Passion and Death," 115.

44. Krister Stendahl, "Anti-Semitism and the New Testament," *Explorations* 7, no. 2 (1993): 7.

45. For much of the historical commentary to follow, I am indebted to Ruether, *Faith and Fratricide;* Flannery, *The Anguish of the Jews;* and Mary C. Boys, "The Cross: Should a Symbol Betrayed Be Reclaimed?" *Cross Currents* (Spring 1994): 9.

46. Flannery, *The Anguish of the Jews,* 3.

47. Ibid., 38.

48. Franklin Littell, *The Crucifixion of the Jews* (Detroit: Wayne State University Press, 1975), 27.

49. Ibid., 28.

50. Williamson and Allen, *Difficult Texts,* 7.

51. Jacob Neusner, *Jews and Christians: The Myth of a Common Tradition* (London: SCM, 1991), 199.

52. Eusebius, *Ecclesiastical History,* quoted in Boys, "The Cross," 9.

53. Heschel, cited in Dresner, *I Asked for Wonder,* 46.

54. Ambrose, cited in Williamson and Allen, *Difficult Texts,* 16.

55. Chrysostom, cited in Ruether, *Faith and Fratricide,* 146f.

56. Augustine, "Reply to Faustus the Manichean," cited in Boys, "A More Faithful Portrait," 6.

57. Augustine, "Reply," cited in Leon Klenicki, ed., *Toward a Theological Encounter: Jewish Understanding of Christianity* (New York: Paulist Press, 1991), 2.

58. John Pawlikowski, "The Vatican-Israeli Accords: Their Implication for Catholic Faith and Teaching," *Professional Approaches for Christian Educators (PACE)* 24 (November 1994): 21.

59. Flannery, *The Anguish of the Jews,* 255.

60. Ruether, *Faith and Fratricide,* 195.

61. Marc Saperstein, *Moments of Crisis in Jewish Christian Relations,* cited in Boys, "The Cross," 13.

62. Ruether, *Faith and Fratricide,* 213ff.

63. Ibid., 204.

64. Flannery, *The Anguish of the Jews,* 138.

65. Martin Luther, "The Jews and Their Lies," in Gerhard Falk, *The Jews in Christian Theology* (Jefferson, N.C.: McFarland Press, 1992), 432.

66. John Murray Cuddihy, *The Ordeal of Civility* (New York: Basic Books, 1974), 206–32.

67. Jules Isaac, *The Teaching of Contempt* (1964), 24.

68. Ibid., 22.

69. Flannery, *The Anguish of the Jews,* 258.

70. Ibid., 258ff.

71. David S. Wyman, *The Abandonment of the Jews* (New York: Pantheon Books, 1984), 191.

72. Ibid., 10ff.

73. Christian Scholars' Group on Judaism and the Jewish People — Catholic Membership, "Statement on the Catechism of the Catholic Church," *Professional Approaches for Christian Educators (PACE)* 24 (September 1994): 43f.

74. Joseph Ratzinger, "Reconciling Gospel and Torah: The Catechism," *Origins* 23, no. 36 (February 24, 1994): 623.

75. William H. Willimon, "What Bible Are Your Children Reading?" *Explorations* 7, no. 1 (1993): 1.

76. Anti-Defamation League, *Farrakhan Unchanged: The Continuing Message of Hate* (New York: ADL, 1994), 15.

77. Anti-Defamation League, *Holocaust Denial* (New York: ADL, 1994), 8f.

78. Eugene Fisher, *Anti-Semitism Is a Sin* (Washington, D.C.: United States Catholic Conference, 1990), 5.

79. Philip Cunningham, "Jews and Judaism in Catholic Religion Textbooks: Progress, Problems and Recommendations," *Professional Approaches for Christian Educators (PACE)* 22 (December 1992): 17–21.

80. Williamson and Allen, *Difficult Texts,* 6f.

81. Charlesworth, *Jews and Christians,* 163.

82. Norman Solomon, "Themes in Christian Jewish Relations," in Klenicki, *Theological Encounter,* 31.

83. Abraham J. Heschel, "What Is Ecumenism?" in Lily Edelman, ed., *Face to Face* (New York: National Conference of Christians and Jews, 1967), 2.

84. Abraham J. Heschel, *The Insecurity of Freedom* (New York: Farrar Straus & Giroux, 1966), 119.

85. Klenicki, *Theological Encounter,* 79.

86. Heschel, "What Is Ecumenism?" 2.

Chapter Two

1. A theologian, most often a Catholic, specializing in the theology of the church.

2. Gordon W. Allport, *The Nature of Prejudice* (Cambridge, Mass.: Addison-Wesley Co., 1954), 413.

3. Sectarianism is the perennial impulse of members of larger institutionalized religious groups to break away and form purer "communions of saints." The history of Christian sectarianism is brilliantly assessed in Ernst Troeltsch's *The Social Forms of the Christian Church,* and in less detail but no less incisively by H. Richard Niebuhr in *Christ and Culture.*

4. Leon Klenicki, ed., *Toward a Theological Encounter: Jewish Understandings of Christianity* (New York: Paulist, 1991), 39.

5. Abraham J. Heschel, *The Insecurity of Freedom* (New York: Farrar, Straus & Giroux, 1966), 9.

6. Karl Barth, *Church Dogmatics,* vol. 1, cited in Paul Knitter, *No Other Name: A Critical Survey of Christian Attitudes Toward the World's Religions* (Edinburgh: T. & T. Clark, 1948), 186.

7. Quoted in Karl Rahner *Theological Investigations,* vol. 5 (Baltimore, Helicon Press), 17.

8. Krister Stendahl, "On Sacred Violence: How to Unmask It and How Not To," *Dialog* 23 (Fall 1993): 261–65.

9. Ibid., 264.

10. E. P. Sanders, *Paul and Palestinian Judaism* (Philadelphia: Fortress Press, 1977), 12.

11. Ibid., 17.

12. William James, cited in David Tracy, *Dialogue with the Other* (Grand Rapids, Mich.: Eerdmans, 1990), 32.

13. Heschel, *The Insecurity of Freedom*, 122.

14. Krister Stendahl, cited in "The Origin of Evil — Elaine Pagels," *New Yorker*, April 3, 1995, 64.

15. Tracy, *Dialogue with the Other*, 4.

16. Raymundo Panikkar, *The Intra-Religious Dialogue* (San Francisco: Harper & Row, 1978), xxvii.

17. Ibid., 2.

18. Ibid., 6.

19. Ibid., 7.

20. Ibid., 6.

21. Langdon Gilkey, "Pluralism: Its Theological Implications," in John Hick and Paul Knitter, eds., *The Myth of Christian Uniqueness: Toward a Pluralist Theology of Religions* (Maryknoll, N.Y.: Orbis Books, 1988), 38.

22. Paul Knitter, *No Other Name*, 9.

23. Ibid., 9.

24. Hick and Knitter, *Christian Uniqueness*, 44.

25. Panikkar, *The Intra-Religious Dialogue*, 6.

26. John Hick, cited in Knitter, *No Other Name*, 34f.

27. Langdon Gilkey, cited in Hick and Knitter, *Christian Uniqueness*, 47.

28. Panikkar, cited in Hick and Knitter, *Christian Uniqueness*, 60.

29. Leonard Swidler, *After the Absolute: The Dialogical Future of Religious Reflection* (Minneapolis: Fortress Press, 1990), 52.

30. Maria Harris is the originator, in my experience, of the observation.

31. Panikkar, *The Intra-Religious Dialogue*, 7.

32. Panikkar, cited in Peter Berger, ed., *The Other Side of God* (Garden City, N.Y.: Doubleday Anchor, 1981), 297.

33. In Hick and Knitter, *Christian Uniqueness*, 184.

34. Swidler, *After the Absolute*, 194.

35. Richard P. McBrien's characterization of the biblical view of the human in his *Catholicism*, vol. 1 (San Francisco: Harper, 1981), 142f.

36. Bernard Lonergan, *Method in Theology* (New York: Herder & Herder, 1972), 253.

37. John Dunne, *The Ways of All the Earth*, cited in Knitter, *No Other Name*, 206.

38. Panikkar, *The Intra-Religious Dialogue*, 10.

39. Leon Klenicki, "The Other Person as God: From Disdain to Recognition," *Dialog* 27 (December 1994), 24.

40. T. S. Eliot, cited in Gabriel Moran, *Uniqueness: Problems and*

Paradox in Jewish and Christian Traditions (Maryknoll, N.Y.: Orbis Books, 1992), 5.

41. Moran, *Uniqueness,* 20.

42. Ibid., 19.

43. Ibid., 20.

44. Ibid.

45. Ibid., 46, 50.

46. Ibid., 58f.

47. Stendahl, "On Sacred Violence," 264.

48. Krister Stendahl, "From God's Perspective We Are All Minorities," *Journal of Religious Pluralism* 2 (1993): 6.

49. Moran, *Uniqueness,* 61.

50. Ibid., 62.

51. Stendahl, "On Sacred Violence," 264.

52. Schubert Ogden, "Problems in the Case of Pluralist Theology," *Journal of Religion* 68 (1988): 496.

53. Paul Tillich, *Christianity and the Encounter of World Religions* (1963; reprint, Minneapolis: Fortress Press, 1994), 62.

54. Ibid., xi.

55. Ibid., 62.

56. Gordon Kaufman, "Religious Diversity, Historical Consciousness and Christian Theology," in Hick and Knitter, *Christian Uniqueness,* 11.

57. Stendahl, "On Sacred Violence," 262f.

58. Stendahl, "From God's Perspective," 9.

59. Martin E. Marty and R. Scott Appleby, *Accounting for Fundamentalism* (Chicago: University of Chicago Press, 1992), 1.

60. Patrick Arnold, SJ, "The Rise of Catholic Fundamentalism," *America,* April 11, 1987, 298.

61. Marty and Appleby, *Accounting for Fundamentalism,* 1.

62. See, for example, Frank Rich, "Shotgun Hearings," *The New York Times,* July 19, 1995, A19.

63. Arnold, "The Rise of Catholic Fundamentalism," 297.

64. Marty and Appleby, *Accounting for Fundamentalism,* 1.

65. Arnold, "The Rise of Catholic Fundamentalism," 300.

66. Marty and Appleby, *Accounting for Fundamentalism,* 18.

67. Charles Davis, cited in Knitter, *No Other Name,* 13.

68. Arnold, "The Rise of Catholic Fundamentalism," 299.

69. David Tracy, *Blessed Rage for Order* (New York: Seabury Press, 1975).

70. Peter Berger, *The Heretical Imperative* (Garden City, N.Y.: Doubleday Anchor, 1979), 155.

71. Ibid., 156.

72. Ibid.

73. Ibid., 153.

74. Gordon W. Allport, *The Individual and His Religion* (New York: Macmillan, 1950), 57–72.

75. Tracy, *Blessed Rage for Order,* 39.

76. Robley Edward Whitson, *The Convergence of World Religion* (New York: Newman Press, 1971), 11f.

77. I am indebted for this typology of modes of theological work to Tracy, *Blessed Rage for Order,* chapter 2.

78. Jaroslav Pelikan commented, "Tradition is the living faith of the dead; traditionalism is the dead faith of the living." Cited in Mary C. Boys, *Educating in Faith* (New York: Harper & Row, 1989), 193.

79. Elizabeth Johnson, *She Who Is* (New York: Crossroad, 1992), 4.

80. Wilfred Cantwell Smith, *The Meaning and End of Religion,* cited in Knitter, *No Other Name,* 45.

81. Heschel, *The Insecurity of Freedom,* 115f.

82. Knitter, *No Other Name,* 121.

83. Ibid., 122.

84. Tracy, *Blessed Rage for Order,* 44.

85. Ibid., 95.

86. Langdon Gilkey, cited in Hick and Knitter, *Christian Uniqueness,* 38.

87. Ibid., 39.

88. Johnson, *She Who Is,* 43.

89. Dorothee Soelle, *The Strength of the Weak,* cited in Johnson, *She Who Is,* 53.

90. Rosemary Radford Ruether, *Sexism and God Talk* (Boston: Beacon Press, 1983), 19.

91. Paul Knitter, "A Liberation Theology of Religions," in Hick and Knitter, *Christian Uniqueness,* 186ff.

92. Harvey Cox, cited in Hick and Knitter, *Christian Uniqueness,* 188.

93. Stendahl, "From God's Perspective," 10.

94. Tracy, *Blessed Rage for Order,* 4.

95. Systematic study of Scripture.

96. Stendahl, "From God's Perspective," 3.

97. Ibid., 4.

98. Ibid., 6.

99. Ibid., 3.

100. Ibid., 4.

101. Ibid., 9.

102. Ibid., 2.

103. "Declaration on the Relation of the Church to non-Christian Religions," *Nostra Aetate,* in *Vatican II: Conciliar and Post-Conciliar Documents,* ed. Austin Flannery, OP (Collegeville, Minn.: The Liturgical Press; Northport, N.Y.: Costello Publishing; Dublin: Dominican Publications, 1965).

104. See Gustavo Gutiérrez, *The Theology of Liberation* (Maryknoll,

N.Y.: Orbis Books, 1972) and *On Job: God Talk and the Suffering of the Innocent* (Maryknoll, N.Y.: Orbis Books, 1986).

105. Gustavo Gutiérrez, *We Drink from Our Own Wells* (Maryknoll, N.Y.: Orbis Books, 1984), 178.

106. Todd Breyfogle and Thomas Levergood, "Conversation with David Tracy," *Cross Currents* (Fall 1994): 293.

107. Abraham Joshua Heschel, *The Insecurity of Freedom* (New York: Farrar, Straus & Giroux, 1972), 117ff.

108. Amos Wilder, *Theopoetic: Theology and the Religious Imagination* (Philadelphia: Fortress Press, 1976), 81.

109. Heschel, *The Insecurity of Freedom,* 119.

110. Abraham Joshua Heschel, "Two Teachers," *A Passion for Truth* (New York: Farrar, Straus & Giroux, 1973), 3–84.

111. Heschel, *The Insecurity of Freedom,* 119.

112. Ibid., 124.

113. Rosemary Haughton, *The Catholic Thing* (Springfield, Ill.: Templegate, 1978), 27.

114. Irenaeus, *Against Heresies,* cited in H. Richard Niebuhr and Waldo Beech, *Christian Ethics* (New York: Ronald Press, 1955), 56ff.

115. McBrien, *Catholicism,* vol. 1 (Minneapolis: Winston Press, 1981), 158.

116. John Calvin, *The Institutes of the Christian Religion,* ed. John T. McNeill (Philadelphia: Westminster Press, 1960).

117. Saint Francis of Assisi, "Canticle of Brother Sun" in *The Writings of St. Francis of Assisi* (Chicago: Franciscan Herald Press, 1976).

118. Helmut Thielicke, *Theological Ethics* (Philadelphia: Fortress Press, 1948), 203ff.

119. Langdon Gilkey, *Catholicism Confronts Modernity* (New York: Seabury Press, 1975), 18f.

120. Haughton, *The Catholic Thing,* 245f.

121. Gilkey, *Catholicism Confronts Modernity,* 18.

122. Haughton, *The Catholic Thing,* 235.

123. Michael J. Himes, "Holiness and Finitude: Creaturely Spirituality," *Professional Approaches for Christian Educators (PACE)* 19 (January 1990), 109.

124. Pierre Teilhard de Chardin, *The Divine Milieu* (New York: Harper & Row, 1958), 55.

125. Haughton, *The Catholic Thing,* 234.

126. Karl Rahner, *Foundations of Christian Faith* (New York: Seabury Press, 1985), 129.

127. William V. Dych, "Theology in a New Key," in Leo J. O'Donovan, ed., *A World of Grace* (New York: Seabury Press, 1987), 7.

128. Karl Rahner, cited by Gerald McCool, ed., in the introduction to *The Rahner Reader* (New York: Seabury Press, 1975), xvii.

129. Dych, "Theology in a New Key," 8.

130. Karl Rahner, *Theological Investigations,* vol. 9, cited in McCool, *The Rahner Reader,* 207.

131. Dych, "Theology in a New Key," 9.

132. Rahner, *Foundations of Christian Faith,* 41.

133. Tracy, *Dialogue with the Other,* 43.

134. Hick and Knitter, *Christian Uniqueness,* 23.

135. Moran, *Uniqueness,* 135.

136. Knitter, *No Other Name,* 6.

137. Walter Brueggemann, " 'Othering, . . .' Random Thoughts on Covenant," *Explorations* 9, no. 1 (1995): 4.

138. Ibid.

139. Stendahl, "From God's Perspective," 2.

Chapter Three

1. David Tracy, *Blessed Rage for Order* (New York: Seabury Press, 1975), 204.

2. Docetism is a heresy that first appears in the early church. It effectively denies the humanity of Jesus. See below.

3. John Macquarrie, *Principles of Christian Theology* (New York: Scribner, 1966), 269.

4. In numerous lectures and conversations, most recently in personal conversation, October 2, 1995.

5. Karl Rahner, *Theological Investigations* (Baltimore: Helicon Press, 1961), 153.

6. David Power, OMI, *The Eucharistic Mystery: Revitalizing the Tradition* (New York: Crossroad, 1992), 56.

7. Tracy, *Blessed Rage for Order,* 206.

8. Paul Tillich, *A History of Christian Thought* (New York: Harper & Row, 1968), 68.

9. Ibid.

10. Richard P. McBrien, glossary in *Catholicism,* vol. 2 (Minneapolis: Winston Press, 1981), xxxviii.

11. Joseph Fitzmyer, SJ, *A Christological Catechism* (New York: Paulist Press, 1981), 63f.

12. See Gerald Sloyan, *The Jesus Tradition* (Winona, Minn.: St. Mary's Press, 1986), 18.

13. Thomas Sheehan, *The First Coming (How the Kingdom of God Became Christianity)* (New York: Random House, 1986), 19.

14. Dietrich Bonhoeffer, *Christ at the Center* (New York: Harper & Row, 1960), 183.

15. McBrien, glossary in *Catholicism,* vol. 2, xxiv.

16. Paula Fredriksen, *From Jesus to Christ* (New Haven: Yale University Press, 1988), 213.

17. Sloyan, *The Jesus Tradition,* 36.

18. Ibid., 35.

19. Ibid., 36.

20. Rahner, *Theological Investigations*, 155.

21. Ibid., 148f.

22. Bede Griffiths, *Return to the Center* (Springfield, Ill.: Templegate, 1976), 26.

23. Norman Pittenger, *Christology Reconsidered* (London: SCM, 1970), 17.

24. Ibid., 11f.

25. John Macquarrie, *Twentieth Century Religious Thought* (New York: Harper & Row, 1963), 373.

26. Not all those socialized into an organized religion really "want" what the particular religion arose to provide, namely, a particular symbolic structure and communal engagement bringing the Holy One, as consolation and challenge, near in this particular way. As William James pointed out, there is a great deal of "secondhandedness" in religion. Thus some believe that they are compelled to "want" what the religion offers, but do not in fact want it.

27. Karl Rahner, *Foundations of Christian Faith* (New York: Seabury Press, 1978), 39.

28. Tracy, *Blessed Rage for Order*, 204.

29. Tillich, *A History of Christian Thought*, 365.

30. Quoted in ibid., 365.

31. See below, David Tracy's discussion of facts as "possibilities actualized" and facts as "possibilities re-presented" in chapter 3.

32. Macquarrie, *Principles of Christian Theology*, 290.

33. Tillich, *A History of Christian Thought*, 249f.

34. Alan Race, *Christians and Religious Pluralism* (London: SCM Press, 1983), 128.

35. Tillich, *A History of Christian Thought*, 172.

36. Macquarrie, *Principles of Christian Theology*, 418.

37. Quoted in Sloyan, *The Jesus Tradition*, 104.

38. Gabriel Moran, *Uniqueness: Problems and Paradox in Jewish and Christian Traditions* (Maryknoll, N.Y.: Orbis Books, 1992), 88.

39. Not "natural" in the sense of divorced from "supernatural," or "human" as if there were a free-standing "humanity" divorced from divinity, but in the sense Macquarrie means when speaking of "the grace of Being not the 'natural' evolution of being." See Macquarrie, *Twentieth Century Religious Thought*, 398.

40. Macquarrie, *Principles of Christian Theology*, 276.

41. Ibid., 270, 275.

42. Quoted in George Maloney, SJ, *The Cosmic Christ* (New York: Sheed & Ward, 1968), 73.

43. Ibid.

44. Paul Tillich, *Systematic Theology*, vol. 2 (Chicago: University of Chicago Press, 1967), 112.

45. Ibid., 125.

46. Macquarrie, *Principles of Christian Theology,* 270.

47. Rahner, *Foundations of the Faith,* 136.

48. Griffiths, *Return to the Center,* 36f, 43f.

49. By "orthodox" I mean the theological formulations, transmuted over time into doctrinal and dogmatic propositions of belief, that over the expanse of time have come to be taken as true by significant majorities of Christians living now, as well as by the official teachers within organized religious institutions.

50. Quoted in Race, *Christians and Religious Pluralism,* 109.

51. Quoted in ibid., 128.

52. Ibid., 127.

53. Quoted in ibid., 110.

54. Quoted in ibid., 109.

55. Moran, *Uniqueness,* 74.

56. Paul Van Buren, *A Theology of Jewish Christian Reality Part III: Christ in Context* (Lanham, Md.: University Press of America, 1988), 85.

57. Quoted from Schillebeeckx, *Jesus,* in Race, *Christians and Religious Pluralism,* 131.

58. Sheehan, *The First Coming,* 115.

59. Rahner, *Foundations of the Faith,* 271.

60. Tillich, *A History of Christian Thought,* 172.

61. Macquarrie, *Principles of Christian Theology,* 284.

62. Ibid., 282.

63. Quoted in Mary C. Boys, "The Cross: Should a Symbol Betrayed Be Reclaimed?" *Cross Currents* (Spring 1994): 17.

64. Macquarrie, *Principles of Christian Theology,* 285.

65. Tillich, *A History of Christian Thought,* 172.

66. Rahner, *Foundations of the Faith,* 268, 283.

67. Ibid., 267.

68. Ibid., 39.

69. Moran, *Uniqueness,* 88.

70. Judith Plaskow, "Feminist Christology and Anti-Jewish Tracings," *Journal of Feminist Studies in Religion* 7, no. 2 (1991): 78.

71. Elisabeth Schüssler Fiorenza, *Jesus: Miriam's Child, Sophia's Prophet* (New York: Continuum, 1994), 18.

72. Ibid., 21.

73. Elizabeth Johnson, *She Who Is* (New York: Crossroad, 1993), 151.

74. Quoted in Schüssler Fiorenza, *Jesus,* 50.

75. Johnson, *She Who Is,* 150.

76. Schüssler Fiorenza, *Jesus,* 53.

77. Johnson, *She Who Is,* 166.

78. Tracy, *Blessed Rage for Order,* 207.

79. Ibid., 215.

80. Ibid., 207.

81. Ibid., 215.

82. David Power, OMI, *The Eucharistic Mystery: Revitalizing the Tradition* (New York: Crossroad, 1992), vii.

83. Ibid., viii.

84. Macquarrie, *Principles of Christian Theology,* 398f.

85. Kenan Osborne, *Sacramental Theology: A General Introduction* (New York: Paulist Press, 1988), 82.

86. Power, *Eucharistic Mystery,* 46.

87. Macquarrie, *Principles of Christian Theology,* 425.

88. Moran, *Uniqueness,* 91.

89. Macquarrie, *Principles of Christian Theology,* 425.

90. I have written of this in *Busy Life, Peaceful Center: A Book of Meditating* (Allan, Tex.: Thomas More Press, 1995), 35.

91. Macquarrie, *Principles of Christian Theology,* 423.

92. Bernard Cooke, *Sacraments and Sacramentality* (Mystic, Conn.: Twenty-Third Publications, 1983), 95.

93. Ibid., 108.

94. Augustine, Sermon 272 in *Commentary on the Lord's Sermon on the Mount and Seventeen Related Sermons,* trans. Denis J. Kavanagh (New York: Fathers of the Church, 1963).

95. Quoted in Samuel Dresner, ed., *I Asked for Wonder* (New York: Schocken Books, 1991), 22.

96. David Stendahl-Rast, OSB, *Gratefulness: The Heart of Prayer* (New York: Paulist Press, 1984), 11.

97. Ibid., 122.

98. Rosemary Haughton, *The Catholic Thing* (Springfield, Ill.: Templegate, 1978), 249.

99. Osborne, *Sacramental Theology,* 42.

100. Sheehan, *The First Coming,* 70.

101. Cooke, *Sacraments and Sacramentality,* 166.

102. Surely the *most* destructive feature is the effort to squelch the movement of the Holy Spirit, which will render women in the church fully available to promote Christian faithfulness in all roles in the church and to fulfill their vocations.

103. Joseph Andreas Jungmann, *The Good News Yesterday and Today* (New York: W. H. Sadlier, 1962), 231.

104. "Doctrinal initiation" is a more adequate phrase for this approach than might first appear, because in this approach religious narrative (Scripture) is subordinate to doctrinal formula and is introduced to show the "truth" of same.

105. For a short course in the accuracy of this statement, peruse the following sections of the Catholic Church. *Catechism of the Catholic Church* (Washington, D.C.: United States Catholic Conference, 1994): 122, 130, 134, 140, 574, 580, 595, 596, 1257, 1334, 1540.

106. Boys, "The Cross," 22.

107. Ibid., 23.

108. Van Buren, *Jewish Christian Reality,* 165.

Chapter Four

1. Gabriel Moran, *No Ladder to the Sky* (San Francisco: Harper & Row, 1987), 177.

2. Gabriel Moran, *Religious Education Development* (Minneapolis: Winston Press, 1983), 183.

3. Ibid., 140.

4. Gabriel Moran, *Interplay: A Theory of Religion and Education* (Winona, Minn.: St. Mary's Press, 1981), 143.

5. Moran, *Religious Education Development,* 182.

6. Gabriel Moran, *Religious Body* (New York: Seabury Press, 1974), 195.

7. Moran, *Religious Education Development,* 134.

8. Ibid., 206.

9. Padraic O'Hare, *The Way of Faithfulness: Contemplation and Formation in the Church* (Valley Forge, Pa.: Trinity Press International, 1993), ix.

10. Moran, *Religious Body,* 24.

11. This distinction between "pastoral" and "religious education" is a functional one for many professional workers in the church. Attention will be given to this distinction in the discussion of teaching later in this chapter.

12. Mary C. Boys, *Educating in Faith* (New York: Harper & Row, 1986), 126.

13. Moran, *Religious Education Development,* 201.

14. Moran, *Religious Body,* 220f.

15. All quotes in this section on revelation are from the twenty-four-page essay under consideration. Therefore no further endnotes citing the essay will appear in this section.

16. Peter Steinfels, "Vatican Says the Ban on Women as Priests Is "Infallible" Doctrine," *The New York Times,* November 19, 1995, 1.

17. Bishop Anthony Pilla, quoted in Steinfels, "Women as Priests."

18. See August Hassler, *How the Pope Became Infallible* (Garden City, N.Y.: Doubleday, 1982).

19. Moran, *Religious Education Development,* 142.

20. Ibid., 143.

21. In John C. Haughey, SJ, ed., *The Faith That Does Justice* (New York: Herder & Herder, 1970), 10–46.

22. Moran, *Religious Body,* 29.

23. Gabriel Moran, *Design for Religion* (New York: Herder & Herder, 1970), 65.

24. Moran, *No Ladder to the Sky,* 13.

25. Ibid.

26. Moran, *Religious Education Development,* 129.

27. Ibid., 130.

28. Maria Harris, *Teaching and the Religious Imagination* (San Francisco: Harper & Row, 1986), chapter 1.

29. Moran, *Interplay,* 193.

30. Moran, *Religious Education Development,* 192.

31. Ibid., 147.

32. All terms will be discussed below, and appropriate endnotes will appear.

33. Moran, *Religious Education Development,* 134, 131.

34. Ibid., 131.

35. Ibid., 145.

36. Ibid., 205.

37. Ibid., 198.

38. Ibid., 148.

39. Ibid., 151.

40. Ibid.

41. Ibid., 204.

42. Ibid., 152.

43. Ibid., 154.

44. Ibid.

45. Ibid., 203f.

46. I have focused on the importance of education in nonviolence in two recent works: in the chapters on work and family in *The Way of Faithfulness: Contemplation and Formation in the Church* and in *Busy Life Peaceful Center: A Book of Meditating.*

47. Gabriel Moran, *Showing How: The Act of Teaching* (Valley Forge, Pa.: Trinity Press International, 1997), 59.

48. Ibid., 54.

49. Ibid., 83.

50. Ibid., 79.

51. In *Religious Education Development,* Moran urges religious educators to give up the arrogance of certain developmental schema and to start "attending to the saints in our midst" (106).

52. Moran, *Showing How,* 111 (page references refer to unpublished manuscript).

53. Ibid., 139.

54. Ibid., 138.

55. Ibid., 170.

56. Ibid., 98.

57. Ibid., 197.

58. See *Religious Education Development,* chapter 7.

59. Moran, *Religious Body,* 50f.

60. Moran, *Showing How,* 87.

61. Gabriel Moran, *Religious Education as a Second Language* (Birmingham: Religious Education Press, 1989), 199.

62. Moran, *Religious Education Development*, 96.

63. Moran, *Uniqueness*, 46.

64. Moran, *Religious Education Development*, 97.

65. Moran, *No Ladder to the Sky*, 61.

66. Moran, *Religious Education Development*, 63.

67. Moran, *Religious Body*, 1.

68. Ibid., 33.

69. Ibid., 44.

70. Ibid., 45.

71. Moran, *Second Language*, 208.

72. Ibid., 200.

73. Moran, *Religious Education Development*, 107.

74. Ibid., 102.

75. Moran, *Religious Body*, 66.

76. Ibid., 86f.

77. Moran, *Religious Education Development*, 140f.

78. Moran, *Religious Body*, 5.

79. Moran, *Interplay*, 136.

80. Moran, *Religious Education Development*, 180.

Chapter Five

1. Jacob Neusner, *Jews and Christians: The Myth of a Common Tradition* (London: SCM, 1991), ix.

2. Jacob Neusner, *The Way of Torah* (Belmont, Calif.: Dickenson Publishing Co., 1970), 68.

3. Joseph Bernardin, "Bernardin Sees Shift in Biblical Scholarship," *National Catholic Reporter*, December 11, 1988, 14.

4. David Tracy, "The Christian Understanding of Salvation-Liberation," *Face to Face (An Interreligious Bulletin)* 14 (Spring 1988): 40.

5. Milton Steinberg, *Basic Judaism* (New York: Harcourt, Brace, 1975), 43.

6. James D. G. Dunn, "What Did Christianity Lose When It Parted from Judaism?" *Explorations* 8, no. 2 (1994): 2.

7. Ibid.

8. Television interview with Carl Stern, on the program, "Lamp Unto My Feet," October 2, 1972.

9. In Steinberg, *Basic Judaism*, 46.

10. Quoted in Margaret Farley, *Personal Commitments* (San Francisco: Harper & Row, 1986), 134.

11. Leo Baeck, *The Essence of Judaism* (New York: Schocken Books, 1961), 86.

12. Steinberg, *Basic Judaism*, 43.

13. Ibid., 44.

14. Television interview with Carl Stern, on the program, "Lamp Unto My Feet," October 2, 1972.

15. Steinberg, *Basic Judaism*, 73.

16. Norman Solomon, "God the Lawgiver — Meditations on the Spirituality of Halakha," in *Spirituality and Prayer: Jewish and Christian Understandings*, Leon Klenicki and Gabe Huck, eds. (New York: Paulist Press, 1983), 70.

17. Gabriel Moran, "Two Languages of Religious Education," *The Living Light* 4, no. 3 (Spring 1974): 120–28.

18. Annie Dillard, *Holy the Firm* (New York: Harper & Row, 1984), 16.

19. Emmanuel Rackman, "What Do All Jews Hold in Common?" pt. 2 of *Jews and Catholics in Conversation* (Boston: American Jewish Committee, Northeast Region, and Catholic Archdiocese of Boston, Catholic Jewish Committee, 1992), 6.

20. In Samuel H. Dresner, ed., *I Asked for Wonder: A Spiritual Anthology — Abraham Joshua Heschel* (New York: Schocken Books, 1991), 49.

21. Ibid., 54.

22. Steinberg, *Basic Judaism*, 71.

23. Leonard Bialles, *Myths, Gods, Heroes and Saviours* (Mystic, Conn.: Twenty-Third Publications, 1984), 65.

24. Steinberg, *Basic Judaism*, 35.

25. In Dresner, *I Asked for Wonder*, 3.

26. Steinberg, *Basic Judaism*, 56f.

27. Ibid., 55.

28. Carol Ochs, *Song of the Self: Biblical Spirituality and Human Holiness* (Valley Forge, Pa.: Trinity Press International, 1994), 71.

29. Ibid., 75.

30. Schocken Books, 1986.

31. Norman Solomon, "God the Lawgiver," 69.

32. Steinberg, *Basic Judaism*, 89.

33. The term was coined by Max Weber to denote loss of rigor, specifically loss of "charism" in religion.

34. Reinhold Niebuhr, *Moral Man and Immoral Society* (New York: Scribner's Sons, 1932), 212.

35. Abraham Joshua Heschel, *The Prophets*, vol. 1 (New York: Harper & Row, 1962), 26.

36. Cornel West, *Race Matters* (Boston: Beacon Press, 1993), chaps. 1 and 2.

37. Heschel, *The Prophets*, vol. 1, 6.

38. Ibid., 159.

39. Beack, *The Essence of Judaism*, 70.

40. Gustavo Gutiérrez, *We Drink from Our Own Wells* (Maryknoll, N.Y.: Orbis Books, 1984), 32.

41. Sherry Blumberg, "Forms of Jewish Spirituality," *Professional Approaches for Christian Educators (PACE)* 22 (December 1992): 4.

42. Ibid.

43. Carol Deutsch, "The Catechism, Jesus and the Law," *Professional Approaches for Christian Educators (PACE)* 24 (February 1995): 13.

44. Leon Klenicki and Eugene J. Fisher, *Roots and Branches: Biblical Judaism, Rabbinic Judaism and Early Christianity* (Winona, Minn.: St. Mary's Press, 1987), 7.

45. Rackman, "What Do All Jews Hold in Common?" 6.

46. Moses Maimonides, *The Guide of the Perplexed* (Indianapolis: Hackett Publishing Co., 1995), 347.

47. Betzah 32b.

48. Leon Klenicki, "The Chosen People: A Contemporary Jewish Perspective," *SIDIC (Service International de Documentation Judeo-Chrétienne)* 23, no. 3, English ed. (1990): unpaginated.

49. Ibid.

50. Heschel, *The Prophets,* vol. 1, 32.

51. Leon Klenicki, "The Promised Land: The Hope of Redemption," *Professional Approaches for Christian Educators (PACE)* 24 (December 1994): 10.

52. Ibid., 12.

53. Walter Brueggemann, *The Land: Place as Gift, Promise and Challenge in Biblical Faith* (Philadelphia: Fortress Press, 1977), 187.

54. Suzannah Heschel, introduction to "Moral Grandeur and Spiritual Audacity: Essays of Abraham Joshua Heschel" in Suzannah Heschel, ed. *Moral Grandeur and Spiritual Audacity* (New York: Farrar, Straus & Giroux, 1996), 6–32.

55. Ibid., 13.

56. Ibid., 22f, 41.

57. Ibid., 23.

58. Dresner, *I Asked for Wonder,* 3.

59. Ibid., 22.

60. S. Heschel, introduction to "Moral Grandeur," 41.

Chapter Six

1. Parker Palmer, *The Promise of Paradox* (Notre Dame, Ind.: Ave Maria Press, 1980), 47.

2. Robert Ludwig, *Reconstructing Catholicism* (New York: Crossroad, 1995).

3. Quoted from "The Star of Redemption," in *Dialogue* 32, no. 1 (Fall 1993): 26.

4. John MacMurray, *Reason and Emotion* (New York: Henry Regnery Co., 1923).

5. Thomas Green, *The Activity of Teaching* (New York: Appleton-Century Co., 1973), 146.

6. John Shea, "Storytelling and Religious Identity," *Chicago Studies* 21 (Spring 1982), 35.

7. Daniel Goldman, *Emotional Intelligence* (New York: Bantam Books, 1995).

8. William Dych, SJ, "Theology and Imagination," *Thought* (March 1992): 23.

9. Paul Ricoeur, *History and Truth* (Evanston, Ill.: Northwestern University Press, 1967), 186.

10. Paul Ricoeur, *The Symbolism of Evil* (Boston: Beacon Press, 1967), 83.

11. Jan Darsa, "Teaching the Holocaust: The Use and Abuse of Media," *Professional Approaches for Christian Educators (PACE)* 23 (October 1993); and "The Challenge of Memories: The Use of Video Testimonies in Teaching the Holocaust," *Professional Approaches for Christian Educators (PACE)* 23 (November 1993).

12. Avery Dulles, "The Problem of Conscience: A Catholic View," in C. Ellis Nelson, ed., *Conscience* (New York: Newman Press, 1973), 146–63.

13. See, for example, Graham Rossiter, "The Place of Faith in Religious Education in Catholic Schools," *The Living Light* 27, no. 1 (October 1987).

14. In personal conversation, Spring 1995.

15. The twelve are: Ave Maria Press; Benzinger Publishing Company; Brown Publishing/Roa Media; The Center for Learning; Hi-Time Publishing; Ignatius Press; Loyola University Press; William H. Sadlier, St. Mary's Press; St Paul's Books and Media; Silver Burdett Ginn; and Winston Press.

16. Collegeville, Minn.: Liturgical Press, 1995.

17. "Facing History and Ourselves" (Brookline, Mass.: Facing History and Ourselves Publishers, 1995), promotional material.

18. Ibid. For information write or call Facing History and Ourselves National Foundation, Inc., 16 Hurd Road, Brookline, MA 02146-6919. Phone 617/232-1595.

19. For examples of praying together see Leon Klenicki and Gabe Huck, eds., *Spirituality and Prayer: Jewish and Christian Understandings* (New York: Paulist Press, 1983).

20. Abraham Joshua Heschel, *A Passion for Truth* (New York: Farrar, Straus & Giroux, 1973), 215.

21. Samuel H. Dresner, ed., *I Asked for Wonder: A Spiritual Anthology — Abraham Joshua Heschel* (New York: Schocken Books, 1991), 21.

22. Both are published by Liturgy Training Publications, Chicago.

23. Thomas Keating, OCSO, *The Heart of the World: A Spiritual Catechism* (New York: Crossroad, 1981), 1.

Afterword

1. See, for example, their essays in Leon Klenicki, ed., *Toward a Theological Encounter: Jewish Understanding of Christianity* (New York: Paulist Press, 1991).

2. Irving Greenberg, "Judaism and Christianity: Their Respective Roles in the Strategy of Redemption," Eugene J. Fisher, ed., *Vision of the Other: Jewish and Christian Theologians Assess the Dialogue* (New York: Paulist Press, 1994), 24.

3. Leon Klenicki, "On Christianity: Toward a Process of Spiritual and Historical Healing — Understanding the Other as a Person of God," *In Dialogue* (November 1992): 21.

4. David Hartman, "Judaism Encounters Christianity Anew," in Fisher, ed., *Vision of the Other,* 79.

Index